BENCHMARK SERIES

Microsoft® Word

2016
Level 3

Rutkosky • Roggenkamp • Rutkosky

PARADIGM
EDUCATION SOLUTIONS

St. Paul

Senior Vice President	Linda Hein
Editor in Chief	Christine Hurney
Director of Production	Timothy W. Larson
Production Editor	Jen Weaverling
Cover and Text Designer	Valerie King
Copy Editors	Communicáto, Ltd.
Senior Design and Production Specialist	Jack Ross
Design and Production Specialist	PerfecType
Assistant Developmental Editors	Mamie Clark, Katie Werdick
Testers	Janet Blum, Fanshawe College; Traci Post
Instructional Support Writers	Janet Blum, Fanshawe College; Brienna McWade
Indexer	Terry Casey
Vice President Information Technology	Chuck Bratton
Digital Projects Manager	Tom Modl
Vice President Sales and Marketing	Scott Burns
Director of Marketing	Lara Weber McLellan

Trademarks: Microsoft is a trademark or registered trademark of Microsoft Corporation in the United States and/or other countries. Some of the product names and company names included in this book have been used for identification purposes only and may be trademarks or registered trade names of their respective manufacturers and sellers. The authors, editors, and publisher disclaim any affiliation, association, or connection with, or sponsorship or endorsement by, such owners.

We have made every effort to trace the ownership of all copyrighted material and to secure permission from copyright holders. In the event of any question arising as to the use of any material, we will be pleased to make the necessary corrections in future printings.

Cover Photo Credits: © Photomall/Dreamstime.com.

Paradigm Publishing is independent from Microsoft Corporation, and not affiliated with Microsoft in any manner. While this publication may be used in assisting individuals to prepare for a Microsoft Office Specialist certification exam, Microsoft, its designated program administrator, and Paradigm Publishing do not warrant that use of this publication will ensure passing a Microsoft Office Specialist certification exam.

ISBN 978-0-76386-762-1 (print)
ISBN 978-0-76386-763-8 (digital)

© 2017 by Paradigm Publishing, Inc.
875 Montreal Way
St. Paul, MN 55102
Email: educate@emcp.com
Website: ParadigmCollege.com

Printed in the United States of America

23 22 21 20 19 18 17 16   1 2 3 4 5 6 7 8 9 10 11 12

Contents

Preface   vii

Chapter 1 Applying Advanced Formatting   1

Applying Character Formatting   2
   Adjusting Character Spacing   2
   Applying OpenType Features   4
   Applying Text Effects   7
   Changing the Default Font   9
Inserting Symbols and Special Characters   10
   Inserting Intellectual Property Symbols   10
   Inserting Hyphens   11
   Inserting Nonbreaking Spaces   12
Finding and Replacing Characters, Styles, and Fonts and Using Wildcard Characters   13
   Finding and Replacing Special Characters   14
   Finding and Replacing Styles   15
   Finding and Replacing Body and Heading Fonts   15
   Finding and Replacing Using Wildcard Characters   17
Merging with Fields and Other Data Source Files   19
   Inserting a Merge Record # Field   20
   Inserting an If… Then… Else… Field   20
   Merging with Other Data Source Files   22
Recording and Running Macros   26
   Running a Macro Automatically   26
   Assigning a Macro to the Quick Access Toolbar   29
   Specifying Macro Security Settings   31
   Saving a Macro-Enabled Document or Template   32
   Copying Macros between Documents and Templates   33
   Recording a Macro with a Fill-in Field   35
   Using File Explorer to Open a Document Based on a Template   37
Chapter Summary   39

Chapter 2 Formatting with Styles   43

Creating a Style   44
   Creating a Style Based on Existing Formatting   44
   Creating a Style Based on an Existing Style   44
   Creating a New Style   45
   Assigning a Keyboard Shortcut to a Style   47
Modifying a Predesigned Style   50
   Saving Styles in a Template   52
   Modifying an Applied Style   54
Displaying All Styles   54
Revealing Style Formatting   55
Saving a Custom Style Set   56
   Changing Default Settings   57
   Deleting a Custom Style Set   58

Creating and Modifying a Multilevel List and a Table Style 59
    Creating a Multilevel List Style 59
    Updating a Template with an Updated Style 60
    Creating a Table Style 63
    Modifying a Multilevel List Style 66
    Modifying a Table Style 66
Using the Style Inspector Task Pane 67
Managing Styles 69
    Copying Styles Between Documents and Templates 72
    Renaming Styles 72
Chapter Summary 74

Chapter 3 Creating Forms **77**
Creating and Using a Form 78
    Designing a Form 78
    Creating a Form Template 79
    Displaying the Developer Tab 80
    Inserting Content Controls 80
    Defining a Group 81
    Displaying a Form in Design Mode 81
    Opening and Filling in a Form Document 83
    Editing Group Data 85
    Inserting Specific Placeholder Text 87
    Creating a Form Using a Table 87
    Protecting a Template 88
    Inserting a Picture Content Control 88
    Inserting a Date Picker Content Control 89
    Inserting a Drop-Down List Content Control 91
    Inserting a Combo Box Content Control 91
    Inserting a Check Box Content Control 91
Setting Content Control Properties 91
    Specifying Drop-Down List Content Control Properties 92
    Customizing Picture Content Control Properties 94
    Customizing Date Picker Content Control Properties 95
Editing a Protected Form Template 96
Chapter Summary 99

Chapter 4 Creating Forms with Legacy Tools **101**
Creating a Form with Legacy Tools 102
    Opening a Document Based on a Template Using File Explorer 102
    Inserting a Text Field Form 103
    Inserting a Check Box Form Field 104
    Protecting a Template 105
    Filling in a Form with Form Fields 106
Printing a Form 106
Customizing Form Field Options 107
    Creating a Drop-Down List Form Field 108
    Customizing Check Box Form Field Options 111
    Customizing Text Form Fields 114
Chapter Summary 116

Chapter 5 Using Outline View and Creating a Table of Authorities   **119**

Managing a Document in Outline View   120
   Displaying a Document in Outline View   120
   Collapsing and Expanding Levels   122
   Promoting and Demoting Heading Levels   124
   Assigning Levels   125
   Organizing a Document in Outline View   126
Assigning Levels at the Paragraph Dialog Box   128
   Navigating in a Document with Assigned Levels   128
   Collapsing and Expanding Levels in Normal View   128
   Moving Collapsed Text   128
   Collapsing Levels by Default   130
Creating a Master Document   131
   Creating a Master Document from an Existing Document   131
   Opening and Closing a Master Document and Its Subdocuments   132
   Expanding and Collapsing Subdocuments   133
   Editing a Subdocument   134
   Inserting a Subdocument   135
   Unlinking a Subdocument   136
   Splitting a Subdocument   136
   Merging Subdocuments   136
Creating a Table of Authorities   138
   Inserting a Table of Authorities   139
   Updating or Deleting a Table of Authorities   140
Chapter Summary   143

Chapter 6 Sharing Documents and Customizing Word Options   **147**

Managing the Accessibility of a Document   148
   Creating Alternate Text for an Image or Table   148
   Establishing a Header Row   150
   Using Built-In Styles   150
Sharing a Document   154
   Using the *Share with People* Option   154
   Using the *Email* Option   157
   Presenting a Document Online   158
Customizing Word Options   160
   Customizing *General* Options   161
   Customizing *Display* Options   163
   Customizing *Proofing* Options   163
   Customizing *Save* Options   164
   Customizing *Advanced* Options   165
   Customizing *Add-Ins and Trust Center* Options   167
Customizing Account Information   168
Chapter Summary   171
Word Level 3 Index   173

Preface

Benchmark Series: Microsoft® Word 2016 is designed for students who want to learn how to use this powerful word processing program to create professional-looking documents for school, work, and personal communication needs. After successfully completing a course using this textbook and digital courseware, students will be able to:

- Create and edit letters, flyers, announcements, and reports of varying complexity
- Apply appropriate formatting elements and styles to a range of document types
- Add graphics and other visual elements to enhance written communication
- Plan, research, write, revise, and publish documents to meet specific information needs
- Given a workplace scenario requiring a written solution, assess the communication purpose and then prepare the materials that achieve the goal efficiently and effectively

Upon completing the text, students can expect to be proficient in using Word to organize, analyze, and present information.

Well-designed textbook pedagogy is important, but students learn technology skills through practice and problem solving. Technology provides opportunities for interactive learning as well as excellent ways to quickly and accurately assess student performance. To this end, this textbook is supported with SNAP 2016, Paradigm's web-based training and assessment learning management system. Details about SNAP as well as additional student courseware and instructor resources can be found on page xii.

Achieving Proficiency in Word 2016

Since its inception several Office versions ago, the *Benchmark Series* has served as a standard of excellence in software instruction. Elements of the *Benchmark Series* function individually and collectively to create an inviting, comprehensive learning environment that produces successful computer users. The following visual tour highlights the structure and features that comprise the highly popular *Benchmark* model.

Student Textbook and eBook

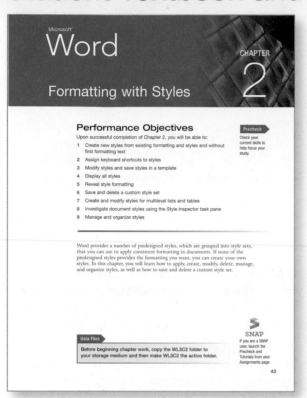

Chapter Openers present the performance objectives and an overview of the skills taught.

Precheck quizzes allow students to check their current skills before starting chapter work.

Data Files are provided for each chapter from the ebook. A prominent note reminds students to copy the appropriate chapter data folder and make it active.

Students with SNAP access are reminded to launch the Precheck quiz and chapter tutorials from their SNAP Assignments page.

Projects Build Skill Mastery within Realistic Context

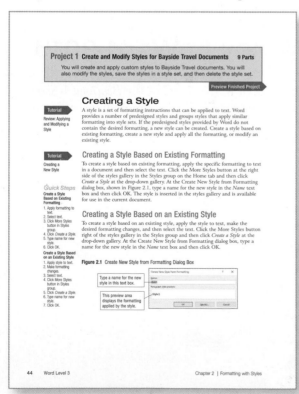

Multipart Projects provide a framework for instruction and practice on software features. A project overview identifies tasks to accomplish and key features to use in completing the work.

Preview Finished Project shows how the file will look after students complete the project.

Tutorials provide interactive, guided training and measured practice.

Quick Steps provide feature summaries for reference and review.

Typically, a file remains open throughout all parts of the project. Students save their work incrementally. At the end of the project, students save and then close the file.

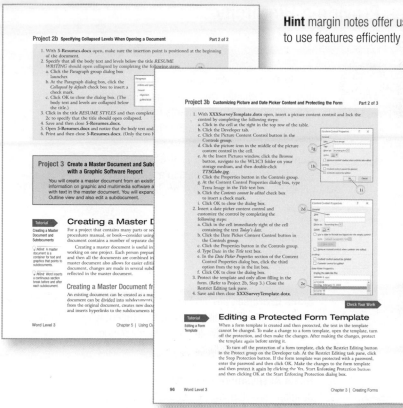

Hint margin notes offer useful tips on how to use features efficiently and effectively.

Step-by-Step Instructions guide students to the desired outcome for each project part. Screen captures illustrate what the screen should look like at key points.

Magenta Text identifies material to type.

Check Your Work allows students to confirm they have completed the project activity correctly.

Between project parts, the text presents instruction on the features and skills necessary to accomplish the next section of the project.

Chapter Review Tools Reinforce Learning

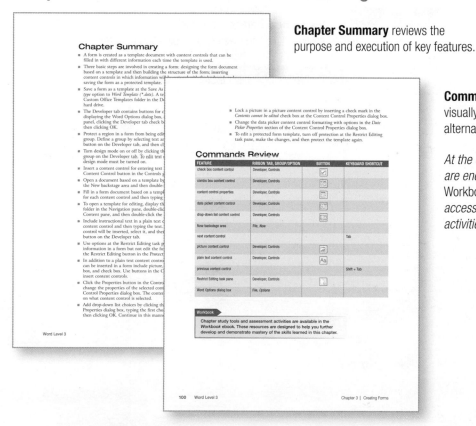

Chapter Summary reviews the purpose and execution of key features.

Commands Review summarizes visually the major features and alternative methods of access.

At the end of each chapter, students are encouraged to go to the Workbook *pages of the ebook to access study tools and assessment activities.*

Workbook eBook Activities Provide a Hierarchy of Learning Assessments

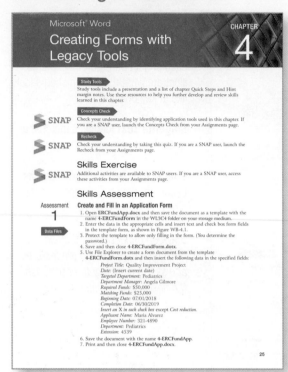

Study Tools are presentations with audio support and a list of chapter Quick Steps and Hint margin notes designed to help students further develop and review skills learned in the chapter.

Concepts Check is an objective completion exercise that allows students to assess their comprehension and recall of application features, terminology, and functions.

Recheck concept quizzes for each chapter enable students to check how their skills have improved after completing chapter work.

Skills Exercises are available to SNAP 2016 users. SNAP will automatically score student work, which is performed live in the application, and provide detailed feedback.

Skills Assessment exercises ask students to develop both standard and customized types of word processing documents without how-to directions.

Visual Benchmark assessments test problem-solving skills and mastery of application features.

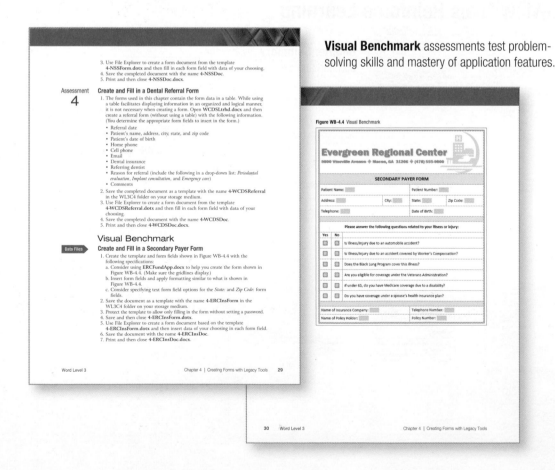

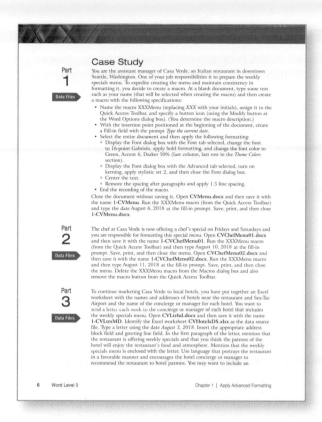

Case Study requires analyzing a workplace scenario and then planning and executing a multipart project.

Students search the web and/or use the program's Help feature to locate additional information required to complete the Case Study.

Capstone Performance Assessments Deliver Cross-Disciplinary, Comprehensive Evaluation

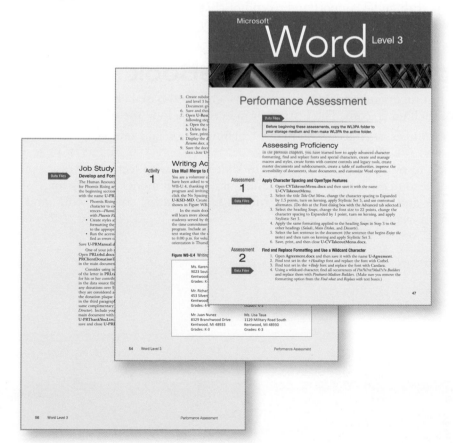

Assessing Proficiency exercises check mastery of features.

Writing Activities involve applying application skills in a communication context.

Internet Research projects reinforce research and information processing skills.

Job Study requires critical thinking and problem solving.

SNAP Training and Assessment

SNAP is a web-based training and assessment program and learning management system (LMS) for learning Microsoft Office 2016. SNAP is comprised of rich content, a sophisticated grade book, and robust scheduling and analytics tools. SNAP courseware supports the *Benchmark Series* content and delivers live-in-the-application assessments for students to demonstrate their skills mastery. Interactive tutorials increase skills-focused moments with guided training and measured practice. SNAP provides automatic scoring and detailed feedback on the many activities, exercises, and quizzes to help identify areas where additional support is needed, evaluating student performance both at an individual and course level. The *Benchmark Series* SNAP course content is also available to export into any LMS system that supports LTI tools.

Paradigm Education Solutions provides technical support for SNAP through 24-7 chat at ParadigmCollege.com. In addition, an online User Guide and other SNAP training tools for using SNAP are available.

Student eBook

The student ebook, available through SNAP or online at Paradigm.bookshelf.emcp.com, provides access to the *Benchmark Series* content from any device (desktop, tablet, and smartphone) anywhere, through a live Internet connection. The versatile ebook platform features dynamic navigation tools including a linked table of contents and the ability to jump to specific pages, search for terms, bookmark, highlight, and take notes. The ebook offers live links to the interactive content and resources that support the print textbook, including the student data files, Precheck and Recheck quizzes, and interactive tutorials. The *Workbook* pages of the ebook provide access to presentations with audio support and to end-of-chapter Concept Check, Skills Assessment, Visual Benchmark, Case Study, and Performance Assessment activities.

Instructor eResources eBook

All instructor resources are available digitally through a web-based ebook at Paradigm.bookshelf.emcp.com. The instructor materials include these items:

- Planning resources, such as lesson plans, teaching hints, and sample course syllabi
- Presentation resources, such as PowerPoint slide shows with lecture notes
- Assessment resources, including live and annotated PDF model answers for chapter work and workbook activities, rubrics for evaluating student work, and chapter-based exam banks

Microsoft®

Word

Applying Advanced Formatting

Performance Objectives

Upon successful completion of Chapter 1, you will be able to:

1 Adjust character spacing, use OpenType features, apply text effects, and change the default font

2 Insert intellectual property symbols, hyphens, and nonbreaking spaces

3 Find and replace special characters, styles, body and heading fonts, and use wildcard characters

4 Insert additional fields in a merge

5 Run a macro automatically

6 Assign a macro to the Quick Access Toolbar

7 Specify macro security settings

8 Save a macro-enabled document or template and copy macros between documents and templates

9 Record a macro with fill-in fields

10 Use File Explorer to open a document based on a template

Precheck ▶

Check your current skills to help focus your study.

Use options at the Font dialog box with the Advanced tab selected to apply advanced character formatting to text. Advanced character formatting options discussed in this chapter include scaling, spacing, and kerning as well as OpenType features such as ligatures, number styles, and stylistic sets. Word's find and replace feature can be used to find and replace text as well as special characters, styles, body and heading fonts, and wildcard characters. Other advanced formatting features covered in this chapter include inserting additional fields when merging documents and recording and copying macros and assigning a macro to the Quick Access Toolbar.

Data Files ▶

Before beginning chapter work, copy the WL3C1 folder to your storage medium and then make WL3C1 the active folder.

SNAP

If you are a SNAP user, launch the Precheck and Tutorials from your Assignments page.

Tutorial

Applying Advanced Character Formatting

Applying Character Formatting

The Font dialog box with the Advanced tab selected contains a number of options for improving the appearance of text in a document. Use options at the dialog box to adjust character spacing, apply OpenType features, and apply text effects to selected text.

Quick Steps

Adjust Character Spacing
1. Click Font group dialog box launcher.
2. Click Advanced tab.
3. Specify scaling, spacing, positioning, and/or kerning.
4. Click OK.

Adjusting Character Spacing

Each typeface is designed with a specific amount of space between characters. This character spacing can be changed with options in the *Character Spacing* section of the Font dialog box with the Advanced tab selected, as shown in Figure 1.1. Display this dialog box by clicking the Font group dialog box launcher on the Home tab and then clicking the Advanced tab at the dialog box.

Figure 1.1 Font Dialog Box with the Advanced Tab Selected

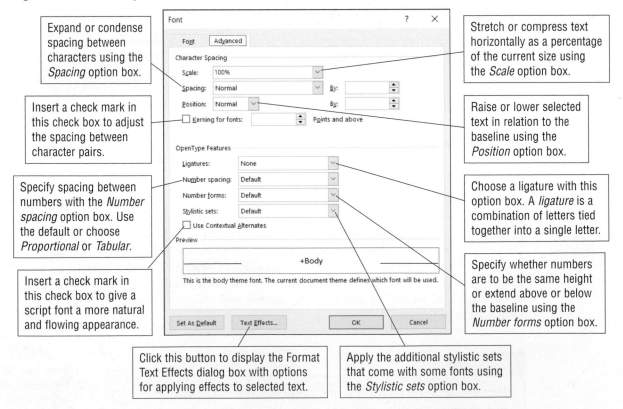

Expand or condense spacing between characters using the *Spacing* option box.

Insert a check mark in this check box to adjust the spacing between character pairs.

Specify spacing between numbers with the *Number spacing* option box. Use the default or choose *Proportional* or *Tabular*.

Insert a check mark in this check box to give a script font a more natural and flowing appearance.

Stretch or compress text horizontally as a percentage of the current size using the *Scale* option box.

Raise or lower selected text in relation to the baseline using the *Position* option box.

Choose a ligature with this option box. A *ligature* is a combination of letters tied together into a single letter.

Specify whether numbers are to be the same height or extend above or below the baseline using the *Number forms* option box.

Click this button to display the Format Text Effects dialog box with options for applying effects to selected text.

Apply the additional stylistic sets that come with some fonts using the *Stylistic sets* option box.

Choose the *Scale* option to stretch or compress text horizontally as a percentage of the current size from 1% to 600%. Expand or condense the spacing between characters with the *Spacing* option box. Choose the *Expanded* or *Condensed* option and then enter a specific point size in the *By* text box. Raise or lower selected text in relation to the baseline with the *Position* option box. Choose the *Raised* or *Lowered* option and then enter the point size in the *By* text box.

Insert a check mark in the *Kerning* check box to apply kerning to selected text in a document. Kerning involves adjusting the spacing between certain character combinations by positioning two characters closer together than normal and uses the shapes and slopes of the characters to improve their appearance. Kerning allows more text to be fit in a specific amount of space; also looks more natural and helps the eye move along the text. Consider kerning text set in larger font sizes, such as 14 points and larger, and text set in italics. Figure 1.2 displays text with and without kerning applied. Notice how the letters *Te* and *Va* are closer together in the kerned text compared with the text that is not kerned.

Turn on automatic kerning by displaying the Font dialog box with the Advanced tab selected and then inserting a check mark in the *Kerning for fonts* check box. Specify the beginning point size to be kerned in the *Points and above* measurement box.

Figure 1.2 Text with and without Kerning Applied

Tennison Valley (kerned)
Tennison Valley (not kerned)

Project 1a Adjusting Character Spacing and Kerning Text

Part 1 of 5

1. Open **PRDonorApp.docx** and then save it with the name **1-PRDonorApp**.
2. Select the title *Donor Appreciation*.
3. With the Home tab active, click the Font group dialog box launcher.
4. At the Font dialog box, click the Advanced tab.
5. Click the *Scale* option box arrow and then click *150%* at the drop-down list.
6. Click the *Spacing* option box arrow and then click *Condensed* at the drop-down list.
7. Click the *Kerning for fonts* check box to insert a check mark.
8. Click OK to close the dialog box.

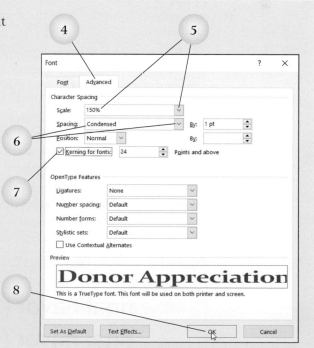

Check Your Work

Text Effects and Typography

Applying OpenType Features

The OpenType font file format was developed by Adobe and Microsoft to work on both Macintosh and Windows computers. The benefits of the OpenType format are cross-platform compatibility, which means font files can be moved between Macintosh and Windows computers; the ability to support expanded character sets and layout figures; and the capability for web page designers to create high-quality, on-screen fonts for online documents.

Microsoft Word offers some advanced OpenType features in the Font dialog box with the Advanced tab selected (refer to Figure 1.1) that desktop publishers and web and graphic designers can use to enhance the appearance of text. At the Font dialog box with the Advanced tab selected, *Ligatures* is the first option box in the *OpenType Features* section. A ligature is a combination of characters joined into a single letter. The OpenType standard specifies four categories of ligatures: *Standard Only*, *Standard and Contextual*, *Historical and Discretionary*, and *All*. The font designer decides which category to support and in which group to put combinations of characters.

With the *Standard Only* option selected, the standard set of ligatures that most typographers and font designers determine are appropriate for the font are applied to text. Common ligatures include letter combinations with the letter *f*, as shown in Figure 1.3. Notice how the *fi* and *fl* letter pairs are combined when ligatures are applied.

Use the other ligature options to specify *Contextual* ligatures, which are ligatures that the font designer believes are appropriate for use with the font but are not standard. Choose the option *Historical and Discretionary* to apply ligatures that were once standard but are no longer commonly used; use them to create a historical or "period" effect. The *All* ligatures option applies all the ligature combinations to selected text. Another method for applying ligatures to selected text is to click the Text Effects and Typography button in the Font group on the Home tab, point to *Ligatures* at the drop-down gallery, and then click an option at the side menu.

The *Number spacing* option box in the *OpenType Features* section will automatically display *Default*, which means the spacing between numbers is determined by the font designer. This can be changed to *Proportional*, which

Figure 1.3 Ligature Combination Examples

final flavor (using ligatures)
final flavor (not using ligatures)

adjusts the spacing for numbers with varying widths. Three Microsoft fonts—Candara, Constantia, and Corbel—use proportional number spacing by default. Use the *Tabular* option to specify that each number is the same width. This is useful in a situation in which the numbers are set in columns and all the numbers need to align vertically. The Cambria, Calibri, and Consolas fonts use tabular spacing by default.

Like the *Number spacing* option, the *Number forms* option box automatically displays *Default*, which means the font designer determines the number form. Change this option to *Lining* if all the numbers should be the same height and not extend below the baseline of the text. Generally, lining numbers are used in tables and forms because they are easier to read. The Cambria, Calibri, and Consolas fonts use lining number forms by default. With the *Old-style* option, the lines of the numbers can extend above or below the baseline of the text. For some fonts, changing the *Number forms* option to *Old-style* results in numbers such as *3* and *5* extending below the baseline or being centered higher on the line. Three fonts that use *Old-style* number forms are Candara, Constantia, and Corbel. The *Number Styles* option at the Text Effects and Typography button drop-down gallery combines number spacing and number forms options and displays the combined options in a side menu. Display the side menu by hovering the mouse pointer over the *Number Styles* option.

Project 1b Applying a Ligature and Number Form

Part 2 of 5

1. With **1-PRDonorApp.docx** open, select the text *Enjoy the "flavor of Tanzania" and an evening of cultural entertainment….*
2. Click the Font group dialog box launcher and, if necessary, click the Advanced tab.
3. At the Font dialog box with the Advanced tab selected, click the *Ligatures* option box arrow and then click *Standard and Contextual* at the drop-down list.
4. Click OK to close the dialog box.
5. Select the text *2019 – 2020* and *$3,500,000.*
6. Click the Text Effects and Typography button in the Font group, point to *Number Styles* at the drop-down gallery, and then click *Tabular Old-style* at the side menu.
7. Save **1-PRDonorApp.docx**.

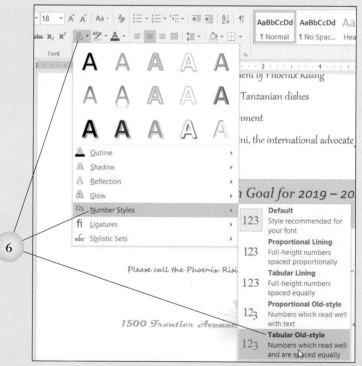

Check Your Work

A font designer may include a number of stylistic sets for a specific font. A different stylistic set may apply additional formatting to the characters in a font. For example, the sentences in Figure 1.4 are set in 16-point Gabriola. Notice the slight variations in characters in some of the stylistic sets. Choose a stylistic set and see a visual representation of the characters with the stylistic set applied in the *Preview* section of the dialog box. A stylistic set can also be selected by clicking the Text Effects and Typography button in the Font group, pointing to *Stylistic Sets* at the drop-down gallery, and then clicking the desired stylistic set at the side menu.

Insert a check mark in the *Use Contextual Alternates* check box in the Font dialog box with the Advanced tab selected to fine-tune letter combinations based on the surrounding characters. Use this feature to give script fonts a more natural and flowing appearance. Figure 1.5 shows text set in 12-point Segoe Script. The first line of text is set with the default setting and the second line of text is set with the *Use Contextual Alternates* option selected. Notice the slight differences in letters such as *t*, *n*, *s*, and *h*.

Not all fonts contain ligature combinations, number spacing and forms, stylistic sets, or contextual alternates. Experiment with fonts using the options in the Font dialog box with the Advanced tab selected to choose the font and font options most suitable for a document.

Figure 1.4 Examples of Gabriola Font Stylistic Sets

Typography refers to the appearance of printed characters on the page. (Default set)

Typography refers to the appearance of printed characters on the page. (Stylistic set 4)

Typography refers to the appearance of printed characters on the page. (Stylistic set 5)

Typography refers to the appearance of printed characters on the page. (Stylistic set 6)

Figure 1.5 Examples of Segoe Script Font without and with *Use Contextual Alternates* Selected

A font designer determines the appearance of each character in a font.

A font designer determines the appearance of each character in a font.

1. With **1-PRDonorApp.docx** open, select the bulleted text.
2. Display the Font dialog box with the Advanced tab selected.
3. Click the *Stylistic sets* option box arrow and then click *4* at the drop-down list.
4. Click OK to close the dialog box.
5. Select the text *Please call the Phoenix Rising office to let us know if you will be joining us.*
6. Display the Font dialog box with the Advanced tab selected.
7. Click the *Use Contextual Alternates* check box to insert a check mark.
8. Click OK to close the Font dialog box.
9. Save **1-PRDonorApp.docx**.

Check Your Work

Applying Text Effects

Applying Text Effects

Click the Text Effects button at the bottom of the Font dialog box with the Advanced tab selected and the Format Text Effects dialog box displays with the Text Fill & Outline icon selected, as shown in Figure 1.6. Click *Text Fill* or *Text Outline* to display the text formatting options. Click the Text Effects icon to display additional effects formatting options. Many of the options available at the dialog box also are available by clicking the Text Effects and Typography button in the Font group on the Home tab.

Quick Steps

Apply Text Effects
1. Click Font group dialog box launcher.
2. Click Text Effects button.
3. Choose options at Format Text Effects dialog box.
4. Click OK.

Figure 1.6 Format Text Effects Dialog Box

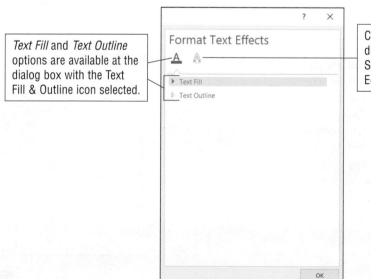

Text Fill and *Text Outline* options are available at the dialog box with the Text Fill & Outline icon selected.

Click the Text Effects icon to display options for applying Shadow, Reflection, Glow, Soft Edges, and 3-D text effects.

1. With **1-PRDonorApp.docx** open, select the title *Donor Appreciation*.
2. Display the Font dialog box.
3. Click the Text Effects button at the bottom of the dialog box.
4. At the Format Text Effects dialog box with the Text Fill & Outline icon selected, click *Text Fill* to expand the options.
5. Click *Gradient fill* to select the option.
6. Click the Preset gradients button and then click the *Medium Gradient - Accent 6* option (last column, third row).
7. Click the Direction button and then click the *Linear Down* option (second column, first row).
8. Scroll down the task pane and then click *Text Outline* to expand the options.
9. Click *Solid line* to select the option.
10. Click the Color button and then click the *Orange, Accent 6, Darker 50%* option (last column, bottom row in the *Theme Colors* section).
11. Click the Text Effects icon.
12. Click *Shadow* to expand the options.
13. Click the Presets button and then click the *Offset Left* option (last column, second row in the *Outer* section).
14. Click *Glow* to expand the options.
15. Click the Presets button in the *Glow* section and then click the *Orange, 5 pt glow, Accent color 6* option (last column, first row in the *Glow Variations* section).
16. Click OK to close the Format Text Effects dialog box.
17. Click OK to close the Font dialog box and then deselect the title.
18. Save **1-PRDonorApp.docx**.

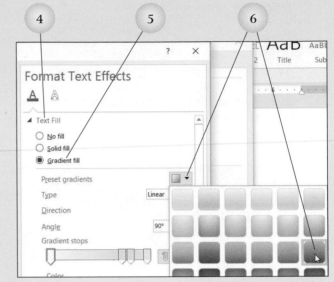

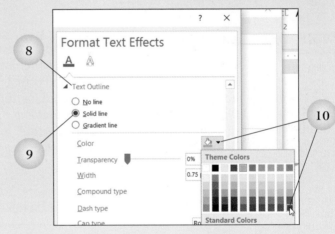

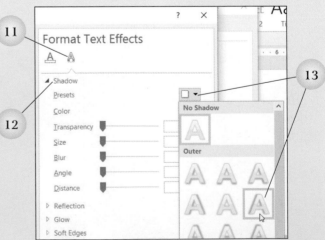

Check Your Work

Changing the Default Font

Quick Steps

Change the Default Font
1. Click Font group dialog box launcher.
2. Change font and/or effects.
3. Click Set As Default button.
4. Click *This document only* or *All documents based on the Normal.dotm template*.
5. Click OK.

If documents are generally created with a font other than the default, the default can be changed with the Set As Default button at the Font dialog box. The default font can be changed for the current document or it can be changed in Normal.dotm, which is the template document on which all new documents are based. To change the default font, display the Font dialog box, make changes to the font and/or effects, and then click the Set As Default button. At the Microsoft Word dialog box that displays, as shown in Figure 1.7, click the *This document only* option to apply the default only to the current document or click the *All documents based on the Normal.dotm template* option to change the default for all new documents based on the default template, Normal.dotm.

Figure 1.7 Microsoft Word Dialog Box

Project 1e **Changing the Default Font**   Part 5 of 5

1. For **1-PRDonorApp.docx**, you decide to change the default font to 12-point Constantia in a brown font color, since this font is used for most documents created for Phoenix Rising. Change the default font by completing the following steps:
   a. Click in the paragraph of text above the bulleted text. (This text is set in 12-point Constantia and in a brown color.)
   b. Click the Font group dialog box launcher.
   c. If necessary, click the Font tab and then notice that *Constantia* is selected in the *Font* list box, *12* is selected in the *Size* list box, and the *Font color* option box displays a brown color.
   d. Click the Set As Default button.
   e. At the Microsoft Word dialog box, click *All documents based on the Normal.dotm template* to select the option.
   f. Click OK.
2. Save, print, and then close **1-PRDonorApp.docx**.
3. Press Ctrl + N to open a new blank document based on the Normal.dotm template. Notice that *Constantia* displays in the *Font* option box and *12* displays in the *Font Size* option box, indicating that it is the default font.
4. Change the font back to the original default by completing the following steps:
   a. Click the Font group dialog box launcher.
   b. Scroll up the *Font* list box and then click *+Body*. (This is the original default font, which applies the Calibri font to body text in a document.)
   c. Click *11* in the *Size* list box.
   d. Click the *Font color* option box arrow and then click the *Automatic* option that displays at the top of the drop-down list.

1d

e. Click the Set As Default button.
f. At the Microsoft Word dialog box, click the *All documents based on the Normal.dotm template* option.
g. Click OK.

5. Close the blank document without saving changes.

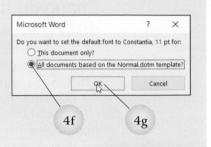
4f
4g

Check Your Work

Project 2 Create a Document with Symbols and Special Characters 3 Parts

You will create a document that includes intellectual property symbols; nonbreaking, em dash, and en dash hyphens; and nonbreaking spaces.

Preview Finished Project

Inserting Symbols and Special Characters

Symbols and special characters can be inserted in a document with options at the Symbol dialog box with either the Symbols tab or Special Characters tab selected. Symbols can also be inserted by typing a sequence of characters or by using keyboard shortcuts. Word creates some special characters automatically as text is typed.

Tutorial

Inserting Intellectual Property Symbols

Inserting Intellectual Property Symbols

Among the symbols that can be inserted in a document are three intellectual property protection symbols: ©, ™, and ®. Insert the © symbol to identify copyrighted intellectual property, use the ™ symbol to identify a trademark, and use the ® symbol to identify a registered trademark.

Insert these symbols with options at the Symbol dialog box with the Special Characters tab selected, by typing a sequence of characters, or by using a keyboard shortcut. Insert a © symbol by typing (c) or pressing Alt + Ctrl + C, insert a ™ symbol by typing (tm) or pressing Alt + Ctrl + T, and insert a ® symbol by typing (r) or pressing Alt + Ctrl + R.

Project 2a Inserting Intellectual Property Symbols

Part 1 of 3

1. At a blank document, type the text shown in Figure 1.8. Insert each intellectual property symbol using the appropriate sequence of characters or keyboard shortcut. To insert (c), (tm), and (r) in the document rather than the corresponding symbol, type the sequence of characters and then immediately click the Undo button. This changes the symbol back to the sequence of characters.
2. Save the document and name it **1-Symbols**.

Check Your Work

Figure 1.8 Project 2a

INTELLECTUAL PROPERTY PROTECTION

A copyright protects original works in areas such as publishing, music, literature, and drama. Use the © symbol to identify copyrighted intellectual property. Create this symbol by typing (c), using the keyboard shortcut Alt + Ctrl + C, or by clicking the symbol in the Symbol dialog box with the Special Characters tab selected.

A trademark identifies a word, symbol, device, or name such as a brand name. Use the ™ symbol to identify a trademarked name or product. Create this symbol by typing (tm), using the keyboard shortcut Alt + Ctrl + T, or by clicking the symbol in the Symbol dialog box with the Special Characters tab selected.

A registered trademark is a trademark that has been registered with the U.S. Patent & Trademark Office. Use the ® symbol to identify a registered trademark. Create this symbol by typing (r), using the keyboard shortcut Alt + Ctrl + R, or by clicking the symbol in the Symbol dialog box with the Special Characters tab selected.

Tutorial

Inserting Hyphens and Nonbreaking Characters

Inserting Hyphens

The Hyphenation button in the Page Setup group on the Layout tab provides options for automatically or manually hyphenating words in a document. In addition to inserting a regular hyphen in a word, an optional hyphen and nonbreaking hyphen can be inserted in a document as well as an en dash and an em dash.

One method for inserting a regular hyphen is to press the hyphen key on the keyboard and use it to create a compound word, such as *fresh-looking* or *sister-in-law*. An optional hyphen is one inserted by Word when a document is automatically hyphenated. An optional hyphen will display only if the word falls at the end of the line and the word is divided across two lines. Word does not display the optional hyphen if the word is not divided across lines. Optional hyphens display as hyphens when the display of nonprinting characters is turned on.

Some text should not be hyphenated and divided across lines. For example, a company name such as *Knowles-Myers Corporation* should not be divided between *Knowles* and *Myers* and set on two lines. To avoid a break like this, insert a nonbreaking hyphen by clicking the *Nonbreaking Hyphen* option at the Symbol dialog box with the Special Characters tab selected or with the keyboard shortcut Ctrl + Shift + -.

Em dashes (—) are used to indicate a break in thought or to highlight a term or phrase by separating it from the rest of the sentence. Em dashes are particularly useful in long sentences and sentences with multiple phrases and commas. For example, the sentence "The main focus of this document is on general-purpose, single-user computers—personal computers—that enable users to complete a variety of computing tasks." contains two em dashes before and after the term *personal computers*.

To create an em dash in a Word document, type the word, type two hyphens, type the next word, and then press the spacebar. When the spacebar is pressed, Word automatically converts the two hyphens to an em dash. If automatic formatting of em dashes is turned off, an em dash can be inserted with the *Em*

Dash option at the Symbol dialog box with the Special Characters tab selected or with the keyboard shortcut Alt + Ctrl + - (on the numeric keypad). (The hyphen key on the numeric keypad rather than the hyphen key, which is located between the 0 key and = key, must be used.)

Hint An em dash is the width of the capital letter M and an en dash is the width of the capital letter N.

En dashes (–) are used between inclusive dates, times, and numbers to mean "through." For example, in the text *9:30–11:00 a.m.*, the numbers should be separated by an en dash rather than a regular hyphen. Word does not automatically convert hyphens to en dashes, as it does with em dashes. To create an en dash, click the *En Dash* option at the Symbol dialog box with the Special Characters tab selected or with the keyboard shortcut Ctrl + - (on the numeric keypad).

Project 2b Inserting Hyphens

Part 2 of 3

1. With **1-Symbols.docx** open, press Ctrl + End, press the Enter key, and then type the text shown in Figure 1.9 with the following specifications:
   a. Type an en dash between the times *9:00* and *10:30 a.m.* by pressing Ctrl + - (on the numeric keypad). If you are working on a laptop that does contain a numeric keypad, insert an en dash by clicking the Insert tab, clicking the Symbol button, and then clicking *More Symbols*. At the Symbol dialog box, click the Special Characters tab, click the *En Dash* option, click the Insert button, and then click the Close button.
   b. Create the em dashes before and after the phrase *Excel, PowerPoint, and Access* by typing hyphens (two hyphens for each em dash).
   c. Insert a nonbreaking hyphen within *Tri-State* by pressing Ctrl + Shift + -.
2. Save **1-Symbols.docx**.

Check Your Work

Figure 1.9 Project 2b

SOFTWARE TRAINING

The Microsoft® Office Word training is scheduled for Thursday, March 10, 2018, from 9:00–10:30 a.m. Additional training for other applications in the Office suite—Excel, PowerPoint, and Access—will be available during the month of April. Contact the Training Department for additional information. All Tri-State employees are eligible for the training.

Inserting Nonbreaking Spaces

As text is typed in a document, Word makes decisions about where to end lines and automatically wraps text to the beginning of new lines. In some situations, a line may break between two words or phrases that should remain together. To control where text breaks across lines, consider inserting nonbreaking spaces between words that should remain together.

Insert a nonbreaking space with the *Nonbreaking Space* option at the Symbol dialog box with the Special Characters tab selected or with the keyboard shortcut Ctrl + Shift + spacebar. If nonprinting characters are turned on, a normal space displays as a dot and a nonbreaking space displays as a degree symbol.

Project 2c Inserting Nonbreaking Spaces

Part 3 of 3

1. With **1-Symbols.docx** open, click the Show/Hide ¶ button in the Paragraph group on the Home tab.
2. Press Ctrl + End, press the Enter key, and then type the text in Figure 1.10. Insert nonbreaking spaces in the keyboard shortcuts by pressing Ctrl + Shift + spacebar before and after each plus (+) symbol.
3. Turn off the display of nonprinting characters.
4. Save, print, and then close **1-Symbols.docx**.

Check Your Work

Figure 1.10 Project 2c

KEYBOARD SHORTCUTS

Microsoft Word includes a number of keyboard shortcuts you can use to access features and commands. The ScreenTip for some buttons displays the keyboard shortcut you can use to execute the command. For example, hovering the mouse over the Font button causes the ScreenTip to display Ctrl + Shift + F as the keyboard shortcut. Additional Home tab Font group keyboard shortcuts include Ctrl + B to bold text, Ctrl + I to italicize text, and Ctrl + U to underline text. You can also press Ctrl + Shift ++ to turn on superscript and press Ctrl + = to turn on subscript.

Project 3 Find and Replace Special Characters, Styles, Body and Heading Fonts, and Use Wildcard Characters in a Lease Agreement

3 Parts

You will open a commercial lease agreement, find and replace special characters, styles, and body and heading fonts and then find and replace text using a wildcard character.

Preview Finished Project

Finding and Replacing Characters, Styles, and Fonts and Using Wildcard Characters

The Find and Replace dialog box can be used to find and replace special characters and styles and find and replace body and heading fonts. The expanded Find and Replace dialog box contains a *Use wildcards* option. With this option selected, a wildcard character can be used to find specific text or characters in a document.

Finding and Replacing Special Characters

Find or find and replace special characters with the Special button at the expanded Find and Replace dialog box. Click the Special button and a drop-down list displays similar to the one shown in Figure 1.11. Click a special character in the drop-down list and a code representing the character is inserted in the text box where the insertion point is positioned. For example, with the insertion point positioned in the *Find what* text box, clicking *Paragraph Mark* at the Special button drop-down list inserts the code $\wedge p$ in the text box. If a character code is known, it can be typed directly in the *Find what* or *Replace with* text box.

Quick Steps

**Find and Replace a
Special Character**
1. Click Replace button.
2. Click More button.
3. Click Special button.
4. Click character at
   drop-down list.
5. Click in *Replace with*
   text box.
6. Insert replacement
   character.
7. Click Replace All
   button.
8. Click OK.

Figure 1.11 Special Button Drop-down List

Project 3a Finding and Replacing Special Characters

Part 1 of 3

1. Open **ComLease.docx** and then save it with the name **1-ComLease**.
2. Search for and delete all continuous section breaks by completing the following steps:
   a. Click the Replace button in the Editing group on the Home tab.
   b. At the Find and Replace dialog box, click the More button.
   c. Click the Special button at the bottom of the dialog box.
   d. Click *Section Break* in the drop-down list. (This inserts $\wedge b$ in the *Find what* text box.)
   e. Click in the *Replace with* text box and make sure the text box is empty.
   f. Click the Replace All button.
   g. At the message indicating that 3 replacements were made, click OK.

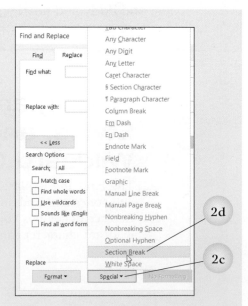

3. With the expanded Find and Replace dialog box open, find all occurrences of regular hyphens and replace them with nonbreaking hyphens by completing the following steps:
a. With ^b selected in the *Find what* text box, type - (a hyphen).
b. Press the Tab key to move the insertion point to the *Replace with* text box.
c. Click the Special button at the bottom of the dialog box.
d. Click *Nonbreaking Hyphen* at the drop-down list.
e. Click the Replace All button.
f. At the message indicating that 19 replacements were made, click OK.
g. Click the Close button to close the Find and Replace dialog box.
4. Save **1-ComLease.docx**.

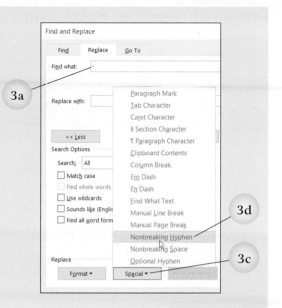

Check Your Work

Quick Steps
Find and Replace a Style
1. Click Replace button.
2. Click More button.
3. Click Format button.
4. Click *Style.*
5. Click style.
6. Click OK.
7. Click in *Replace with* text box and then repeat steps 4-6 to specify replacement style.
8. Click Replace All button.
9. Click OK.

Finding and Replacing Styles

The Find and Replace dialog box can be used to find specific styles in a document and replace them with other styles. To find styles, display the Find and Replace dialog box and then click the More button. At the expanded Find and Replace dialog box, click the Format button and then click *Style* at the drop-down list. At the Find Style dialog box that displays, click the style in the *Find what style* list box and click OK. Click in the *Replace with* text box at the Find and Replace dialog box, click the Format button and then click *Style*. At the Replace Style dialog box, click the replacement style in the *Replace With Style* list box and then click OK.

Tutorial

Finding and Replacing Body and Heading Fonts

Finding and Replacing Body and Heading Fonts

By default, a Word document has the Office theme applied, which applies that set of colors, fonts, and effects. The theme fonts include a body font and heading font. The default settings for theme fonts are *Calibri (Body)* and *Calibri Light (Headings)*. These fonts display at the beginning of the *Font* option drop-down gallery. If a different theme has been applied, other body and heading fonts will be used; they can be viewed at the *Font* option drop-down gallery.

A document can be searched for one body or heading font and then replaced with a different font. To do this, display the Find and Replace dialog box with the Replace tab selected. Expand the dialog box, click the Format button, and then click *Font* at the drop-down list. At the Find Font dialog box, scroll up the *Font* list box and then click *+Body* if searching for the body font or click *+Headings* if searching for the heading font. Click in the *Replace with* text box and then complete the steps to insert the replacement font.

Quick Steps
Find and Replace Body or Heading Font
1. Click Replace button.
2. Click More button.
3. Click Format button.
4. Click *Font.*
5. Click *+Body* or *+Headings* in Font list box.
6. Click OK.
7. Click in *Replace with* text box.
8. Insert replacement font.
9. Click Replace All button.
10. Click OK.

1. Search for Heading 3 styles and replace them with Heading 2 styles by completing the following steps:
   a. Click the Replace button in the Editing group on the Home tab.
   b. At the Find and Replace dialog box, if necessary, click the More button. (If a check mark displays in any of the check boxes, click the option to remove it.)
   c. If necessary, clear any text and formatting from the *Find what* and *Replace with* text boxes.
   d. With the insertion point positioned in the *Find what* text box, click the Format button near the bottom of the dialog box and then click *Style* at the drop-down list.
   e. At the Find Style dialog box, scroll down the *Find what style* list box and then click *Heading 3*.
   f. Click OK to close the Find Style dialog box.

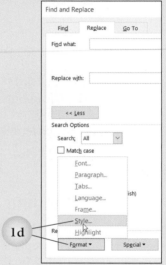

   g. At the Find and Replace dialog box, click in the *Replace with* text box.
   h. Click the Format button near the bottom of the dialog box and then click *Style* at the drop-down list.
   i. At the Replace Style dialog box, scroll down the *Replace With Style* list box, click *Heading 2*, and then click OK.
   j. At the Find and Replace dialog box, click the Replace All button.
   k. At the message indicating that 6 replacements were made, click OK.

2. With the Find and Replace dialog box open, search for the +Body font and replace it with Constantia by completing the following steps:
   a. With the insertion point positioned in the *Find what* text box, click the No Formatting button near the bottom of the dialog box.
   b. Click the Format button and then click *Font* at the drop-down list.
   c. At the Find Font dialog box, scroll up the *Font* list box and then click *+Body*.

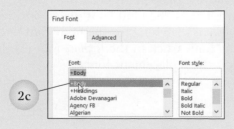

d. Click OK to close the Find Font dialog box.

e. At the Find and Replace dialog box, click in the *Replace with* text box, and then click the No Formatting button near the bottom of the dialog box.

f. Click the Format button and then click *Font* at the drop-down list.

g. At the Replace Font dialog box, scroll down the *Font* list box and then click *Constantia*.

h. Click OK to close the Replace Font dialog box.

i. At the Find and Replace dialog box, click the Replace All button.

j. At the message indicating that 13 replacements were made, click OK.

3. With the Find and Replace dialog box open, search for the +Headings font and replace it with Corbel and then change the paragraph alignment to center by completing the following steps:

a. With the insertion point positioned in the *Find what* text box, click the No Formatting button near the bottom of the dialog box.

b. Click the Format button near the bottom of the dialog box and then click *Font* at the drop-down list.

c. At the Find Font dialog box, click *+Headings* in the *Font* list box.

d. Click OK to close the Find Font dialog box.

e. At the Find and Replace dialog box, click in the *Replace with* text box.

f. Click the No Formatting button near the bottom of the dialog box.

g. Click the Format button near the bottom of the dialog box and then click *Font* at the drop-down list.

h. At the Replace Font dialog box, scroll down the *Font* list box and then click *Corbel*.

i. Click OK to close the Replace Font dialog box.

j. At the Find and Replace dialog box, click the Format button and then click *Paragraph* at the drop-down list.

k. At the Replace Paragraph dialog box, click the *Alignment* option box arrow and then click *Centered* at the drop-down list.

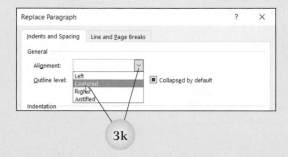

3k

l. Click OK to close the Replace Paragraph dialog box.

m. Click the Replace All button.

n. At the message indicating that 7 replacements were made, click OK.

4. Click the Less button and then close the Find and Replace dialog box.

5. Scroll through the document and notice that the text with the Heading 1 style and Heading 2 style applied are now set in Corbel and centered.

6. Save **1-ComLease.docx**.

Check Your Work

Tutorial

Finding and Replacing Using Wildcard Characters

Finding and
Replacing Text
Using a Wildcard
Character

The expanded Find and Replace dialog box contains a *Use wildcards* check box. Insert a check mark in this check box to use wildcard characters in a search to find or find and replace data. For example, suppose the company name *Hansen Products*

Quick Steps

Finding and Replacing Text Using a Wildcard Character
1. Click Replace button.
2. Click More button.
3. Click *Use wildcards* check box.
4. Click in *Find what* text box.
5. Type find text using a wildcard character.
6. Click in *Replace with* text box.
7. Type replacement text.
8. Click Replace All button.
9. Click OK.

also mistakenly appears in a document as *Hanson Products*. Both spellings can be found by typing *Hans?n* in the *Find what* text box. Word will find *Hansen* and *Hanson* if the *Use wildcards* check box contains a check mark. If the *Use wildcards* check box does not contain a check mark, Word will try to find the exact spelling *Hans?n* and not find either spelling in the document. Table 1.1 identifies some common wildcard characters along with the functions they perform. For additional wildcard characters, use the Help feature.

Table 1.1 Wildcard Characters

Wildcard Character	Function
*	Indicates any characters. For example, type le*s and Word finds *less*, *leases,* and *letters*.
?	Indicates one character. For example, type gr?y and Word finds *gray* and *grey*.
@	Indicates any occurrence of the previous character. For example, type cho@se and Word finds *chose* and *choose*.
<	Indicates the beginning of a word. For example, type <(med) and Word finds *medical*, *medicine*, and *media*.
>	Indicates the ending of a word. For example, type (tion)> and Word finds *election*, *deduction*, and *education*.

Project 3c Finding and Finding and Replacing Using a Wildcard Character   Part 3 of 3

1. With **1-ComLease.docx** open, use a wildcard character to search for words beginning with *leas* by completing the following steps:
   a. Click the Find button arrow in the Editing group on the Home tab and then click *Advanced Find* at the drop-down list.

   b. At the Find and Replace dialog box, click the More button.
   c. Click the No Formatting button.
   d. Click the *Use wildcards* check box to insert a check mark.
   e. Click in the *Find what* text box and then type <(leas).

f. Click the Find Next button to find the first occurrence of a word that begins with *leas*.

g. Click the Find Next button four more times.

h. Press the Esc key to end the find and close the Find and Replace dialog box.

2. The name *Arigalason* is spelled a variety of ways in the document. Use a wildcard character to search for all the versions of the name and replace them with the correct spelling by completing the following steps:

a. Press Ctrl + Home to move the insertion point to the beginning of the document.

b. Click the Replace button in the Editing group on the Home tab.

c. At the Find and Replace dialog box, delete the text in the *Find what* text box and then type Ar?galas?n.

d. Make sure that the dialog box is expanded and the *Use wildcards* check box contains a check mark.

e. Press the Tab key.

f. Click the No Formatting button.

g. Type Arigalason (the correct spelling) in the *Replace with* text box.

h. Click the Replace All button.

i. At the message indicating that 23 replacements were made, click OK.

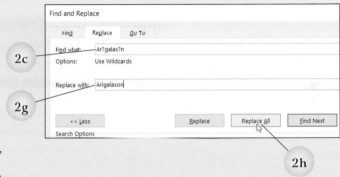

3. Close the Find and Replace dialog box.

4. Save, print, and then close **1-ComLease.docx**.

Check Your Work

Project 4 Insert Merge Fields in a Main Document   1 Part

You will insert an If...Then...Else... field and a Merge Record # field in a City of Edgewood main document and then merge it with a data source file.

Preview Finished Project

Merging with Fields and Other Data Source Files

The Mail Merge feature provides a number of methods for inserting fields into a main document. In a previous chapter, the Fill-in field from the Rules button drop-down list on the Mailings tab was used during a merge. The Rules button drop-down list contains additional fields for merging documents, such as the Merge Record # field, which inserts a record number in each merged document, and the If...Then...Else... field, which compares two values and inserts one set of text or another depending on the comparison.

In addition to merging a main document with a data source file with the *.mdb* file extension, a main document can be merged with other data source files. Other data source files include a Word table, an Excel worksheet, an Access database table, and an Outlook contacts list.

Inserting a Merge Record # Field

Ọuick Steps

Insert a Record Number Field
1. In main document, click Mailings tab.
2. Click Rules button.
3. Click *Merge Record #*.

After merging a small number of records, it is easy to determine if all the records were merged and printed. When merging a large number of records in a data source file, consider inserting a Merge Record # field to ensure that each document merges and prints. This field will insert a record number in each merged document. To insert a Merge Record # field, click the Rules button in the Write & Insert Fields group on the Mailings tab and then click *Merge Record #* at the drop-down list. This inserts the field «*Merge Record #*» in the document.

Inserting an If…Then…Else… Field

Tutorial

Inserting an If… Then…Else… Field

Ọuick Steps

Insert If…Then… Else… Field
1. In main document, click Mailings tab.
2. Click Rules button.
3. Click *If…Then… Else…*.
4. Click *Field name* option box arrow.
5. Click field at drop-down list.
6. If necessary, specify compare value.
7. Type text in *Insert this text* text box if field entry is matched.
8. Type text in *Otherwise insert this text* text box if field entry is not matched.
9. Click OK.

Hint Alt + F9 displays or hides fields in a document.

Use an If…Then…Else… field to tell Word to compare two values and then, depending on what is determined, enter one set of text or the other. Click *If… Then…Else…* at the Rules button drop-down list and the Insert Word Field: IF dialog box displays, as shown in Figure 1.12.

Specify the field Word is to compare with the *Field name* option. Click the *Field name* option box arrow and then click the field at the drop-down list. The drop-down list displays all the fields specified when the data source file was created. Use the *Comparison* option to identify how Word is to compare values. By default, *Equal to* displays in the *Comparison* option box. Click the *Comparison* option box arrow and a drop-down list displays with a variety of value options, such as *Not equal to, Less than, Greater than*, and so on. In the *Compare to* text box, type the specific field value Word is to use. For example, to include a statement in a letter for all customers with the zip code *98405*, click the *Field name* option box arrow and then click *ZIP_Code* at the drop-down list. Type the zip code in the *Compare to* text box.

After specifying the field name and field entry, type in the *Insert this text* text box the text to be inserted if the field entry is matched, and type in the *Otherwise insert this text* text box the text to be inserted if the field entry is not matched. The *Otherwise insert this text* text box can be left empty. This tells Word not to insert any text if the specific entry value is not matched.

By default, an If…Then…Else… field does not display in the document. To make the field visible, press Alt + F9. To turn off the display, press Alt + F9 again. Turning on the display of field codes also expands other merge codes.

Figure 1.12 Insert Word Field: IF Dialog Box

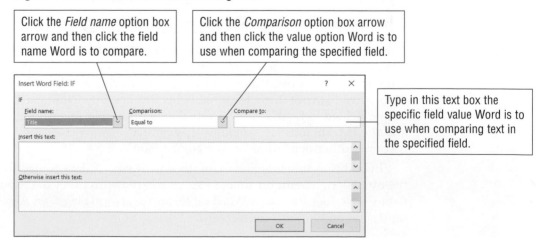

Click the *Field name* option box arrow and then click the field name Word is to compare.

Click the *Comparison* option box arrow and then click the value option Word is to use when comparing the specified field.

Type in this text box the specific field value Word is to use when comparing text in the specified field.

1. Open **CofEMD.docx** and then save it with the name **1-CofEMD**. At the message indicating that opening the document will run the SQL command, click the Yes button, navigate to the WL3C1 folder on your storage medium, and then double-click the file named *CofEDS.mdb*. (If the message does not appear, identify the data source file by clicking the Mailings tab, clicking the Select Recipients button, and then clicking *Use an Existing List*. At the Select Data Source dialog box, navigate to your WL3C1 folder and then double-click *CofEDS.mdb*.)

2. Insert an If...Then...Else... field that tells Word to add text if the membership is equal to *Platinum* by completing the following steps:
    a. Position the insertion point right of the period that ends the second paragraph and then press the spacebar.
    b. Click the Mailings tab.
    c. Click the Rules button in the Write & Insert Fields group and then click *If...Then...Else...* at the drop-down list.
    d. At the Insert Word Field: IF dialog box, click the *Field name* option box arrow and then click *Membership* at the drop-down list. (Scroll down the list box to display this field.)
    e. Click in the *Compare to* text box and then type Platinum.
    f. Click in the *Insert this text* text box and then type We hope you will continue your Platinum membership and enjoy the benefits of supporting your local community.
    g. Click OK to close the dialog box.

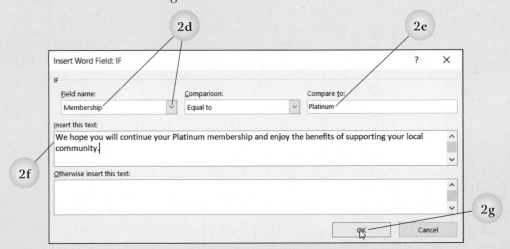

    h. View the If...Then...Else... field code (and expand the other merge codes) by pressing Alt + F9.
    i. After viewing the expanded fields, press Alt + F9 again to turn off the display.
3. Replace the letters *XX* that display near the bottom of the letter with your initials and then change the file name after your initials to **1-CofEMD**.

4. Insert a Merge Record # field by completing the following steps:
   a. Position the insertion point immediately right of the letters *MD* in the document name **1-CofEMD.docx**.
   b. Type a hyphen.
   c. Click the Rules button in the Write & Insert Fields group and then click *Merge Record #* at the drop-down list.
5. Save **1-CofEMD.docx**.
6. Merge the main document with the data source file by completing the following steps:
   a. Click the Finish & Merge button and then click *Edit Individual Documents* at the drop-down list.
   b. At the Merge to New Document dialog box, make sure *All* is selected and then click OK.
7. Save the merged document with the name **1-CofELetters**.
8. Print and then close **1-CofELetters.docx**.
9. Save and then close **1-CofEMD.docx**.

Check Your Work

Project 5 Merge Data Source Files with a Travel Letter   3 Parts

You will merge a Bayside Travel main document with different data source files, including a Word table, an Excel worksheet, and an Access database table.

Preview Finished Project

Tutorial

Merging a Main Document with Other Data Source Files

Merging with Other Data Source Files

Word saves a data source file as an Access database with the *.mdb* file extension. (In Access 2016, a database file is saved with the *.accdb* file extension.) A main document can also be merged with other data source files, such as a Word document containing data in a table, an Excel worksheet, an Access database table, and an Outlook contacts list. Select the data source file—such as a Word document, Excel worksheet, or Access database table—in the same manner as selecting a data source file with the *.mdb* file extension.

Project 5a Merging a Main Document with a Word Table Data Source File   Part 1 of 3

1. Open **BTTourLtr.docx** and then save it with the name **1-BTTourLtrMD**.
2. Open **BTClientTable.docx** from the WL3C1 folder on your storage medium. Notice that the document, which will be used as a data source file, contains only a table with data in columns and rows. After viewing the document, close it.
3. Identify **BTClientTable.docx** as the data source file by completing the following steps:
   a. Click the Mailings tab.
   b. Click the Select Recipients button in the Start Mail Merge group and then click *Use an Existing List* at the drop-down list.
   c. At the Select Data Source dialog box, navigate to the WL3C1 folder on your storage medium and then double-click **BTClientTable.docx**.

4. Press the Down Arrow key four times and then click the Address Block button in the Write & Insert Fields group.
5. At the Insert Address Block dialog box, click OK.
6. Press the Enter key two times.
7. Insert the greeting line fields by completing the following steps:
   a. Click the Greeting Line button in the Write & Insert Fields group.
   b. At the Insert Greeting Line dialog box, click the option box arrow for the option box containing the comma (the box right of the box containing *Mr. Randall*).
   c. At the drop-down list that displays, click the colon.
   d. Click OK to close the Insert Greeting Line dialog box.
8. Scroll to the end of the letter and then replace the *XX* with your initials.
9. Merge the document by clicking the Finish & Merge button in the Finish group and then clicking *Edit Individual Documents* at the drop-down list. At the Merge to New Document dialog box, click OK.
10. Save the merged letters with the name **1-BTTourMergedLtrs**.
11. Print the first two pages (letters) of the document and then close it.
12. Save and then close **1-BTTourLtrMD.docx**.

Check Your Work

 Match Fields

If the fields in a data source file do not match the fields in the address block, use options at the Match Fields dialog box to match the field names. Display the Match Fields dialog box by clicking the Match Fields button in the Write & Insert group or by clicking the Match Fields button in the Insert Address Block dialog box or the Greeting Line dialog box. To match the fields, click the option box arrow at the right side of the field to be matched and then click the field at the drop-down list of fields in the data source file.

For example, in Project 5b, you will use an Excel worksheet as a data source file. One of the fields, *MailingAddress*, does not have a match in the address block, so you will use the Match Fields button to match the *Address 1* field in the address block to the *MailingAddress* field in the Excel worksheet.

Project 5b Merging a Main Document with an Excel Worksheet Data Source File   Part 2 of 3

1. Open **BTTourLtr.docx** and then save it with the name **1-BTMD**.
2. Identify an Excel worksheet as the data source file by completing the following steps:
   a. Click the Mailings tab.
   b. Click the Select Recipients button in the Start Mail Merge group and then click *Use an Existing List* at the drop-down list.
   c. At the Select Data Source dialog box, navigate to the WL3C1 folder on your storage medium and then double-click **BTClientsExcel.xlsx**.
   d. At the Select Table dialog box, click OK.

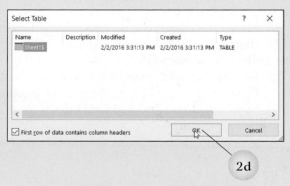

2d

3. Press the Down Arrow key four times and then insert the address block by completing the following steps:
   a. Click the Address Block button in the Write & Insert Fields group.
   b. At the Insert Address Block dialog box, click the Match Fields button.

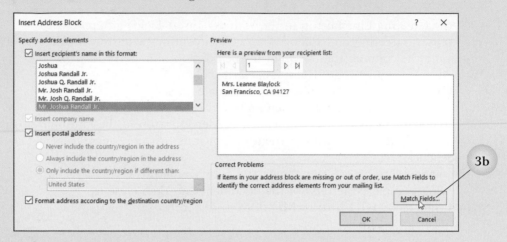

c. At the Match Fields dialog box, click the *Address 1* field option box arrow and then click *MailingAddress* at the drop-down list.
   d. Click OK to close the Match Fields dialog box.
   e. Click OK to close the Insert Address Block dialog box.
4. Press the Enter key two times.
5. Insert the greeting line fields by completing the following steps:
   a. Click the Greeting Line button in the Write & Insert Fields group.
   b. At the Insert Greeting Line dialog box, click the option box arrow right of the option box containing the comma (the box right of the box containing *Mr. Randall*).
   c. At the drop-down list that displays, click the colon.
   d. Click OK to close the Insert Greeting Line dialog box.

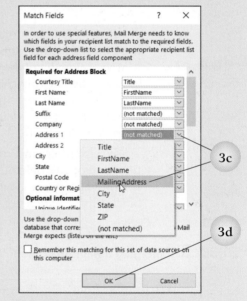

6. Scroll to the end of the letter and then replace the *XX* with your initials.
7. Merge the document by clicking the Finish & Merge button in the Finish group and then clicking *Edit Individual Documents* at the drop-down list. At the Merge to New Document dialog box, click OK.
8. Save the merged letters with the name **1-BTExcelMergedLtrs**.
9. Print the first two pages (letters) of the document and then close it.
10. Save and then close **1-BTMD.docx**.

Check Your Work

In addition to a Word table or Excel worksheet, an Access database table can be used as a data source file. To choose an Access database table, display the Select Data Source dialog box, navigate to the desired folder, and then double-click the Access database file. At the Select Table dialog box, select the specific table and then click OK.

Project 5c **Merging a Main Document with an Access Database Table Data Source File**   Part 3 of 3

1. Open **BTTourLtr.docx** and then save it with the name **1-BTLtrMD**.
2. Identify an Access table as the data source file by completing the following steps:
    a. Click the Mailings tab.
    b. Click the Select Recipients button in the Start Mail Merge group and then click *Use an Existing List* at the drop-down list.
    c. At the Select Data Source dialog box, navigate to the WL3C1 folder on your storage medium and then double-click *BaysideTravel.accdb*.
    d. At the Select Table dialog box, click the *Clients* table and then click OK.

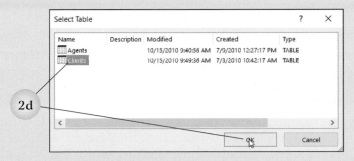

3. Press the Down Arrow key four times.
4. Click the Address Block button in the Write & Insert Fields group and then click OK at the Insert Address Block dialog box.
5. Press the Enter key two times.
6. Insert the greeting line fields by completing the following steps:
    a. Click the Greeting Line button in the Write & Insert Fields group.
    b. At the Insert Greeting Line dialog box, click the option box arrow right of the option box containing the comma (the option box right of the option box containing *Joshua Randall Jr.*).
    c. At the drop-down list that displays, click the colon.
    d. Click OK to close the Insert Greeting Line dialog box.
7. Scroll to the end of the letter and then replace the *XX* with your initials.
8. Merge the document by clicking the Finish & Merge button in the Finish group and then clicking *Edit Individual Documents* at the drop-down list. At the Merge to New Document dialog box, click OK.
9. Save the merged letters with the name **1-BTAccessMergedLtrs**.
10. Print the first two pages (letters) of the document and then close it.
11. Save and then close **1-BTLtrMD.docx**.

Check Your Work

You will record a macro that runs automatically and a macro that formats heading text. You will then open a document, which runs the automatic macro, insert a resume document into the open document, and then run the heading macro for each heading.

Preview Finished Project

Quick Steps

Display the Developer Tab
1. Click File tab.
2. Click *Options*.
3. Click *Customize Ribbon*.
4. Click *Developer* check box.
5. Click OK.

Record a Macro
1. Click Developer tab.
2. Click Record Macro button.
OR
1. Click View tab.
2. Click Macros button arrow.
3. Click *Record Macro*.
4. Make changes at Record Macro dialog box.
5. Click OK.
6. Complete macro steps.
7. Click Stop Recording button.
OR
7. Click macro icon on Status bar.

 Record Macro

 Macros

Recording and Running Macros

As discussed in an earlier chapter, macros are time-saving tools that automate the formatting of Word documents. Two basic steps are involved in working with macros: recording a macro and running a macro.

Recording a macro involves turning on the macro recorder, performing the steps to be recorded, and then turning off the recorder. Both the View tab and Developer tab contain buttons for recording a macro. If the Developer tab does not appear on the ribbon, turn on the display by opening the Word Options dialog box, clicking *Customize Ribbon* in the left panel, inserting a check mark in the *Developer* check box in the list box at the right, and then clicking OK to close the dialog box.

To record a macro, click the Record Macro button in the Code group on the Developer tab or click the View tab, click the Macros button arrow in the Macros group, and then click *Record Macro* at the drop-down list. At the Record Macro dialog box, type a name and description for the macro.

By default, Word stores a macro in the Normal template. Macros stored in this template are available for any document based on it. In a company or school setting, where computers may be networked, consider storing macros in personalized documents or templates. Specify the location for storing macros with the *Store macro in* option at the Record Macro dialog box.

Running a Macro Automatically

A macro can be created that starts automatically when a certain action is performed, such as opening or closing a document or closing Word. To use a macro that starts automatically, the macro must be saved in the Normal template and contain one of the names listed in Table 1.2.

Table 1.2 Automatic Macros

Automatic Macro Name	Action
AutoExec	Runs when Word is opened.
AutoOpen	Runs when a document is opened.
AutoNew	Runs when a new document is opened.
AutoClose	Runs when a document is closed.
AutoExit	Runs when Word is closed.

To create a macro that runs automatically, display the Record Macro dialog box, type the macro name from the list in Table 1.2 in the *Macro name* text box, and then click OK. Complete the steps for the macro and then end the recording.

Project 6 **Recording Macros and Running a Macro Automatically**

1. Open **MacroText.docx** and then create a macro that changes the font and view and runs automatically when a new document is opened by completing the following steps:
   a. Click the View tab.
   b. Click the Macros button arrow in the Macros group and then click *Record Macro* at the drop-down list.

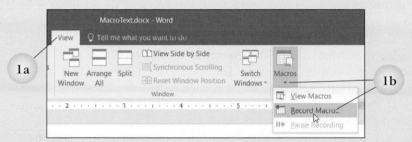

   c. At the Record Macro dialog box, type AutoNew in the *Macro name* text box.
   d. Click inside the *Description* text box and then type Runs automatically when a new document is opened and changes the font and document view. (If text displays in the *Description* text box, select the text and then type the description.)
   e. Click OK.

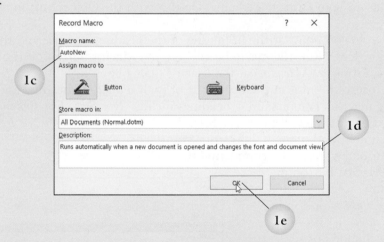

   f. Click the Home tab, click the *Font* option box arrow, and then click *Constantia* at the drop-down gallery.
   g. Click the View tab and then click the Draft button in the Views group.
   h. Press the spacebar and then press the Backspace key. (To save the document in Draft view, an action must appear in the *Undo* drop-down list. Pressing the spacebar and then pressing the Backspace key will create the action in the *Undo* list.)
   i. Click the macro icon on the Status bar to turn off the macro recording.

2. Record a macro that applies formatting to a heading by completing the following steps:
   a. Move the insertion point to the beginning of the text *Heading*.
   b. Click the View tab.
   c. Click the Macros button arrow in the Macros group and then click *Record Macro* at the drop-down list.
   d. At the Record Macro dialog box, type XXXHeading in the *Macro name* text box (typing your initials in place of the *XXX*).
   e. Click in the *Description* text box and then type Select text, change font size, turn on bold and italic, and insert bottom border line. (If text displays in the *Description* text box, select the text and then type the description.)
   f. Click OK.
   g. At the document screen, press the F8 function key and then press the End key.
   h. Click the Home tab.
   i. Click the Bold button in the Font group.
   j. Click the Italic button in the Font group.
   k. Click the *Font Size* option box arrow and then click *12* at the drop-down gallery.
   l. Click the Border button arrow and then click *Bottom Border* at the drop-down list.
   m. Press the Home key. (This moves the insertion point back to the beginning of the heading and deselects the text.)
   n. Click the macro icon on the Status bar to turn off the macro recording.
3. Close the document without saving it and then close Word.
4. Open Word and then open a blank document. Notice that the blank document contains the new settings (11-point Constantia and Draft view) because the AutoNew macro ran automatically.
5. Insert into the current document the document **ResumeStandards.docx** located in the WL3C1 folder on your storage medium. (Do this with the Object button arrow on the Insert tab.)
6. Position the insertion point at the beginning of the heading *Typestyle* and then run the XXXHeading macro. (Run the macro by clicking the Macros button on the View tab and then double-clicking *XXXHeading* at the Macros dialog box.)
7. Position the insertion point at the beginning of each remaining heading and run the XXXHeading macro. (The remaining headings include *Type Size*, *Type Enhancements*, *Page Length*, *Paper Color*, *Graphics*, and *White Space*.)
8. Save the document and name it **1-ResumeStandards**.
9. Delete the AutoNew macro by completing the following steps:
   a. Click the Macros button on the View tab.
   b. Click the *AutoNew* option in the *Macro name* list box at the Macros dialog box.
   c. Click the Delete button.
   d. At the message asking if you want to delete the macro, click the Yes button.
   e. Click the Close button to close the Macros dialog box.

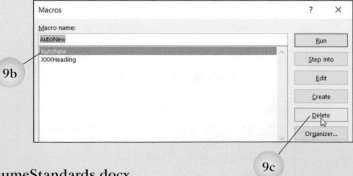

10. Save, print, and then close **1-ResumeStandards.docx**.

Check Your Work

You will create a macro that sets tabs and then assign the macro to the Quick Access Toolbar. You will then create a table of contents document and run the macro to format text in columns.

Preview Finished Project

Tutorial

Assigning a Macro to the Quick Access Toolbar

Quick Steps

Assign a Macro to the Quick Access Toolbar
1. Click View tab.
2. Click Macros button arrow.
3. Click *Record Macro*.
4. Type macro name.
5. Click Button button.
6. Click macro name in left list box.
7. Click Add button.
8. Click Modify button.
9. Click symbol.
10. Click OK.
11. Click OK.

Assigning a Macro to the Quick Access Toolbar

If a macro is used on a regular basis, consider assigning it to the Quick Access Toolbar. To run a macro from the Quick Access Toolbar, just click the button. To assign a macro to the toolbar, click the Button button at the Record Macro dialog box. This displays the Word Options dialog box with the *Quick Access Toolbar* option selected in the left panel. Click the macro name in the left list box and then click the Add button between the two list boxes. This adds the macro name in the right list box.

Specify a button icon by clicking the Modify button, clicking the desired icon at the Modify Button dialog box, and then clicking OK. Click OK to close the Word Options dialog box and a Macro button is inserted on the Quick Access Toolbar. To remove a Macro button from the Quick Access Toolbar, right-click the button on the toolbar and then click *Remove from Quick Access Toolbar* at the shortcut menu.

Project 7 Assigning a Macro to the Quick Access Toolbar   Part 1 of 1

1. At a blank document, create a macro and assign it to the Quick Access Toolbar by completing the following steps:
   a. Click the View tab.
   b. Click the Macros button arrow and then click *Record Macro* at the drop-down list.
   c. At the Record Macro dialog box, type XXXTab (use your initials in place of the *XXX*) in the *Macro name* text box.
   d. Click in the *Description* text box and then type Set left tabs at 0.5 and 1.0 and right tab with leaders at 5.5.
   e. Click the Button button.
   f. At the Word Options dialog box, click the macro *Normal. NewMacros.XXXTab* in the left list box.
   g. Click the Add button.

h. Click the Modify button in the lower right corner of the dialog box.

i. At the Modify Button dialog box, click the fourth button from the left in the top row.

j. Click OK to close the Modify Button dialog box.

k. Click OK to close the Word Options dialog box.

l. At the blank document, click the Home tab and then click the Paragraph group dialog box launcher.

m. At the Paragraph dialog box, click the Tabs button in the lower left corner of the dialog box.

n. At the Tabs dialog box, type 0.5 and then click the Set button.

o. Type 1 and then click the Set button.

p. Type 5.5, click the *Right* option in the *Alignment* section, click *2 ....* in the *Leader* section, and then click the Set button.

q. Click OK to close the dialog box.

r. At the blank document, click the macro icon on the Status bar to turn off recording.

2. Close the document without saving it.

3. At a new blank document, create the document shown in Figure 1.13 by completing the following steps:

   a. Click the Macro button on the Quick Access Toolbar.

   b. Type the text as shown in Figure 1.13. (Type the first column of text at the first tab stop, not the left margin.)

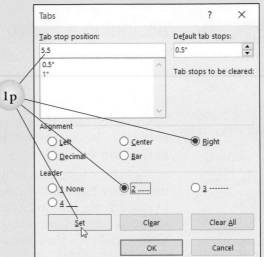

4. Select the title *COMPUTER CONCEPTS* and apply bold formatting and center the title.

5. Save the document and name it **1-TofC**.

6. Print and then close **1-TofC.docx**.

7. Remove the Macro button from the Quick Access Toolbar by right-clicking the button and then clicking *Remove from Quick Access Toolbar* at the shortcut menu.

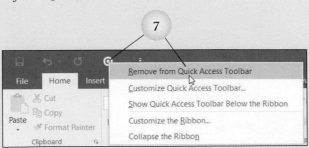

Figure 1.13 Project 7

COMPUTER CONCEPTS

Computer Hardware 3

    Types of Computers 4

    Hardware Components 8

Computer Software 14

    Operating Systems 16

    Application Software..20

Networking 25

    Types of Networks 27

    Uses of Networks...30

    Network Topologies 34

Project 8   Manage Macros and Record and Run a Macro with Fill-in Fields   3 Parts

You will change macro security settings, copy macros, and save a macro-enabled document. You will also record and run a macro with fill-in fields in a legal document.

Preview Finished Project

Specifying Macro Security Settings

Some macros pose a security risk because they have the potential to introduce and spread viruses on a computer or network. For this reason, Microsoft Word provides macro security settings to specify what actions occur with macros in a document. To display the macro security settings, click the Macro Security button in the Code group on the Developer tab. If the Developer tab is not visible, display it by clicking the File tab, clicking *Options*, and then clicking the *Customize Ribbon* option in the left panel. In the list box at the right, click the *Developer* check box to insert a check mark and then click OK to close the dialog box. Clicking the Macro Security button on the Developer tab displays the Trust Center dialog box with *Macro Settings* selected in the left panel, as shown in Figure 1.14.

 Macro Security

Figure 1.14 Trust Center Dialog Box

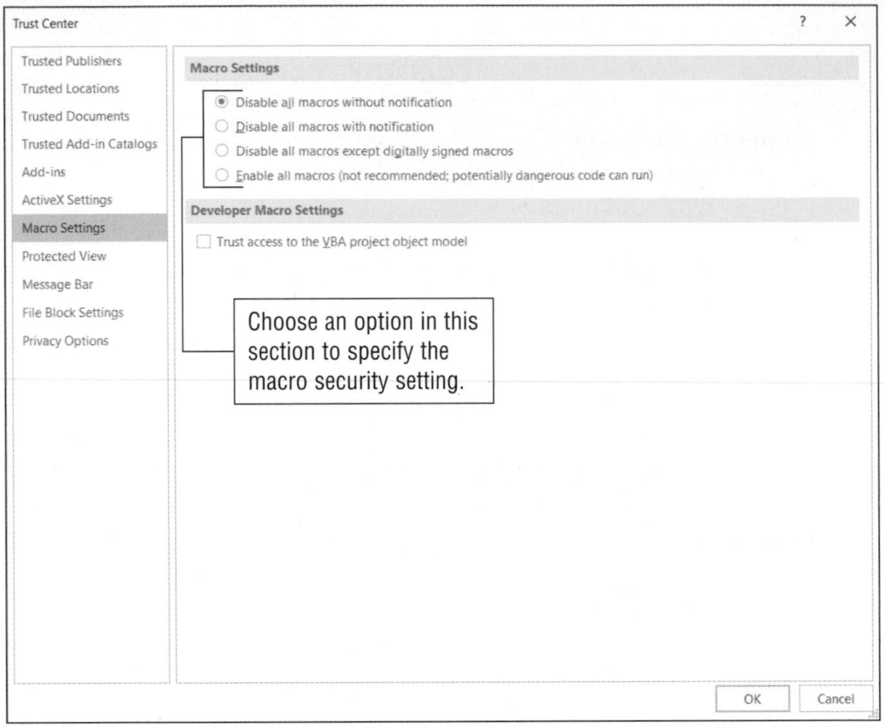

Choose an option in this section to specify the macro security setting.

Choose the first option, *Disable all macros without notification*, and all macros and security alerts are disabled. The second option, *Disable all macros with notification,* is the default setting. At this setting, a security alert appears if a macro is present that asks if the macro should be enabled. Choose the third option, *Disable all macros except digitally signed macros,* and a digitally signed macro by a trusted publisher will automatically run. (However, a digitally signed macro will still need to be enabled for a publisher that is not trusted.) The last option, *Enable all macros (not recommended; potentially dangerous code can run),* allows all macros to run but, as the option implies, this is not recommended.

Changes made to the macro security settings in Word only apply to Word. The macro security settings do not change in the other programs in the Office suite.

Saving a Macro-Enabled Document or Template

By default, macros are saved in Normal.dotm. The extension *.dotm* identifies the template as "macro-enabled." A template or document must be macro enabled for a macro to be saved in it.

In addition, macros can be saved in a specific document or template to make them available when that document or template is opened. To specify a location for saving a macro, display the Record Macro dialog box, click the *Store macro in* option box arrow, and then click the specific document or template.

Save a document containing macros as a macro-enabled document. To do this, display the Save As dialog box and then change the *Save as type* option to *Word Macro-Enabled Document (*.docm)*. Save a template containing macros as a macro-enabled template by changing the *Save as type* option at the Save As dialog box to *Word Macro-Enabled Template (*.dotm)*.

Copying Macros between Documents and Templates

Macros saved in a document can be copied to other documents or templates at the Organizer dialog box with the Macro Project Items tab selected. Display this dialog box by clicking the Macros button in the Code group on the Developer tab and then clicking the Organizer button at the Macros dialog box. The Macros dialog box can also be displayed by clicking the Macros button in the Macros group on the View tab.

Macros created in a document or template are saved in the NewMacros project. At the Organizer dialog box with the Macro Project Items tab selected, copy the NewMacros project from a document or template to another document or template. To copy the NewMacro project, click *NewMacro* in the list box at the left or right and then click the Copy button between the two list boxes.

By default, the Organizer dialog box displays the NewMacro project for the open document in the list box at the left and the NewMacro project for Normal.dotm in the list box at the right. Choose a different document or template by clicking the Close File button. This changes the Close File button to the Open File button. Choose a different document or template by clicking the Open File button. At the Open dialog box, navigate to the folder containing the document or template and then double-click the document or template.

The Organizer dialog box contains buttons for renaming and deleting macro projects. To rename the NewMacro project, click *NewMacro* in the list box and then click the Rename button between the two list boxes. At the Rename dialog box, type the new name and then press the Enter key. Delete a macro project by clicking the project name in the list box and then clicking the Delete button between the two list boxes.

Project 8a Changing Macro Security Settings, Copying Macros, and Saving a Macro-Enabled Document

Part 1 of 3

1. At a blank screen, display the Developer tab by completing the following steps:
   a. Click the File tab and then click *Options*.
   b. At the Word Options dialog box, click *Customize Ribbon* in the left panel.
   c. Click the *Developer* check box in the list box at the right side of the dialog box to insert a check mark.
   d. Click OK.
2. Change macro security settings by completing the following steps:
   a. Click the Developer tab and then click the Macro Security button in the Code group.
   b. At the Trust Center dialog box, click the *Enable all macros (not recommended; potentially dangerous code can run)* option.

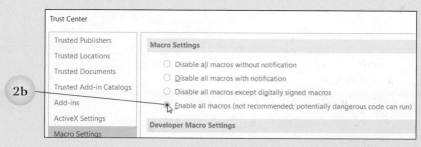

   c. Click OK.

3. Press Ctrl + N to display a blank document.
4. Save the document as a macro-enabled document in the WL3C1 folder on your storage medium by completing the following steps:
   a. Press the F12 function key to display the Save As dialog box.
   b. Type 1-LegalMacros in the *File name* text box.
   c. Click the *Save as type* option box and then click *Word Macro-Enabled Document (*.docm)* at the drop-down list.

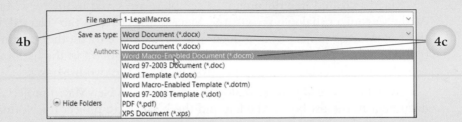

d. Click the Save button.
5. The WL3C1 folder contains a macro-enabled document named **MacroDocument.docm** that contains two macros. Copy the macros from the **MacroDocument.docm** document to the current document by completing the following steps:
   a. Make sure the Developer tab is active and then click the Macros button in the Code group.
   b. At the Macros dialog box, click the Organizer button.
   c. At the Organizer dialog box with the Macro Project Items tab selected, click the Close File button below the right list box (the list box containing *NewMacros*).
   d. Click the Open File button (previously the Close File button).
   e. At the Open dialog box, click the option box that displays right of the *File name* text box and then click *All Files (*.*)* at the drop-down list.
   f. Navigate to the WL3C1 folder and then double-click ***MacroDocument.docm***.
   g. At the Organizer dialog box with *NewMacros* selected in the list box at the right, click the Copy button between the list boxes.
   h. Click the Close button to close the Organizer dialog box.

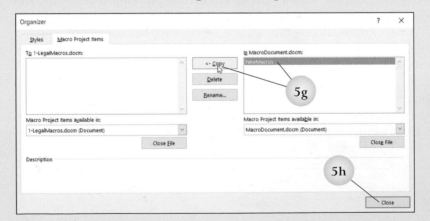

6. Save **1-LegalMacros.docm**.

Quick Parts

Recording a Macro with a Fill-in Field

A macro can be recorded that requires input from the keyboard using the Fill-in field. To insert a Fill-in field in a macro, begin recording the macro. At the point when the Fill-in field is to be inserted, click the Insert tab, click the Quick Parts button in the Text group, and then click *Field* at the drop-down list. At the Field dialog box with *(All)* selected in the *Categories* list box, as shown in Figure 1.15, scroll down the *Field names* list and then click the *Fill-in* field. Add information telling the operator what text to enter at the keyboard by clicking in the *Prompt:* text box and then typing the message. When running the macro, type the text specified by the prompt message.

Figure 1.15 Field Dialog Box

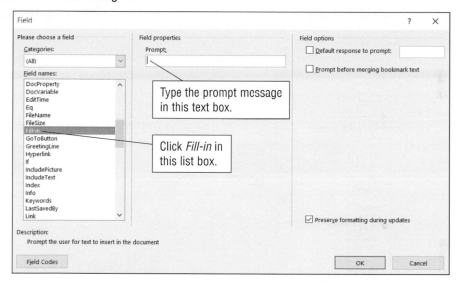

Project 8b Recording a Macro with Fill-in Fields

Part 2 of 3

1. With **1-LegalMacros.docm** open, create a macro that is saved in the current document. Begin by clicking the Developer tab and then clicking the Record Macro button in the Code group.
2. At the Record Macro dialog box, type Notary in the *Macro name* text box.
3. Click the *Store macro in* option box arrow and then click *1-LegalMacros.docm (document)* at the drop-down list.
4. Click in the *Description* text box and then type Notary signature information.
5. Click the Keyboard button.
6. At the Customize Keyboard dialog box with the insertion point positioned in the *Press new shortcut key* text box, press Alt + Shift + S.
7. Click the Assign button.
8. Click the Close button.

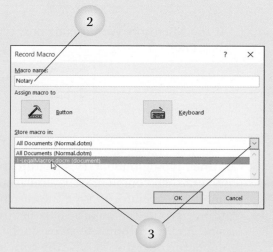

9. At the document, click the Home tab and then click the *No Spacing* style in the Styles group.

10. Set three left tabs by completing the following steps:
    a. Make sure the alignment button above the vertical ruler displays with the left tab symbol.
    b. Click the 0.5-inch mark on the horizontal ruler.
    c. Click the 2-inch mark on the horizontal ruler.
    d. Click the 2.5-inch mark on the horizontal ruler.

11. Type the text shown in Figure 1.16 up to *(name of person)*. (Do not type the text *(name of person)*.)

12. Insert a Fill-in field by completing the following steps:
    a. Click the Insert tab.
    b. Click the Quick Parts button in the Text group and then click *Field* at the drop-down list.
    c. At the Field dialog box with *(All)* selected in the *Categories* list box, scroll down the list and then click *Fill-in*.
    d. Click in the *Prompt:* text box and then type Type name of person signing.
    e. Click OK.

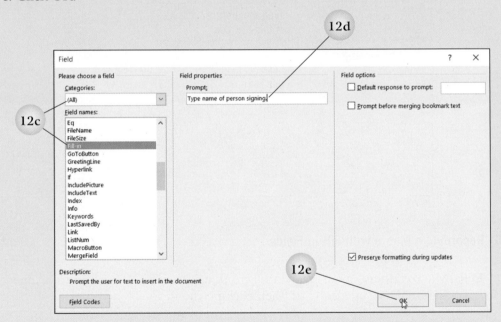

    f. At the Microsoft Word dialog box, type (name of person) in the text box and then click OK.

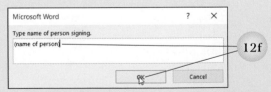

13. Continue typing the notary signature information shown in Figure 1.16 up to the text *(day)* and then complete steps similar to those in Step 12 to insert a Fill-in field that prompts the operator to type the current day.

14. Continue typing the notary signature information shown in Figure 1.16 up to the text *(month)* and then complete steps similar to those in Step 12 to insert a Fill-in field that prompts the operator to type the current month.

15. Continue typing the notary signature information shown in Figure 1.16 up to the text *(expiration date)* and then complete steps similar to those in Step 12 to insert a Fill-in field that prompts the operator to type the expiration date.
16. After inserting the expiration date information, press the Enter key.
17. End the recording by clicking the macro icon on the Status bar.
18. Click the Save button on the Quick Access Toolbar to save the document.
19. Press Ctrl + A to select the entire document and then press the Delete key. (The document should not contain any text.)
20. Save the document as a macro-enabled template by completing the following steps:
    a. Press the F12 function key to display the Save As dialog box.
    b. At the Save As dialog box, click the *Save as type* option box and then click *Word Macro-Enabled Template (*.dotm)* at the drop-down list.
    c. Select the text in the *File name* text box and then type XXX-LegalMacrosTemplate (typing your initials in place of the *XXX*).
    d. Click the Save button. (The template will be saved in the Custom Office Templates folder in the Documents folder on the computer's hard drive.)
21. Save the template in the WL3C1 folder on your storage medium with the name **1-LegalMacrosTemplate**. (Make sure it is saved as a macro-enabled template.)
22. Close **1-LegalMacrosTemplate.dotm**.

Figure 1.16 Project 8b

STATE OF CALIFORNIA   )
) ss.

COUNTY OF LOS ANGELES   )

      On this day personally appeared before me (name of person), known to me to be the individual described in and who executed the aforesaid instrument, and acknowledged that he/she signed as his/her free and voluntary act and deed for the uses and purposes therein mentioned.
      Given under my hand and official seal this (day) day of (month), 2018.

_____

NOTARY PUBLIC in and for the State of California
My appointment expires (expiration date)

Using File Explorer to Open a Document Based on a Template

Quick Steps
Use File Explorer to Open a Document Based on a Template
1. Click File Explorer icon on taskbar.
2. Navigate to folder containing template.
3. Double-click template.

When a document is saved as a template, Word saves it in the Custom Office Templates folder. If a template is saved in another folder or location, it will not display when the *PERSONAL* option is clicked at the New backstage area. However, a document can be opened based on a template saved in a location other than the Custom Office Templates folder by opening the template in File Explorer. To do this, click the File Explorer icon on the taskbar, navigate to the folder containing the template, and then double-click the template. Instead of the template opening, a blank document opens that is based on the template.

In Project 8b, you saved the legal macros template in the Custom Office Templates folder and also the WL3C1 folder. In the next project, you will use File Explorer to open a blank document based on the legal macros template you saved to the WL3C1 folder.

Project 8c Running a Macro with Fill-in Fields

1. Open a document based on **1-LegalMacrosTemplate.dotm** in the WL3C1 folder on your storage medium using File Explorer by completing the following steps:
   a. Click the File Explorer icon on the taskbar. (The taskbar displays along the bottom of the screen.)
   b. Navigate to the WL3C1 folder and then double-click *1-LegalMacrosTemplate.dotm*.
2. Use the Object button on the Insert tab to insert the document **Affidavit.docx**, located in the WL3C1 folder, into the current document.
3. Position the insertion point at the beginning of the title *AFFIDAVIT OF TRUST* and then run the Title macro.
4. Select the numbered paragraphs of text (paragraphs 1 through 6) and then run the Indent macro.
5. Complete the following finds and replaces:
   a. Find all occurrences of *NAME* and replace them with *LOREN HOUSTON*. (Be sure to replace only the occurrences of *NAME* in all uppercase letters.) **Hint: Expand the Find and Replace dialog box and insert a check mark in the Match case check box.**
   b. Find the one occurrence of *ADDRESS* and replace it with *102 Marine Drive, Los Angeles, CA*. (Be sure to replace only the occurrence of *ADDRESS* in all uppercase letters.)
6. Press Ctrl + End to move the insertion point to the end of the document and then run the Notary macro by completing the following steps:
   a. Press Alt + Shift + S.
   b. When the macro stops and prompts you for the name of a person, type LOREN HOUSTON and then click OK.

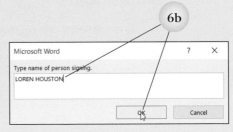

   c. When the macro stops and prompts you for the day, type 9th and then click OK.
   d. When the macro stops and prompts you for the month, type March and then click OK.
   e. When the macro stops and prompts you for the expiration date, type 12/31/2020 and then click OK.
7. Save the document and name it **1-Affidavit**.
8. Print and then close **1-Affidavit.docx**.
9. At a blank screen, change the macro security settings by completing the following steps:
   a. Click the Developer tab and then click the Macro Security button in the Code group.
   b. At the Trust Center dialog box, click the *Disable all macros with notification* option.
   c. Click OK.

Check Your Work

Chapter Summary

- Use options in the *Character Spacing* section of the Font dialog box with the Advanced tab selected to adjust character spacing and turn on kerning.

- The OpenType features available at the Font dialog box with the Advanced tab selected include options for choosing a ligature style, specifying number spacing and form, and applying stylistic sets.

- The Text Effects and Typography button in the Font group on the Home tab contains options for applying text effects such as outline, shadow, reflection, and glow effects as well as typography options such as number styles, ligatures, and stylistic sets.

- Click the Text Effects button at the Font dialog box to display the Format Text Effects dialog box. Use options at this dialog box to apply text fill and text outline effects to selected text.

- Change the default font with the Set As Default button at the Font dialog box. The default font can be changed for the current document or all documents based on Normal.dotm.

- Use the © symbol to identify copyrighted intellectual property, use the ™ symbol to identify a trademark, and use the ® symbol to identify a registered trademark.

- Insert regular, optional, and nonbreaking hyphens, as well as en dashes and em dashes, for specific purposes.

- Insert a nonbreaking hyphen by clicking the *Nonbreaking Hyphen* option at the Symbol dialog box with the Special Characters tab selected or by using the keyboard shortcut Ctrl + Shift + -.

- Use em dashes to indicate a break in a thought or to highlight a term or phrase by separating it from the rest of the sentence. To insert an em dash, type a word, type two hyphens, type the next word, and press the spacebar. An em dash also can be inserted with the keyboard shortcut Alt + Ctrl + - (on the numeric keypad) or at the Symbol dialog box with the Special Characters tab selected.

- Use an en dash to indicate inclusive dates, times, and numbers. To insert an en dash, click the *En Dash* option at the Symbol dialog box with the Special Characters tab selected or use the keyboard shortcut Ctrl + - (on the numeric keypad).

- Insert nonbreaking spaces between words that should not be separated across a line break. Insert a nonbreaking space by clicking the *Nonbreaking Space* option at the Symbol dialog box with the Special Characters tab selected or with the keyboard shortcut Ctrl + Shift + spacebar.

- Use the Special button at the expanded Find and Replace dialog box to find special characters and replace with other characters.

- The Office theme is applied to a Word document by default. The theme fonts are Calibri (Body) and Calibri Light (Headings).

- Search for a specific style and replace it with another style with options at the expanded Find and Replace dialog box. Click the Format button, click, *Style*, and then specify the search style at the Find Style dialog box and the replacement style at the Replace Style dialog box.

- Search a document for a body or heading font and then replace it with a different font. Display the Find and Replace dialog box with the Replace tab selected, click the Format button, and then click *Font*. At the Find Font dialog box, scroll up the *Font* list box and then click +*Body* to search for the body font or click +*Headings* to search for the heading font. Click in the *Replace with* text box and then complete the steps to insert the replacement font.

- Wildcard characters can be used to find text in a document. To use wildcard characters in a search to find or find and replace, display the expanded Find and Replace dialog box and then click the *Use wildcards* check box to insert a check mark.

- Insert a Merge Record # field in a main document to insert a record number in each merged document. Insert the field by clicking the Rules button in the Write & Insert Fields group on the Mailings tab and then click *Merge Record #* at the drop-down list.

- Use an If...Then...Else... field to compare two values and then, depending on what is determined, enter one set of text or another. To insert this field, click the Rules button in the Write & Insert Fields group on the Mailings tab and then click *If...Then...Else...* at the drop-down list. At the Word Field: IF dialog box, make the desired changes and then click OK.

- A main document can be merged with data source files such as a Word table, an Excel worksheet, an Access database table, or an Outlook contacts list.

- If the fields in a data source file do not match the fields used in the address block, use options at the Match Fields dialog box to match the field names.

- A macro can be recorded that starts automatically when Word is opened, when a document is opened, when a new document is opened, when a document is closed, or when Word is closed.

- A regularly used macro can be assigned to the Quick Access Toolbar using the Button button at the Record Macro dialog box.

- Specify macro settings at the Trust Center dialog box with *Macro Settings* selected in the left panel. Display the Trust Center dialog box by clicking the Macro Security button in the Code group on the Developer tab.

- Save a document as a macro-enabled document or a template as a macro-enabled template with the *Save as type* option at the Save As dialog box.

- Macros saved in a document can be copied to other documents or templates at the Organizer dialog box with the Macro Project Items tab selected. Display this dialog box by clicking the Macros button in the Code group on the Developer tab and then clicking the Organizer button at the Macros dialog box.

- A macro can be recorded that requires input from the keyboard when running the macro. When recording a macro, use the Fill-in field at the location that keyboard entry is required. The Fill-in field is available in the Field dialog box with *(All)* selected in the *Categories* list box.

- File Explorer can be used to open a document based on a template. To do this, click the File Explorer icon on the taskbar, navigate to the folder containing the template, and then double-click the template.

Commands Review

FEATURE	RIBBON TAB, GROUP	BUTTON, OPTION	KEYBOARD SHORTCUT
copyright symbol	Insert, Symbols	Ω, More Symbols	Alt + Ctrl + C
em dash	Insert, Symbols	Ω, More Symbols	Alt + Ctrl + - (on numeric keypad)
en dash	Insert, Symbols	Ω, More Symbols	Ctrl + - (on numeric keypad)
Field dialog box	Insert, Text	, Field	
Find and Replace dialog box with Find tab selected	Home, Editing	, Advanced Find	
Find and Replace dialog box with Replace tab selected	Home, Editing	, Replace	Ctrl + H
Font dialog box	Home, Font		Ctrl + D
insert merge fields	Mailings, Write & Insert Fields		
Insert Word Field: IF dialog box	Mailings, Write & Insert Fields	, If...Then...Else...	
Macros dialog box	Developer, Code OR View, Macros		Alt + F8
Merge Record # field	Mailings, Write & Insert Fields	, Merge Record #	
nonbreaking hyphen	Insert, Symbols	Ω, More Symbols	Ctrl + Shift + -
nonbreaking space	Insert, Symbols	Ω, More Symbols	Ctrl + Shift + spacebar
Record Macro dialog box	Developer, Code OR View, Macros		
registered trademark symbol			Alt + Ctrl + R
Symbol dialog box	Insert, Symbols	Ω, More Symbols	
Text Effects and Typography button	Home, Font	A ▾	
trademark symbol	Insert, Symbols	Ω, More Symbols	Alt + Ctrl + T
Trust Center dialog box	Developer, Code		

Workbook

Chapter study tools and assessment activities are available in the *Workbook* ebook. These resources are designed to help you further develop and demonstrate mastery of the skills learned in this chapter.

Microsoft®
Word

Formatting with Styles

CHAPTER 2

Performance Objectives

Upon successful completion of Chapter 2, you will be able to:

1 Create new styles from existing formatting and styles and without first formatting text

2 Assign keyboard shortcuts to styles

3 Modify styles and save styles in a template

4 Display all styles

5 Reveal style formatting

6 Save and delete a custom style set

7 Create and modify styles for multilevel lists and tables

8 Investigate document styles using the Style Inspector task pane

9 Manage and organize styles

Precheck

Check your current skills to help focus your study.

Word provides a number of predesigned styles, which are grouped into style sets, that you can use to apply consistent formatting in documents. If none of the predesigned styles provides the formatting you want, you can create your own styles. In this chapter, you will learn how to apply, create, modify, delete, manage, and organize styles, as well as how to save and delete a custom style set.

Data Files

Before beginning chapter work, copy the WL3C2 folder to your storage medium and then make WL3C2 the active folder.

SNAP

If you are a SNAP user, launch the Precheck and Tutorials from your Assignments page.

Project 1 **Create and Modify Styles for Bayside Travel Documents** **9 Parts**

You will create and apply custom styles to Bayside Travel documents. You will also modify the styles, save the styles in a style set, and then delete the style set.

Preview Finished Project

Creating a Style

Tutorial

Review: Applying and Modifying a Style

A style is a set of formatting instructions that can be applied to text. Word provides a number of predesigned styles and groups styles that apply similar formatting into style sets. If the predesigned styles provided by Word do not contain the desired formatting, a new style can be created. Create a style based on existing formatting, create a new style and apply all the formatting, or modify an existing style.

Creating a Style Based on Existing Formatting

Tutorial

Creating a New Style

To create a style based on existing formatting, apply the specific formatting to text in a document and then select the text. Click the More Styles button at the right side of the styles gallery in the Styles group on the Home tab and then click *Create a Style* at the drop-down gallery. At the Create New Style from Formatting dialog box, shown in Figure 2.1, type a name for the new style in the *Name* text box and then click OK. The style is inserted in the styles gallery and is available for use in the current document.

Quick Steps

Create a Style Based on Existing Formatting
1. Apply formatting to text.
2. Select text.
3. Click More Styles button in Styles group.
4. Click *Create a Style*.
5. Type name for new style.
6. Click OK.

Creating a Style Based on an Existing Style

To create a style based on an existing style, apply the style to text, make the desired formatting changes, and then select the text. Click the More Styles button right of the styles gallery in the Styles group and then click *Create a Style* at the drop-down gallery. At the Create New Style from Formatting dialog box, type a name for the new style in the *Name* text box and then click OK.

Create a Style Based on an Existing Style
1. Apply style to text.
2. Make formatting changes.
3. Select text.
4. Click More Styles button in Styles group.
5. Click *Create a Style*.
6. Type name for new style.
7. Click OK.

Figure 2.1 Create New Style from Formatting Dialog Box

Type a name for the new style in this text box.

This preview area displays the formatting applied by the style.

1. Open **BTStyles.docx** and then save it with the name **2-BTStyles**.
2. Create a style based on the formatting of the text *CustomTitle* by completing the following steps:
    a. Click the Show/Hide ¶ button in the Paragraph group on the Home tab to turn on the display of nonprinting characters.
    b. Select the text *CustomTitle*. (Make sure you select the paragraph symbol [¶] after *Title*.)
    c. Click the More Styles button right of the styles gallery in the Styles group.
    d. Click the *Create a Style* option.
    e. At the Create New Style from Formatting dialog box, type CustomTitle in the *Name* text box.
    f. Click OK.
    g. Click the Show/Hide ¶ button to turn off the display of nonprinting characters.
3. Save **2-BTStyles.docx**.

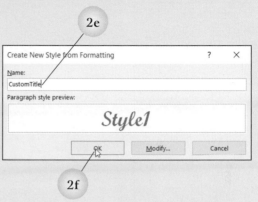

Creating a New Style

A new style can be created without first applying formatting to text. To do this, click the More Styles button right of the styles gallery in the Styles group and then click *Create a Style* at the drop-down gallery. At the Create New Style from Formatting dialog box, click the Modify button. This displays an expanded Create New Style from Formatting dialog box, as shown in Figure 2.2. At this dialog box, type a name for the new style in the *Name* text box and then use the *Style type* option box to specify the type of style being created. Click the *Style type* option box arrow and a drop-down list displays with options for creating a paragraph style, character style, linked style (both paragraph and character styles), table style, or list style. Choose the option that identifies the type of style being created.

The *Style based on* option has a default setting of *¶ Normal*. A new style can be based on an existing style. To do this, click the *Style based on* option box arrow and then click the desired style at the drop-down list. For example, a new style can be based on a predesigned style, such as the Heading 1 style. Click *Heading 1* style at the drop-down list and the formatting settings of the Heading 1 style display in the Create New Style from Formatting dialog box. Apply additional formatting at the dialog box to modify the formatting of the Heading 1 style. If a predesigned style contains some of the formatting for the new style, choosing the predesigned style at the *Style based on* option box drop-down list saves formatting time.

Use the *Style for following paragraph* option to specify what style to use for the next paragraph in the document when the Enter key is pressed. For example, a style can be created that formats a caption heading and is then followed by a style that applies paragraph formatting to the text after the caption heading (such as italic formatting or a specific font and font size). In this situation, the style would be created that applies the desired paragraph formatting to the text that follows a caption heading. The caption heading style would be created and then the *Style for following paragraph* option would specify that the paragraph style is applied when the Enter key is pressed after applying the caption heading style.

Figure 2.2 Expanded Create New Style from Formatting Dialog Box

Type a name for the style in this text box.

Choose a style type in this option box, such as paragraph, character (or both), table, or list.

Choose a style in this option box on which to base the new style.

Use option boxes and buttons in this section to apply formatting to the style.

Click this button to display a list of formatting options.

Create New Style from Formatting ? ×

Properties

Name: Style1

Style type: Linked (paragraph and character)

Style based on: ¶ Normal

Style for following paragraph: ¶ Style1

Formatting

Calibri (Body) 11 B I U Automatic

Previous Paragraph Previous Paragraph Previous Paragraph Previous Paragraph Previous Paragraph Previous Paragraph Previous Paragraph Previous Paragraph Previous Paragraph Previous Paragraph

Sample Text Sample Text Sample Text Sample Text Sample Text Sample Text Sample Text Sample Text Sample Text Sample Text Sample Text Sample Text Sample Text Sample Text Sample Text Sample Text Sample Text Sample Text Sample Text Sample Text

Following Paragraph Following Paragraph

Style: Show in the Styles gallery
Based on: Normal

☑ Add to the Styles gallery ☐ Automatically update
⦿ Only in this document ○ New documents based on this template

Format ▾ OK Cancel

The Create New Style from Formatting dialog box contains a number of options for specifying formatting for the new style. Use options in the *Formatting* section to apply character and paragraph formatting, such as changing the font, font size, font color, and font effects and changing paragraph alignment, spacing, and indenting. Click the Format button in the lower left corner of the dialog box and a drop-down list displays with a number of formatting options. Use options at this drop-down list to specify formatting for the style with options in dialog boxes such as the Font, Paragraph, Tabs, Borders, Language, and Frame dialog boxes.

Unless the Create New Style from Formatting dialog has been customized, the *Add to the Styles gallery* check box in the lower left corner of the dialog box contains a check mark. With this option active, the new style will display in the Styles group on the Home tab. Additionally, the *Only in this document* option is active. With this option active, the new style is saved only with the current document. To make the style available for new documents based on the Normal template (or any other template on which the current document is based), click the *New documents based on this template* option. The *Automatically update* check box is empty by default. Insert a check mark in the check box for this option and a style applied to text will be updated when changes are made to the style. Keep this option inactive if text should retain the original style formatting.

Assigning a Keyboard Shortcut to a Style

Consider assigning a keyboard shortcut to a style that is applied on a regular basis. A keyboard shortcut can be assigned to a style using any of the following combinations:

Alt + letter

Alt + Ctrl + letter

Alt + Shift + letter

Ctrl + Shift + letter

Alt + Ctrl + Shift + letter

Word already uses many combinations for Word functions. For example, pressing Ctrl + Shift + F displays the Font dialog box.

Assign a keyboard shortcut to a style at the expanded Create New Style from Formatting dialog box by clicking the Format button and then clicking *Shortcut key* at the drop-down list. This displays the Customize Keyboard dialog box, shown in Figure 2.3. With the insertion point positioned in the *Press new shortcut key* text box, press the desired keys. Word inserts the message *Currently assigned to* below the *Current keys* list box. If the keyboard shortcut is already assigned to a command, the command is indicated after the *Currently assigned to* message. If Word is not already using the keyboard shortcut, *[unassigned]* displays after the *Currently assigned to* message. When assigning a keyboard shortcut, use an unassigned combination of keystrokes.

Figure 2.3 Customize Keyboard Dialog Box

Press the shortcut keys on the keyboard and the key names display in this text box.

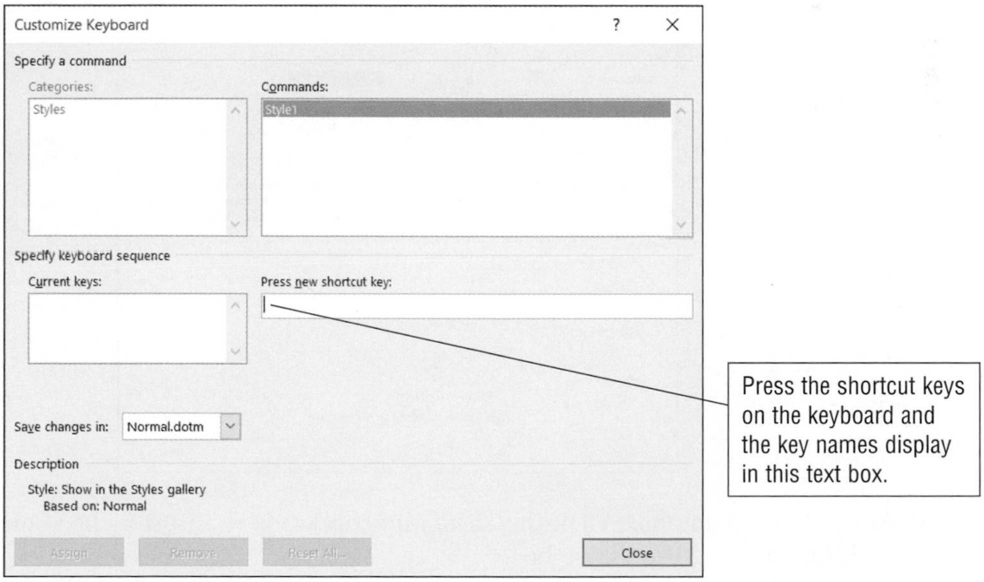

1. With **2-BTStyles.docx** open, press Ctrl + End to move the insertion point to the end of the document.
2. Click the More Styles button right of the styles gallery in the Styles group.
3. Click *Create a Style* at the drop-down gallery.
4. At the Create New Style from Formatting dialog box, type CustomEmphasis in the *Name* text box.
5. Click the Modify button.

6. At the expanded Create New Style from Formatting dialog box, make the following changes:
   a. Click the *Font Size* option box arrow and then click *12* at the drop-down list.
   b. Click the *Font Color* option box arrow and then click the *Dark Blue* color (ninth option in the *Standard Colors* section).
   c. Click the Format button at the bottom of the Create New Style from Formatting dialog box and then click *Font* at the drop-down list.

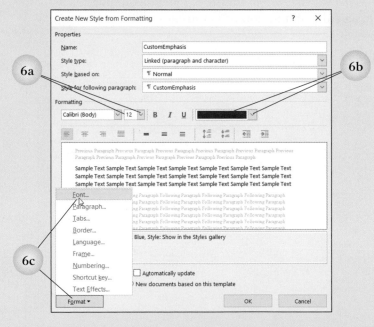

   d. At the Font dialog box, click the *Small caps* check box to insert a check mark and then click OK to close the dialog box.
   e. Click the Format button and then click *Paragraph* at the drop-down list.
   f. At the Paragraph dialog box with the Indents and Spacing tab selected, click the *Left* measurement box up arrow in the *Indentation* section until *0.3″* displays.
   g. Select the current measurement in the *After* measurement box in the *Spacing* section and then type 3.
   h. Click OK to close the Paragraph dialog box.
   i. Click OK to close the Create New Style from Formatting dialog box.

7. Create a character style and assign a keyboard shortcut to it by completing the following steps:

a. Click the *No Spacing* style in the Styles group on the Home tab.

b. Click the More Styles button at the right side of the styles gallery in the Styles group and then click *Create a Style* at the drop-down gallery.

c. At the Create New Style from Formatting dialog box, type Zenith in the *Name* text box.

d. Click the Modify button.

e. At the Create New Style from Formatting dialog box, click the *Style type* option box arrow and then click *Character* at the drop-down list.

f. Click the *Font* option box arrow, scroll down the drop-down list, and then click *Imprint MT Shadow*.

g. Click the Format button at the bottom of the dialog box and then click *Font* at the drop-down list.

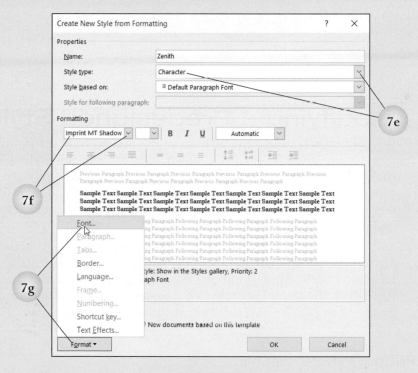

h. At the Font dialog box, click the *Small caps* check box (displays with a solid square inside) to insert a check mark.

i. Click OK to close the dialog box.

j. Click the Format button and then click *Shortcut key* at the drop-down list.

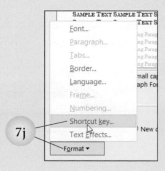

k. At the Customize Keyboard dialog box with the insertion point positioned in the *Press new shortcut key* text box, press the keys Alt + Z.

l. Check to make sure *[unassigned]* displays after *Currently assigned to*.

m. Click the Assign button.

n. Click the Close button to close the Customize Keyboard dialog box.

o. Click OK to close the Create New Style from Formatting dialog box.

8. Save **2-BTStyles.docx**.

Modifying a Predesigned Style

Quick Steps

Modify a Predesigned Style
1. Right-click style in Styles group or Styles drop-down gallery.
2. Click *Modify*.
3. Type new name for style.
4. Make changes.
5. Click OK.

If a predesigned style contains most of the desired formatting, modify the style to create a new style. To do this, right-click the style in the Styles group and then click *Modify* at the shortcut menu. This displays the Modify Style dialog box, which contains the same options as the Create New Style from Formatting dialog box. Type a new name in the *Name* text box, make the desired changes, and then click OK.

Another method for modifying a predesigned style is to update the style to match selected text. To do this, apply a predesigned style to text, such as the Heading 1 style. Apply additional formatting to the text and then select the text. Right-click the *Heading 1* style in the Styles group and then click the *Update Heading 1 to Match Selection* option at the shortcut menu.

Project 1c **Modifying a Predesigned Style** Part 3 of 9

1. With **2-BTStyles.docx** open, modify the Heading 2 style by completing the following steps:

a. Right-click the *Heading 2* style in the Styles group on the Home tab and then click *Modify* at the shortcut menu.

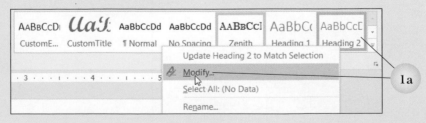

b. At the Modify Style dialog box, type CustomHeading in the *Name* text box.

c. Click the *Font* option box arrow and then click *Candara* at the drop-down list.

d. Click the Italic button.

e. Click the *Font Color* option box arrow and then click the *Dark Blue* color (ninth option in the *Standard Colors* section).

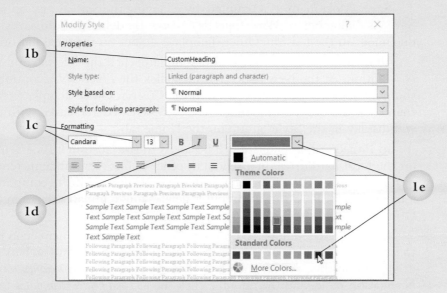

f. Click the Format button at the bottom of the dialog box and then click *Paragraph* at the drop-down list.

g. At the Paragraph dialog box with the Indents and Spacing tab selected, select the current measurement in the *After* measurement box in the *Spacing* section and then type 6.

h. Click OK to close the Paragraph dialog box.

i. Click the Format button at the bottom of the dialog box and then click *Border* at the drop-down list.

j. At the Borders and Shading dialog box, click the Shading tab.

k. Click the *Fill* option box arrow and then click the *Blue, Accent 1, Lighter 80%* color (fifth column, second row in the *Theme Colors* section).

l. Click OK to close the Borders and Shading dialog box.

m. Click OK to close the Modify Style dialog box.

2. Save **2-BTStyles.docx**.

Saving Styles in a Template

Quick Steps

Open a Document Based on a Template
1. Click File tab.
2. Click *New* option.
3. Click PERSONAL option.
4. Click template thumbnail.

The styles created in 2-BTStyles.docx are saved only in that document. To make the styles available for future Bayside Travel documents, save the document containing the styles as a template. With the styles saved in a template, a document can be opened based on the template and the styles are available.

Save a document as a template by changing the *Save as type* option at the Save As dialog box to *Word Template (*.dotx)*. By default, Word saves a template document in the Custom Office Templates folder on the local hard drive.

To open a document based on a template, click the File tab and then click the *New* option. At the New backstage area, click the *PERSONAL* option to display thumbnails of the templates saved in the Custom Office Templates folder and then click the desired thumbnail. The styles created and saved with the template will display in the Styles group on the Home tab.

In Project 1d, a template will be saved to the Custom Office Templates folder on the local hard drive. In a school or other public environment, templates saved in the Custom Office Templates folder may be deleted if the computer is reset on a regular basis. Resetting a computer deletes any templates saved in the Custom Office Templates folder.

If you are working on a computer in a public environment, you may want to save a backup of your template on your storage medium (such as a USB flash drive). To do this, display the Open dialog box, click the *Documents* folder in the Navigation pane, and then double-click the *Custom Office Templates* folder that displays in the Content pane. Right-click the template you want to copy and then click *Copy* at the shortcut menu. Click the drive representing your USB flash drive (or other storage device) and then double-click the *WL3C2* folder. Right-click in a blank area of the Content pane and then click *Paste* at the shortcut menu. Complete similar steps to copy a template from your storage device to the Custom Office Templates folder on the local hard drive.

Project 1d   Saving Styles in a Template and Applying Custom Styles   Part 4 of 9

1. With **2-BTStyles.docx** open, press Ctrl + A to select all the text in the document (except the header and footer) and then press the Delete key.
2. Click the *No Spacing* style in the Styles group on the Home tab.
3. Save the document as a template by completing the following steps:
   a. Press the F12 function key to display the Save As dialog box.
   b. Click the *Save as type* option box and then click *Word Template (*.dotx)* at the drop-down list.
   c. Click in the *File name* text box, type your three initials followed by a hyphen, and then type BTTemplate.
   d. Click the Save button. (This saves the template in the Custom Office Templates folder.)
4. Save **XXX-BTTemplate.dotx** to the WL3C2 folder on your storage medium by pressing the F12 function key to display the Save As dialog box, navigating to the WL3C2 folder, and then clicking the Save button.
5. Close **XXX-BTTemplate.dotx** (where your initials display in place of the *XXX*).

6. Open a document based on **XXX-BTTemplate.dotx** by completing the following steps:
   a. Click the File tab and then click the *New* option.
   b. At the New backstage area, click the *PERSONAL* option.
   c. Click the *XXX-BTTemplate* thumbnail (where your initials display in place of the *XXX*).
7. Insert a document into the existing document by completing the following steps:
   a. Press the Enter key, click the Insert tab, and then click the Object button arrow in the Text group.
   b. Click *Text from File* at the drop-down list.
   c. Navigate to the WL3C2 folder and then double-click **BTZenith.docx**.
8. Apply the CustomTitle style by completing the following steps:
   a. Click in the title *Extreme Adventures*.
   b. Click the Home tab and then click the *CustomTitle* style in the Styles group.
   c. Scroll to the end of the document, click in the title *Volunteer Adventures,* and then click the *CustomTitle* style.
9. Apply the CustomHeading style by completing the following steps:
   a. Press Ctrl + Home to move the insertion point to the beginning of the document.
   b. Click in the heading *Antarctic Adventures*.
   c. Click the *CustomHeading* style in the Styles group. (Note that the style name begins with *Heading2* when you hover the mouse pointer over the style thumbnail.)

   d. Apply the CustomHeading style to the headings *Tall-Ship Adventures* and *Bicycling Adventures*.
10. Apply the CustomEmphasis style by completing the following steps:
    a. Select the lines of text in the *Antarctic Adventures* section that contain money amounts.
    b. Click the *CustomEmphasis* style in the Styles group.
    c. Apply the CustomEmphasis style to the lines of text in the *Tall-Ship Adventures* section that contain money amounts.
    d. Apply the CustomEmphasis style to the lines of text in the *Bicycling Adventures* section that contain money amounts.
11. Select the text *Zenith Adventures* in the first sentence in the first paragraph of text below the *Extreme Adventures* title and then press Alt + Z. (This applies the Zenith style.)
12. Press Ctrl + End to move the insertion point to the end of the document. Select the text *Zenith Adventures* in the first sentence of the last paragraph of text and then press Alt + Z to apply the Zenith style.
13. Save the document and name it **2-BTZenith.docx**.

Check Your Work

Modifying an Applied Style

One of the advantages of applying styles in a document is that modifying the formatting of a style will automatically update all the text in the document to which that style has been applied. Using styles streamlines formatting and maintains consistency in documents.

1. With **2-BTZenith.docx** open, edit the CustomTitle style to change the font size and alignment by completing the following steps:
   a. Right-click the *CustomTitle* style in the *Styles* gallery in the Styles group on the Home tab.
   b. Click *Modify* at the shortcut menu.
   c. At the Modify Style dialog box, change the font size to 22 points.
   d. Click the Align Left button in the *Formatting* section.
   e. Click OK to close the Modify Style dialog box.
2. Scroll through the document and notice that the custom title style is applied to both titles in the document.
3. Save **2-BTZenith.docx**.

Check Your Work

Displaying All Styles

Each style set contains a title style and body text style, a number of heading level styles, and other styles that are designed to work together in a single document. Only the styles for the currently selected style set display in the *Styles* drop-down gallery or Styles task pane. Display all available styles with options at the Style Pane Options dialog box, shown in Figure 2.4. Display this dialog box by clicking

Figure 2.4 Style Pane Options Dialog Box

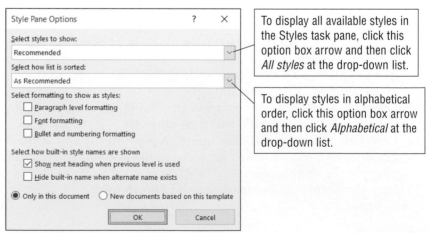

To display all available styles in the Styles task pane, click this option box arrow and then click *All styles* at the drop-down list.

To display styles in alphabetical order, click this option box arrow and then click *Alphabetical* at the drop-down list.

the Styles group task pane launcher or pressing the keyboard shortcut Alt + Ctrl + Shift + S to display the Styles task pane and then clicking the Options hyperlink in the lower right corner of the task pane.

To display all available styles, click the *Select styles to show* option box arrow and then click *All styles* at the drop-down list. Specify how the styles are sorted in the Styles task pane with the *Select how list is sorted* option.

1. With **2-BTZenith.docx** open, display all available styles in the Styles task pane by completing the following steps:
   a. Click the Styles group task pane launcher.
   b. Click the Options hyperlink in the lower right corner of the Styles task pane.
   c. At the Style Pane Options dialog box, click the *Select styles to show* option box arrow and then click *All styles* at the drop-down list.
   d. Click the *Select how list is sorted* option box arrow and then click *Alphabetical* at the drop-down list.
   e. Click OK to close the dialog box.
2. Apply styles by completing the following steps:
   a. Select the lines of text in the *Antarctic Adventures* section that contain money amounts.
   b. Click the *Body Text Indent* style.
   c. Click the *Book Title* style.
   d. Apply the Body Text Indent and Book Title styles to the two other sections of text that contain money amounts.
3. Save and then print **2-BTZenith.docx**.

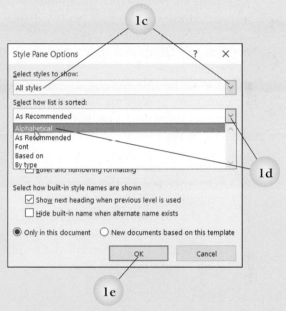

Check Your Work

Revealing Style Formatting

Hovering the mouse pointer over a style in the Styles task pane causes a ScreenTip to display with information about the formatting applied by the style and the styles in the styles gallery in the Styles group display with a visual representation of the formatting applied by the style. Other methods for displaying a visual representation of styles include inserting a check mark in the *Show Preview* check box in the Styles task pane and displaying the Reveal Formatting task pane by pressing Shift + F1.

1. With **2-BTZenith.docx** open, view the styles in the Styles task pane by completing the following steps:
   a. With the Styles task pane open, click the *Show Preview* check box to insert a check mark.
   b. Scroll through the list box to see how styles display with the preview feature turned on.
   c. Click the *Show Preview* check box to remove the check mark.
   d. Close the Styles task pane by clicking the Close button in the upper right corner of the task pane.
2. Display style formatting in the Reveal Formatting task pane by completing the following steps:
   a. Press Shift + F1 to turn on the display of the Reveal Formatting task pane.
   b. Click the *Distinguish style source* check box to insert a check mark.
   c. Click in the title *Extreme Adventures* and notice the formatting applied by the style displayed in the Reveal Formatting task pane.
   d. Click in the heading *Antarctic Adventures* and notice the formatting applied by the style displayed in the Reveal Formatting task pane.
   e. Click other text in the document and view the formatting.
   f. Click the *Distinguish style source* check box to remove the check mark.
   g. Press Shift + F1 to turn off the display of the Reveal Formatting task pane.

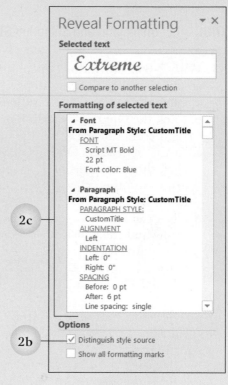

Saving a Custom Style Set

Word provides a number of predesigned styles and groups styles that apply similar formatting into style sets. These style sets are available in the Document Formatting group on the Design tab. In addition to the style sets provided by Word, styles can be created and then saved into a custom style set. For example, the styles saved in the template XXX-BTTemplate.dotx can be saved as a custom style set. The advantage to creating a custom style set is that the set is saved in Normal.dotm and is available for all documents, not just documents based on a specific template.

Quick Steps

Save a Custom Style Set
1. Click Design tab.
2. Click More Style Sets button in Document Formatting group.
3. Click *Save as a New Style Set*.
4. Type custom style set file name.
5. Click Save button.

To save styles in a custom style set, click the Design tab, click the More Style Sets button at the right side of the style sets gallery in the Document Formatting group, and then click *Save as a New Style Set* at the drop-down gallery. This displays the Save as a New Style Set dialog box and makes the QuickStyles subfolder on the local hard drive the active folder. The *Save as type* option at the dialog box is set at *Word Template (*.dotx)*. The custom style set is saved as a template that is available with the Normal.dotm template, which is the default template that most documents are based on. Type a name for the style set in the *File name* text box and then press the Enter key or click the Save button. The custom style set will be available in the style sets gallery in the Document Formatting group on the Design tab for all documents.

Changing Default Settings

If a predesigned or custom style set is applied to most documents, it can be specified as the default style set for all future documents. Change the default style set with the Set as Default button in the Document Formatting group on the Design tab. In addition to changing the default style set, default settings can be changed by making changes to the theme, theme colors, theme fonts, theme effects, and paragraph spacing in a document. Click the Set as Default button and a confirmation message displays asking if the current style set and theme should be the default. At this message, click the Yes button.

When the current style set, themes, theme colors, theme fonts, theme effects, and paragraph spacing are specified as the default, the changes are made to the Normal.dotm template. To return to the original default settings, open a document that was created before the default settings were changed, click the Set as Default button in the Document Formatting group on the Design tab, and then click the Yes button at the confirmation message.

Project 1h Saving Styles in a Custom Style Set   Part 8 of 9

1. With **2-BTZenith.docx** open, save the styles in a custom style set by completing the following steps:
   a. Click the Design tab.
   b. Click the More Style Sets button at the right side of the style sets gallery in the Document Formatting group.
   c. Click the *Save as a New Style Set* option at the drop-down gallery.
   d. At the Save as a New Style Set dialog box, type XXX-BTStyles (typing your initials in place of the *XXX*) and then press the Enter key.

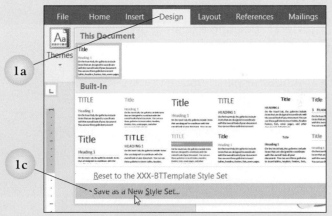

2. Save, print, and then close **2-BTZenith.docx**.
3. Open **BTVacations.docx** and then save it with the name **2-BTVacations**.
4. Apply the XXX-BTStyles custom style set (where your initials display in place of the *XXX*) by completing the following steps:
   a. Click the Design tab.
   b. Click the More Style Sets button at the right side of the style sets gallery in the Document Formatting group.
   c. Click the *XXX-BTStyles* custom style set (where your initials display in place of the *XXX*) in the *Custom* section of the drop-down gallery.

5. Click the Home tab and then apply the following styles to the specified text:
   a. Apply the CustomTitle style to the title *Vacation Adventures*.
   b. Apply the CustomHeading style to the headings *Disneyland Adventure*, *Florida Adventure*, and *Cancun Adventure*.
   c. Apply the CustomEmphasis style to the bulleted text below the *Disneyland Adventure* heading, *Florida Adventure* heading, and *Cancun Adventure* heading.
6. Save and then print **2-BTVacations.docx**.

Check Your Work

Deleting a Custom Style Set

Quick Steps
Delete a Custom Style Set
1. Click Design tab.
2. Click More Style Sets button in the Document Formatting group.
3. Right-click custom style set in *Custom* section.
4. Click *Delete*.
5. Click Yes.

If a custom style set is no longer needed, delete it at the style sets drop-down gallery. To do this, click the Design tab and then click the More Style Sets button at the right side of the style sets gallery in the Document Formatting group. At the drop-down gallery, right-click the custom style set in the *Custom* section and then click *Delete* at the shortcut menu. At the confirmation message, click the Yes button.

Project 1i Deleting a Custom Style Set   **Part 9 of 9**

1. With **2-BTVacations.docx** open, delete the XXX-BTStyles custom style set (where your initials display in place of the *XXX*) by completing the following steps:
   a. Click the Design tab.
   b. Click the More Style Sets button at the right side of the style sets gallery in the Document Formatting group.
   c. Right-click the *XXX-BTStyles* custom style set (where your initials display in place of the *XXX*) in the *Custom* section of the drop-down gallery.
   d. Click *Delete* at the shortcut menu.
   e. At the message that displays, click the Yes button.
2. Save and then close **2-BTVacations.docx**.

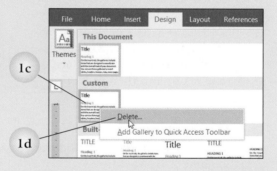

Project 2 Create, Apply, and Modify a Multilevel List and Table Style for Bayside Travel Documents   6 Parts

You will create, apply, and modify a multilevel list style and table style for Bayside Travel documents. You will also copy styles between templates at the Organizer dialog box.

Preview Finished Project

Creating and Modifying a Multilevel List and a Table Style

Custom character and paragraph styles are available in the Styles group on the Home tab and custom style sets are available in the style sets gallery in the Document Formatting group on the Design tab. Other types of styles can also be created, such as multilevel list styles and table styles, but these styles cannot be saved in the Styles group on the Home tab or in the style sets gallery in the Document Formatting group. However, multilevel list styles and table styles can be saved in the current document or a template document.

Tutorial

Creating a
Multilevel List
Style

Creating a Multilevel List Style

Word provides a number of predesigned list styles that can be applied to text in a document. These styles are generally paragraph styles that apply formatting to text such as paragraph indenting and spacing and that apply formatting only to one level of the list. To create a multilevel list style that applies formatting to more than one level, create the style at the Define New List Style dialog box, shown in Figure 2.5. Display this dialog box by clicking the Multilevel List button in the Paragraph group on the Home tab and then clicking *Define New List Style* at the drop-down list. A multilevel list style can also be created at the Create New Style from Formatting dialog box by changing the *Style type* to *List*.

The Define New List Style dialog box (and the Create New Style from Formatting dialog box with *List* selected as the *Style type* option) contains the same options as the Create New Style from Formatting dialog box with *Paragraph*, *Character*, or *Linked (paragraph and character)* selected along with some additional

Figure 2.5 Define New List Style Dialog Box

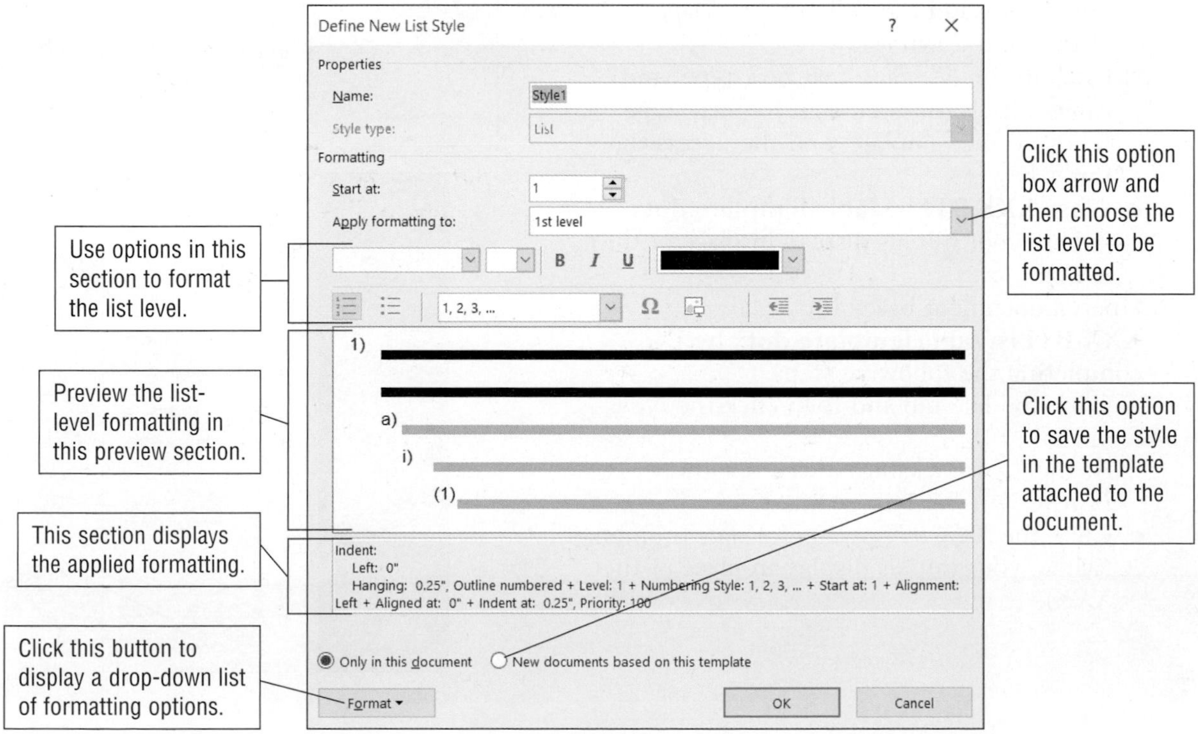

options, such as the *Start at* and *Apply formatting to* options. By default, the *Apply formatting to* option is set at *1st level*. With this option selected, apply the formatting for the letter, number, or symbol that begins the first level of the list. (The formatting applied affects only the letter, number, or symbol—not the following text.)

After specifying formatting for the first level, click the *Apply formatting to* option box arrow, click *2nd level* at the drop-down list, and then apply the formatting for the second level. Continue in this manner until formatting has been applied to the desired number of levels.

Updating a Template with an Updated Style

Create a style in a document based on a template and the style can be saved in the template, making it available for any future documents created with that template. A document based on a template is attached to the template. To save a style in a template, open a document based on the template, create the style, and then click the *New documents based on this template* option at the Create New Style dialog box. When the document is saved, a message displays asking if the attached document template should be updated. At this message, click the Yes button.

Project 2a **Saving a Document as a Template and Creating and Applying a Multilevel List Style**   **Part 1 of 6**

1. Open **BTListTableTemplate.docx** and then save it as a template by completing the following steps:
   a. Press the F12 function key to display the Save As dialog box.
   b. At the Save As dialog box, click the *Save as type* option box and then click *Word Template (*.dotx)* at the drop-down list.
   c. Click in the *File name* text box, type your three initials followed by a hyphen, type BTListTableTemplate, and then press the Enter key.
   d. Close **XXX-BTListTableTemplate.dotx** (where your initials display in place of the *XXX*).
2. Open a document based on **XXX-BTListTableTemplate.dotx** by completing the following steps:
   a. Click the File tab and then click the *New* option.
   b. At the New backstage area, click the *PERSONAL* option.
   c. Click the *XXX-BTListTableTemplate* thumbnail (where your initials display in place of the *XXX*).

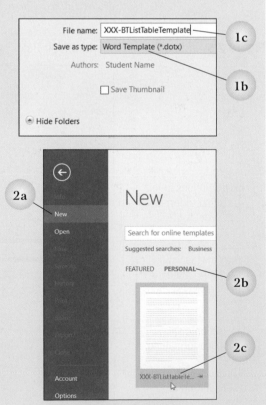

3. At the document based on the template, create a multilevel list style by completing the following steps:
   a. Click the Multilevel List button in the Paragraph group on the Home tab.
   b. Click the *Define New List Style* option at the bottom of the drop-down list.
   c. At the Define New List Style dialog box, type BTMultilevelList in the *Name* text box.
   d. Click the Bold button.
   e. Click the option box arrow right of the option box containing *1, 2, 3, …* and then click *A, B, C, …* at the drop-down list.
   f. Click the *Font Color* option box arrow and then click the *Blue* color (eighth option in the *Standard Colors* section).
   g. Click the *Apply formatting to* option box arrow and then click *2nd level* at the drop-down list.

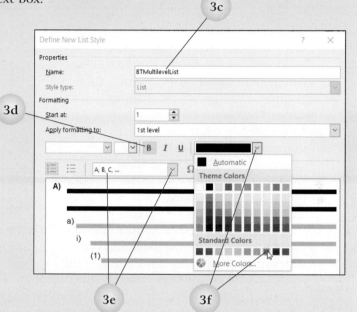

   h. Click the Symbol button below the *Font Color* option.
   i. At the Symbol dialog box, change the font to Wingdings, double-click the current number in the *Character code* text box, type 173 to select the ✸ symbol, and then click OK.
   j. At the Define New List Style dialog box, click the Bold button and then change the font color to standard blue.
   k. Click the *Apply formatting to* option box arrow and then click *3rd level* at the drop-down list.
   l. Click the Symbol button.
   m. At the Symbol dialog box, make sure that Wingdings is selected as the font, double-click the current number in the *Character code* text box, type 252 to select the ✓ symbol, and then click OK.
   n. At the Define New List Style dialog box, click the Bold button and then make sure the font color is standard blue.
   o. Click the *New documents based on this template* option at the bottom of the dialog box.
   p. Click OK to close the Define New List Style dialog box.
4. Close the document without saving it. At the message that displays asking if you want to save changes to **XXX-BTListTableTemplate.dotx**, click the Save button.
5. Open a document based on the template by completing the following steps:
   a. Click the File tab and then click the *New* option.
   b. At the New backstage area, click the *PERSONAL* option.
   c. Click the *XXX-BTListTableTemplate* thumbnail.
6. Insert a document into the current document by completing the following steps:
   a. Click the Insert tab.
   b. Click the Object button arrow and then click *Text from File* at the drop-down list.
   c. Navigate to the WL3C2 folder on your storage medium and then double-click **BTTourList.docx**.

7. Apply the multilevel style you created by completing the following steps:
   a. Select the text that was just inserted.
   b. Click the Home tab and then click the Multilevel List button in the Paragraph group.
   c. If necessary, scroll down the drop-down list and then click the multilevel list style you created (located in the *List Styles* section). (Hover the mouse pointer over the multilevel list and a ScreenTip will display with the style name.)
8. Add the text shown in Figure 2.6 to the document by completing the following steps:
   a. Move the insertion point so it is immediately right of the text *Double-occupancy rate: $2,755* and then press the Enter key. (This moves the insertion point down to the next line and inserts a check mark bullet.)
   b. Click the Decrease Indent button in the Paragraph group on the Home tab two times to move the insertion point to the left margin. (This inserts *B)* in the document.)

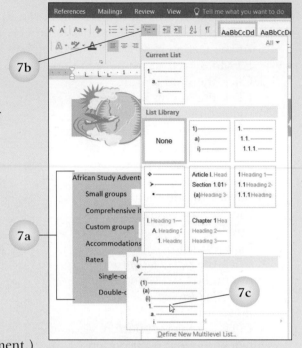

   c. Type the text shown in Figure 2.6. (When typing the text, click the Increase Indent button to move the insertion point to the next level or click the Decrease Indent button to move the insertion point to the previous level.)
9. Click the Design tab, click the Paragraph Spacing button in the Document Formatting group, and then click *Double* at the drop-down gallery.
10. Save the document in the WL3C2 folder on your storage medium and name it **2-BTTours**.
11. Print and then close **2-BTTours.docx**.
12. If you are working on a computer in a public environment, such as a school, make a backup of **XXX-BTListTableTemplate.dotx** by copying **XXX-BTListTableTemplate.dotx** from the Custom Office Templates folder in the Documents folder on the local hard drive to the WL3C2 folder.

Check Your Work

Figure 2.6 Project 2a

Southwest Sun Adventure
   Small groups
   Guided day trips
   Grand Canyon vistas
   Bilingual tour guides
   Rates
      Single-occupancy rate: $1,450
      Double-occupancy rate: $1,249

Creating a Table Style

The Table Tools Design tab contains a number of predesigned styles that can be applied to a table. If none of these styles applies the desired formatting to a table, create a custom table style.

Create a table style at the Create New Style from Formatting dialog box with *Table* selected in the *Style type* option box, as shown in Figure 2.7. Display this dialog box by clicking the More Styles button at the right side of the styles gallery in the Styles group on the Home tab and then clicking *Create a Style*. At the Create New Style from Formatting dialog box, click the Modify button. Click the *Style type* option box arrow and then click *Table* at the drop-down list. This dialog box can also be displayed by inserting a table in the document, clicking the More Table Styles button at the right side of the table styles gallery in the Table Styles group on the Table Tools Design tab, and then clicking *New Table Style* at the drop-down list.

The Create New Style from Formatting dialog box with *Table* selected as the style type contains options for formatting the entire table or specific portions of the table. By default, *Whole table* is selected in the *Apply formatting to* option. With this option selected, any formatting options that are chosen will affect the entire table. To format a specific part of the table, click the *Apply formatting to* option box arrow and then click the desired option at the drop-down list. Use options at this drop-down list to specify formatting for sections in the table, such as the header row, total row, first column, last column, odd banded rows, even banded rows, and so on.

Figure 2.7 Create New Style from Formatting Dialog Box with the Table Style Type Selected

Use options in this section to format the whole table or specific parts of the table.

Click this option box arrow and then choose the part of the table to format.

Preview the table formatting in this section.

Review the applied formatting in this section.

Click this button to display a drop-down list of formatting options.

1. Open **XXX-BTListTableTemplate.dotx** from the Custom Office Templates folder in the Documents folder on the local hard drive. If your template does not appear in the Custom Office Templates folder, open the template from the WL3C2 folder on your storage medium. (Open the template at the Open dialog box [not through the New backstage area].)
2. Create a table style by completing the following steps:
   a. Click the More Styles button at the right side of the styles gallery in the Styles group on the Home tab and then click *Create a Style* at the drop-down list.
   b. At the Create New Style from Formatting dialog box, type BTTable in the *Name* text box.
   c. Click the Modify button.
   d. At the Create New Style from Formatting dialog box, click the *Style type* option box arrow and then click *Table* at the drop-down list.

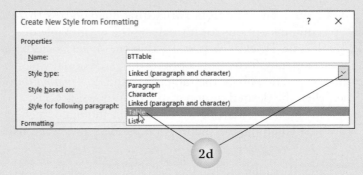

2d

   e. Make sure *Whole table* is selected in the *Apply formatting to* option.
   f. Click the *Font* option box arrow and then click *Constantia* at the drop-down list.
   g. Click the *Font Size* option box arrow and then click *12* at the drop-down list.
   h. Click the *Font Color* option box arrow and then click the *Dark Blue* color (ninth color option in the *Standard Colors* section).
   i. Click the Border button arrow and then click *All Borders* at the drop-down list. (See the image below to locate the button.)

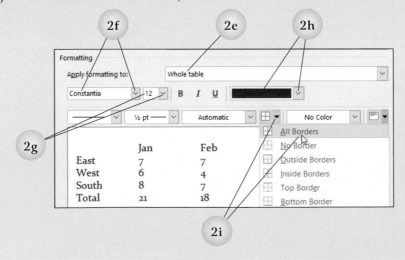

j. Click the *Apply formatting to* option box arrow and then click *Header row* at the drop-down list.
k. Click the *Font Size* option box arrow and then click *14* at the drop-down list.
l. Click the Bold button.
m. Click the *Fill Color* option box arrow and then click *Orange, Accent 2, Lighter 40%* (sixth column, fourth row in the *Theme Colors* section).
n. Click the Alignment button arrow immediately right of the *Fill Color* option and then click *Align Center* at the drop-down list.

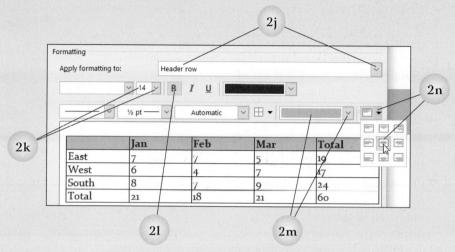

o. Click the *Apply formatting to* option box arrow and then click *Even banded rows* at the drop-down list.
p. Click the *Fill Color* option box arrow and then click *Orange, Accent 2, Lighter 60%* (sixth column, third row in the *Theme Colors* section).
q. Click OK to close the Create New Style from Formatting dialog box.
3. If you opened the template from the WL3C2 folder, click the Save button on the Quick Access Toolbar.
4. Save the template to the Custom Office Templates folder by completing the following steps:
   a. Press the F12 function key to display the Save As dialog box.
   b. Click the *Save as type* option box and then click *Word Document (*.docx)*.
   c. Click the *Save as type* option box again and then click *Word Template (*.dotx)*. (This ensures that the Custom Office Templates folder is active.)
   d. Click the Save button and then click the Yes button if a message displays asking if you want to replace the existing template.
   e. Close **XXX-BTListTableTemplate.dotx**.
5. Open a document based on the template by completing the following steps:
   a. Click the File tab and then click the *New* option.
   b. At the New backstage area, click the *PERSONAL* option.
   c. Click the *XXX-BTListTableTemplate* thumbnail (where your initials display in place of the *XXX*).
6. Insert a document into the current document by completing the following steps:
   a. Press the Enter key two times and then click the Insert tab.
   b. Click the Object button arrow in the Text group and then click *Text from File* at the drop-down list.
   c. Navigate to the WL3C2 folder and then double-click **BTAdvTables.docx**.
7. Apply the table style you created by completing the following steps:
   a. Click in any cell in the top table.
   b. Click the Table Tools Design tab.

c. In the Table Styles group, click the table style you created. (Your table style should be the first thumbnail in the group. If it is not, click the More Table Styles button at the right side of the table styles gallery and then click your table style at the drop-down gallery. To find your table style, hover the mouse pointer over a table and wait for the ScreenTip to display the style name.)

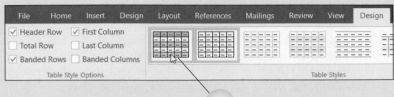

8. Apply your table style to the two other tables in the document.
9. Save the document and name it **2-BTTables.docx**.
10. Print and then close the document.

Check Your Work

Modifying a Multilevel List Style

Quick Steps

Modify a Multilevel List Style
1. Click Multilevel List button.
2. Right-click style.
3. Click *Modify*.

Modify a Table Style
1. Click in table.
2. Click Table Tools Design tab.
3. Right-click table style in table style gallery.
4. Click *Modify Table Style*.

Like other styles, a multilevel list style can be modified. To do this, click the Multilevel List button, scroll down the drop-down list to display the style to be modified, right-click the style, and then click *Modify* at the shortcut menu. This displays the Modify Style dialog box, which contains the same formatting options as the Create New Style from Formatting dialog box.

Modifying a Table Style

A custom table style or one of the predesigned table styles can be modified. To modify a table style, open the document containing the table style. Click in a table with that style applied or insert a new table in the document. Click the Table Tools Design tab, right-click the table style, and then click *Modify Table Style* at the shortcut menu. (If the table style is not visible, click the More Table Styles button that displays at the right side of the table styles gallery.) This displays the Modify Style dialog box, which contains the same formatting options as the Create New Style from Formatting dialog box.

Project 2c Modifying a Table Style   Part 3 of 6

1. Open **2-BTTables.docx** and then save it with the name **2-BTTablesModified**.
2. Modify the table style you created by completing the following steps:
   a. Click in any cell in the top table.
   b. Click the Table Tools Design tab. (Your table style should be the first thumbnail in the Table Styles group. If your table style is not visible, click the More Table Styles button at the right side of the table styles gallery and then locate your table style.)
   c. Right-click your table style and then click *Modify Table Style* at the shortcut menu.

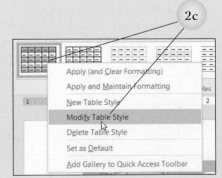

d. At the Modify Style dialog box, click the Format button in the lower left corner of the dialog box and then click *Table Properties* at the drop-down list.

e. At the Table Properties dialog box with the Table tab selected, click the *Center* option in the *Alignment* section.

f. Click OK to close the Table Properties dialog box.

g. Click the *Apply formatting to* option box arrow and then click *Odd banded rows* at the drop-down list.

h. Click the *Fill Color* option box arrow and then click *Blue, Accent 1, Lighter 80%* (fifth column, second row in the *Theme Colors* section).

i. Click the *New documents based on this template* option (at the bottom of the dialog box).

j. Click OK to close the Modify Style dialog box. (Notice that the formatting changes for all three tables in the document because the table style is applied to each table.)

3. Select the second row in the top table of the document, press Ctrl + B to apply bold formatting, and then press Ctrl + E to center the text in the cells.

4. Apply bold formatting to and center-align the second row in the middle table and the second row in the bottom table.

5. Save and then print **2-BTTablesModified.docx**. (At the message asking if you want to save the changes to the template, click the Yes button.)

6. Close **2-BTTablesModified.docx**.

7. If you are working on a public computer, copy **XXX-BTListTableTemplate.dotx** from the Custom Office Templates folder in the Documents folder on the local hard drive to the WL3C2 folder on your storage medium.

Check Your Work

Using the Style Inspector Task Pane

When working with styles and creating and applying styles to documents, a situation may arise in which multiple styles have been applied to the text. If multiple styles are applied and the formatting is not what is intended, investigate the document styles using the Style Inspector task pane.

Quick Steps

Display the Style Inspector Task Pane
1. Click Styles group task pane launcher.
2. Click Style Inspector button.

Display the Style Inspector task pane by clicking the Styles group task pane launcher to display the Styles task pane and then clicking the Style Inspector button at the bottom of the task pane. The Style Inspector task pane displays paragraph- and text-level formatting for the paragraph where the insertion point is positioned. Figure 2.8 displays the Style Inspector task pane with the insertion point positioned in the title in 2-BTZenith.docx.

The *Paragraph formatting* option box and the *Text level formatting* option box display style formatting applied to the selected text or character where the insertion point is positioned. A box displays below each option that contains the word *Plus:* followed by any additional formatting that is not specific to the style formatting.

Hover the mouse pointer over the *Paragraph formatting* option box or *Text level formatting* option box and a down-pointing arrow displays. Click the arrow and a drop-down list displays with options for clearing the formatting applied to the text, applying a new style, and displaying the Reveal Formatting task pane. Click

Figure 2.8 Style Inspector Task Pane

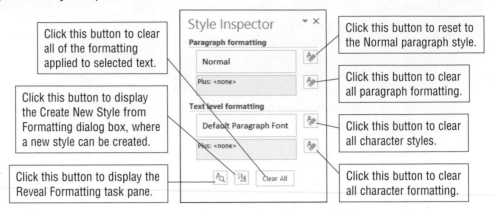

Click this button to clear all of the formatting applied to selected text.

Click this button to reset to the Normal paragraph style.

Click this button to display the Create New Style from Formatting dialog box, where a new style can be created.

Click this button to clear all paragraph formatting.

Click this button to clear all character styles.

Click this button to display the Reveal Formatting task pane.

Click this button to clear all character formatting.

the New Style button right of the Reveal Formatting button and the Create New Style from Formatting dialog box displays.

Use the buttons right of the *Paragraph formatting* option box to return the paragraph style back to the Normal style and clear any paragraph formatting applied to the text. Use the buttons right of the *Text level formatting* option box to clear character formatting applied to text.

Project 2d Using the Style Inspector Task Pane

Part 4 of 6

1. Open **2-BTZenith.docx** and then save it with the name **2-BTZenithAdvs**.
2. Click in the title *Extreme Adventures*.
3. Click the Styles group task pane launcher. (This displays the Styles task pane.)
4. Display the Style Inspector task pane by clicking the Style Inspector button at the bottom of the Styles task pane.
5. At the Style Inspector task pane, hover the mouse pointer over the *Paragraph formatting* option box and then look at the information about the custom title style that displays in the ScreenTip.
6. Click in the heading *Antarctic Adventures*.
7. Hover the mouse pointer over the *Paragraph formatting* option and then look at the information that displays about the custom heading.
8. Remove paragraph and character styles and apply a style to the text in the document by completing the following steps:
   a. Select the lines of text in the *Antarctic Adventures* section that contain money amounts.

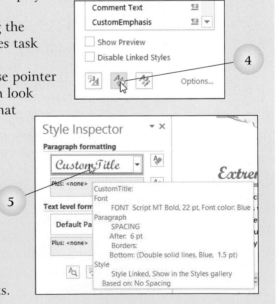

b. Remove the paragraph style from the text by clicking the Reset to Normal Paragraph Style button right of the *Paragraph formatting* option box.

c. Remove the character style from the text by clicking the Clear Character Style button right of the *Text level formatting* option box.

d. Click the *Block Text* style in the Styles task pane.

9. Select the lines of text in the *Tall-Ship Adventures* section that contain money amounts and then complete Steps 8b through 8d to remove styles and apply a style.

10. Select the lines of text in the *Bicycling Adventures* section that contain money amounts and then complete Steps 8b through 8d to remove styles and apply a style.

11. Close the Style Inspector task pane by clicking the Close button (contains an *X*) in the upper right corner of the task pane. (Leave the Style task pane open.)

12. Save **2-BTZenithAdvs.docx**.

Check Your Work

Tutorial

Managing
Styles

Paragraph
Spacing

Quick Steps

Display the Manage Styles Dialog Box
1. Click Styles group task pane launcher.
2. Click Manage Styles button.

Managing Styles

The Manage Styles dialog box provides one location for managing all styles. Display this dialog box, shown in Figure 2.9, by clicking the Manage Styles button at the bottom of the Styles task pane or by clicking the Paragraph Spacing button in the Document Formatting group on the Design tab and then clicking *Custom Paragraph Spacing* at the drop-down gallery.

Figure 2.9 Manage Styles Dialog Box

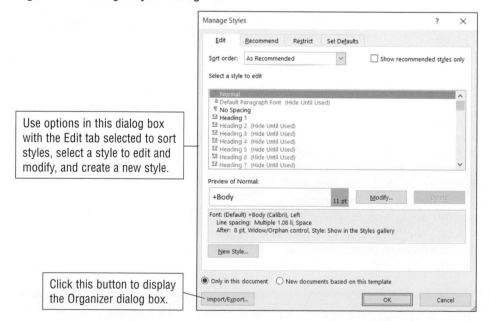

Use options in this dialog box with the Edit tab selected to sort styles, select a style to edit and modify, and create a new style.

Click this button to display the Organizer dialog box.

The options available in the Manage Styles dialog box vary depending on which tab is selected. Select the Edit tab and options are available to sort styles, select a style to edit and modify, and create a new style.

Click the Recommend tab and options display for specifying which styles to display in the Styles pane and in what order. With the Recommend tab selected, styles display in the list box preceded by priority numbers. Styles display in ascending order, with the styles preceded by the lowest numbers displaying first. The priority of a style can be changed by clicking the style in the list box and then clicking the Move Up button, Move Down button, or Move Last button, or a value number can be assigned with the Assign Value button.

With the Restrict tab selected, access to styles can be permitted or restricted. This allows control over which styles other individuals can apply or modify in a document.

Click the Set Defaults tab to display character and formatting options and specify whether changes made in the dialog box will affect the current document or all documents based on the current document. If the default document is being used, changes will affect the Normal.dotm template.

Project 2e Managing Styles   Part 5 of 6

1. With **2-BTZenithAdvs.docx** open, make sure the Styles task pane displays. (If not, click the Styles group task pane launcher.)
2. Click in the first paragraph of text. (Do not click a title or heading.)
3. Click the Manage Styles button at the bottom of the Styles task pane.
4. At the Manage Styles dialog box, make sure the Edit tab is active. (If it is not, click the Edit tab.)
5. Click the *Show recommended styles only* check box to insert a check mark. (This causes only the styles recommended by Word [along with your custom styles] to display in the *Select a style to edit* list box.)
6. Make sure *As Recommended* is selected in the *Sort order* option box. (If it is not, click the *Sort order* option box arrow and then click *As Recommended* at the drop-down list.)
7. Create a new style by completing the following steps:
   a. Click the New Style button near the lower left corner of the dialog box.

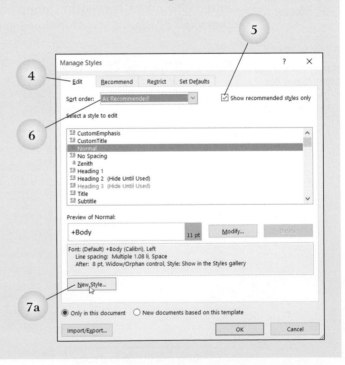

b. At the Create New Style from Formatting dialog box, type your two initials in the *Name* text box followed by CoNameEmphasis.

c. Click the *Style type* option box arrow and then click *Character* at the drop-down list.

d. Click the Bold button in the *Formatting* section of the dialog box.

e. Click the Italic button.

f. Click the *Font Color* option box arrow and then click the *Dark Blue* color (ninth option in the *Standard Colors* section).

g. Click the *Add to the Styles gallery* check box in the lower left corner of the dialog box to insert a check mark. (Skip this step if the check box already contains a check mark.)

h. Click OK to close the Create New Style from Formatting dialog box.

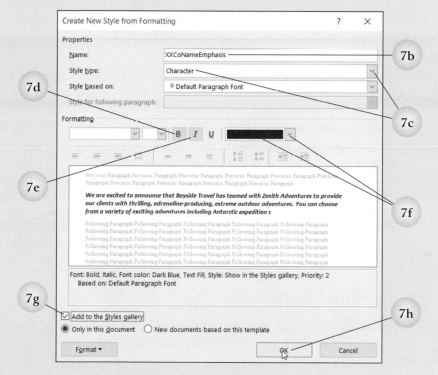

8. Specify that you want the XXCoNameEmphasis style to be prioritized as number 1 by completing the following steps:

a. At the Manage Styles dialog box, click the Recommend tab.

b. Make sure the XXCoNameEmphasis style is selected in the list box.

c. Click the Move Up button. (Notice that the XXCoNameEmphasis style moves to near the top of the list.)

d. Click OK to close the Manage Styles dialog box.

9. Select the company name *Bayside Travel* in the first paragraph of the document and then apply the XXCoNameEmphasis style (where your initials display in place of the *XX*).

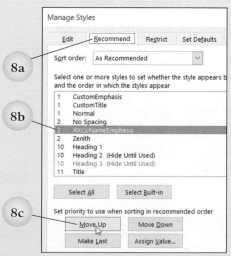

10. Select the company name *Bayside Travel* in the last paragraph of the document and then apply the XXCoNameEmphasis style (where your initials display in place of the *XX*).
11. Close the Styles task pane.
12. Save, print, and then close **2-BTZenithAdvs.docx**.

Check Your Work

Copying Styles Between Documents and Templates

Quick Steps

Display the Organizer Dialog Box
1. Click Styles group task pane launcher.
2. Click Manage Styles button.
3. Click Import/Export button.

A style (or styles) created for a specific document or template can be copied to the default template, Normal.dotm, or another template. Copy the style using the Organizer dialog box with the Styles tab selected, as shown in Figure 2.10. Display this dialog box by clicking the Import/Export button at the Manage Styles dialog box.

At the Organizer dialog box with the Styles tab selected, copy a style from a document or template to another document or template and delete and rename styles. To copy a style, click the style in the list box at the left and then click the Copy button between the two list boxes. Complete similar steps to delete a style.

By default, the Organizer dialog box displays styles available in the open document in the list box at the left and styles available in the Normal.dotm template in the list box at the right. Choose a different document or template by clicking the Close File button. This removes the styles from the list box and changes the Close File button to the Open File button. Choose a different document or template by clicking the Open File button. At the Open dialog box, navigate to the folder containing the desired document or template and then double-click the document or template.

Renaming Styles

To rename a style, click the style in the list box and then click the Rename button between the two list boxes. At the Rename dialog box, type the new name and then press the Enter key.

Figure 2.10 Organizer Dialog Box

The styles available in the current document or template display in this list box.

The styles available in the Normal.dotm template display in this list box.

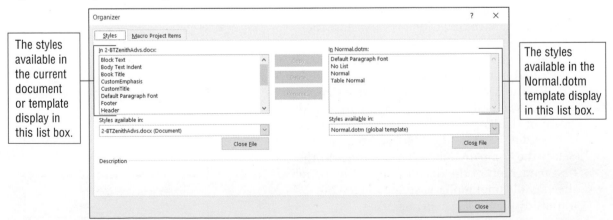

1. The templates **XXX-BTTemplate.dotx** and **XXX-BTListTableTemplate.dotx** both contain styles for formatting Bayside Travel documents. Copy the Bayside Travel styles in **XXX-BTListTableTemplate.dotx** to **XXX-BTTemplate.dotx** by completing the following steps:

   a. Press Ctrl + N to display a blank document.
   b. Display the Styles task pane.
   c. Click the Manage Styles button at the bottom of the Styles task pane.
   d. At the Manage Styles dialog box, click the Import/Export button in the lower left corner of the dialog box.
   e. At the Organizer dialog box, click the Close File button below the left list box.
   f. Click the Open File button (previously the Close File button).
   g. At the Open dialog box, click the *Documents* folder in the Navigation pane and then double-click the *Custom Office Templates* folder in the Content pane. (Be sure to click the *Documents* folder to display the Custom Office Templates folder.)
   h. Double-click **XXX-BTListTableTemplate.dotx** in the Content pane (where your initials display in place of the *XXX*). (If your template is not available in the Custom Office Templates folder, navigate to the WL3C2 folder on your storage medium and then double-click **XXX-BTListTableTemplate.dotx**.)
   i. Click the Close File button below the right list box.
   j. Click the Open File button (previously the Close File button).
   k. At the Open dialog box, click the *Documents* folder in the Navigation pane and then double-click the *Custom Office Templates* folder in the Content pane.
   l. Double-click **XXX-BTTemplate.dotx** in the Content pane (where your initials display in place of the *XXX*). (If your template is not available in the Custom Office Templates folder, navigate to the WL3C2 folder and then double-click **XXX-BTTemplate.dotx**.)
   m. Click the *BTTable* style in the left list box.
   n. Click the Copy button between the two list boxes.

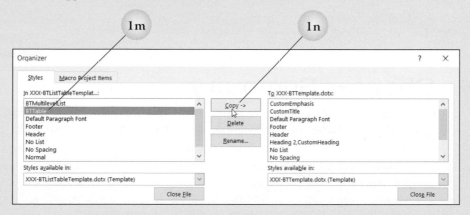

   o. Click the *BTMultiLevelList* style in the left list box.
   p. Click the Copy button between the two list boxes.
   q. Click the Close button to close the Organizer dialog box.
   r. If a message displays asking if you want to save the changes made to **XXX-BTTemplate.dotx**, click the Save button.

2. If you copied styles from templates from the WL3C2 folder, copy **XXX-BTTemplate.dotx** from the WL3C2 folder to the Custom Office Templates folder in the Documents folder on the local hard drive.

3. Open a document based on **XXX-BTTemplate.dotx** by completing the following steps:
   a. Click the File tab and then click the *New* option.
   b. Click the *PERSONAL* option.
   c. Click the *XXX-BTTemplate* thumbnail (where your initials display in place of the *XXX*).

4. Insert a document into the existing document by completing the following steps:
   a. Click the Insert tab.
   b. Click the Object button arrow and then click *Text from File* at the drop-down list.
   c. Navigate to the WL3C2 folder and then double-click **BTEastAdventures.docx**.

5. Apply the following styles to the document:
   a. Apply the CustomTitle style to the title *Eastern Adventures*.
   b. Apply the CustomHeading style to the two headings in the document.
   c. Apply the BTTable style to the two tables in the document.

6. Save the document and name it **2-BTEastAdventures**. If a message displays asking if you want to save the changes to the document template, click the Yes button.

7. Print and then close **2-BTEastAdventures.docx**.

8. Delete any templates you have saved in the Custom Office Templates folder by completing the following steps:
   a. Press Ctrl + F12 to display the Open dialog box.
   b. Click the *Documents* folder in the Navigation pane.
   c. Double-click the *Custom Office Templates* folder in the Content pane.
   d. Click the first template in the Content pane that begins with your initials.
   e. Press and hold down the Ctrl key, click any other templates that begin with your initials, and then release the Ctrl key.
   f. Click the Organize button on the toolbar.
   g. Click *Delete* at the drop-down list.
   h. Click the Cancel button to close the Open dialog box.
   i. If necessary, close the Styles task pane.

Check Your Work

Chapter Summary

- A style is a set of formatting instructions that can be applied to text. Word provides a number of predesigned styles that are grouped into style sets.

- A style can be created based on existing formatting or style formatting or by modifying an existing style. A new style can also be created without first applying formatting to text.

- Create a style at the Create New Style from Formatting dialog box. Display this dialog box by clicking the More Styles button at the right side of the styles gallery in the Styles group on the Home tab and then clicking *Create a Style* at the drop-down gallery.

- Use options at the expanded Create New Style from Formatting dialog box to name the style and specify the style type and style formatting.

- Assign a keyboard shortcut to a style with options at the Customize Keyboard dialog box. Display this dialog box by clicking the Format button at the expanded Create New Style from Formatting dialog box and then clicking *Shortcut key* at the drop-down list.

- To make the styles in a document available for future documents, save the document as a template. Do this by displaying the Save As dialog box, changing the *Save as type* option to *Word Template (*.dotx)*, and then clicking the Save button.

- Open a document based on a template by clicking the File tab and then clicking the *New* option. At the New backstage area, click the *PERSONAL* option and then click the template thumbnail.

- Display all available styles with options at the Style Pane Options dialog box. Display the dialog box by clicking the Options hyperlink that displays in the Styles task pane. Display the Styles task pane by clicking the Styles group task pane launcher.

- Modify a predesigned style by right-clicking the style in the Styles group and then clicking *Modify*. Type a name for the style at the Modify Style dialog box, make formatting changes, and then click OK.

- Reveal style formatting by hovering the mouse pointer over a style in the Styles task pane, inserting a check mark in the *Show Preview* check box in the Styles task pane, or by pressing Shift + F1 to turn on the display of the Reveal Formatting task pane.

- Save styles in a custom style set by clicking the Design tab, clicking the More Style Sets button at the right side of the style sets gallery in the Document Formatting group, and then clicking *Save as a New Style Set* at the drop-down gallery. At the Save as a New Style Set dialog box, type a name for the new style set and then click the Save button. The custom style set will be available for all future documents based on the Normal.dotm template.

- Change default settings by choosing a style set, theme, theme colors, theme fonts, theme effects, and/or paragraph spacing and then clicking the Set as Default button in the Document Formatting group on the Design tab.

- Delete a custom style set by clicking the More Style Sets button at the right side of the style sets gallery in the Document Formatting group on the Design tab, right-clicking the custom style set, and then clicking *Delete* at the shortcut menu.

- Create a multilevel list style at the Define New List Style dialog box. Display this dialog box by clicking the Multilevel List button in the Paragraph group on the Home tab and then clicking *Define New Style List*.

- A multilevel list style can also be created at the Create New Style from Formatting dialog box with the *Style type* option changed to *List*. Specify formatting for each desired level in the list.

- A multilevel list style displays in the *List Styles* section of the Multilevel List button drop-down list.

- Create a table style at the Create New Style from Formatting dialog box with *Table* selected in the *Style type* option box. Specify formatting for the entire table or specific parts of the table.

- A custom table style displays in the Table Styles group on the Table Tools Design tab.

- Modify a multilevel list style by clicking the Multilevel List button, right-clicking the style, and then clicking *Modify* at the shortcut menu. This displays the Modify Style dialog box with options for specifying changes to the style.

- Modify a table style by clicking in a table, clicking the Table Tools Design tab, right-clicking the table style, and then clicking *Modify Table Style* at the shortcut menu. This displays the Modify Style dialog box with options for specifying changes to the style.
- Use the Style Inspector task pane to investigate the styles applied to text in a document. Display the Style Inspector task pane by displaying the Styles task pane and then clicking the Style Inspector button at the bottom of the task pane.
- The Manage Styles dialog box provides one location for managing all styles. Display this dialog box by clicking the Manage Styles button at the bottom of the Styles task pane, or by clicking the Paragraph Spacing button in the Document Formatting group on the Design tab and then clicking *Custom Paragraph Spacing*.
- Copy styles from one template or document to another with options at the Organizer dialog box. Display this dialog box by clicking the Import/Export button in the bottom left corner of the Manage Styles dialog box. Styles can also be deleted or renamed at the Organizer dialog box.

Commands Review

FEATURE	RIBBON TAB, GROUP	BUTTON, OPTION	KEYBOARD SHORTCUT
Create New Style from Formatting dialog box	Home, Styles	▼ , *Create a Style*	
Manage Styles dialog box	Home, Styles	⌷ , A⁄	
Organizer dialog box	Home, Styles	⌷ , A⁄ , Import/Export...	
Reveal Formatting task pane			Shift + F1
Style Inspector task pane	Home, Styles	⌷ , A⁄	
Style Pane Options dialog box	Home, Styles	⌷ , Options	
Styles task pane	Home, Styles	⌷	Alt + Ctrl + Shift + S

Workbook

Chapter study tools and assessment activities are available in the *Workbook* ebook. These resources are designed to help you further develop and demonstrate mastery of the skills learned in this chapter.

Creating Forms

Performance Objectives

Precheck

Check your
current skills to
help focus your
study.

Upon successful completion of Chapter 3, you will be able to:

1 Design and create a form and save the form as a template

2 Insert content controls in a form

3 Define a group and edit text and content controls in design
mode

4 Open and fill in a form based on a template

5 Edit a form template

6 Insert and edit placeholder text

7 Create a form using a table

8 Restrict editing of a template

9 Set properties for content controls

10 Edit a protected form template

Many businesses have preprinted forms that respondents fill in by hand or with a
computer. Using these forms involves a printing cost and requires space for storage.
With Word, you can create your own forms and eliminate the need to buy and
store preprinted forms. In this chapter, you will learn how to create forms using
content controls such as plain text, drop-down list, combo box, picture, and date
picker content controls. In addition, you will save group text and content controls
in a form, save a form as a template, restrict editing in a form, create documents
based on form templates, and fill in forms.

Data Files

Before beginning chapter work, copy the WL3C3 folder to
your storage medium and then make WL3C3 the active folder.

SNAP

If you are a SNAP
user, launch the
Precheck and
Tutorials from your
Assignments page.

You will create a mailing list template for Terra Travel Services, insert plain text controls in the template, group the text and content controls, and then create a mailing list form based on the template.

Preview Finished Project

Tutorial

Creating a Form and Defining a Group with Content Controls

Creating and Using a Form

In Word, the term *form* refers to a protected document that includes user-defined sections into which a user (respondent) enters information. These user-defined sections are made up of content controls. Content controls limit response options to ensure the collection of desired data.

The Developer tab, shown in Figure 3.1, contains options for inserting content controls. The Developer tab also contains options for creating forms with legacy tools, which are tools for developing forms that were available in previous versions of Word. Creating forms with legacy tools is covered in Chapter 4.

Designing a Form

Designing a form involves two goals: gathering all the information necessary to meet a specific objective and gathering information that is useful and accurate. Thus, the first step in designing a form is to determine its purpose. To do so, make a list of all the information needed to meet the purpose of the form. Be careful not to include unnecessary or redundant information, which will clutter the appearance of the form and frustrate the person completing it.

The next step is to plan the layout of the form. The simplest way to design a form is to find an existing form that requests similar information or serves a similar purpose and then mimic it. Finding a similar form is not always easy, however, and in many cases, a form may need to be designed from scratch. When starting from scratch, first sketch out the form. This will provide a guide to follow when creating the form in Word. Here are some other points to consider when designing a form:

- Group like items in the form. This makes providing complete and accurate information easier for the respondent.

- Place the most important information at the top of the form to increase the likelihood of obtaining it. Many respondents fail to complete a form entirely before submitting it.

Figure 3.1 Developer Tab

- Leave plenty of space for respondent input. The respondent may become frustrated if a field does not contain enough space for the data to be entered.

- Use fonts, colors, lines, and graphics purposefully and sparingly. Overusing such design elements tends to clutter a form and make it difficult to read.

- Separate sections of the form using white space, lines, and shading. Each section should be clearly defined.

Creating a Form Template

A form is created as a template, so a respondent who fills it in is working in a copy of the form, rather than the original. That way, a form can be used again and again without changing the original. When a form is created from a form template, information can be typed only in the content controls that are designated when the form was created.

Figure 3.2 shows an example of a form template created with content controls. (This form will be created in Project 1a.) Forms can be created that contain content controls for text, such as the *First Name:*, *Last Name:*, *Address:*, and so on. Forms can also be created that contain drop-down lists, date pickers, and pictures.

Quick Steps

Save a Form as a Template

1. Open blank document.
2. Display Save As dialog box.
3. Change *Save as type* option to *Word Template (*.dotx)*.
4. Click Save button.

Create a new form template by opening an existing document or a blank document, displaying the Save As dialog box, changing the *Save as type* option to *Word Template (*.dotx)*, and then clicking the Save button. This saves the template in the Custom Office Templates folder in the Documents folder on the computer's hard drive. To use the template, display the New backstage area, click the *PERSONAL* option, and then click the template thumbnail.

If you are working on a computer in a public environment, you should save a backup of your template on your storage medium (such as a USB flash drive). That way, if the computer is reset on a regular basis, you can copy your template back to the Custom Office Templates folder.

Figure 3.2 Project 1a

Another option for managing templates is to change the default location that templates are saved from the Custom Office Templates folder to another location, such as a disk drive. To change the default location for templates, display the Word Options dialog box, click *Save* in the left panel, and then specify the folder or drive in which to save templates with the *Default personal templates location* option. The folder or drive specified at this option will be the folder or drive that displays when the *PERSONAL* option is clicked at the New backstage area.

The projects in this chapter are based on the assumption that you are saving to the default Custom Office Templates folder. Please check with your instructor to determine if you should save your templates to a different location. Also determine if you need to make backup copies of your templates.

Displaying the Developer Tab

Quick Steps

Display the Developer Tab
1. Click File tab.
2. Click *Options*.
3. Click *Customize Ribbon*.
4. Click Developer tab check box to insert check mark.
5. Click OK.

A number of buttons for creating a form are available in the Controls group on the Developer tab. To display the Developer tab on the ribbon, click the File tab and then click *Options*. At the Word Options dialog box, click *Customize Ribbon* in the left panel. In the list box at the right, click the Developer tab check box to insert a check mark and then click OK to close the dialog box. The Developer tab is positioned right of the View tab.

Inserting Content Controls

The Controls group on the Developer tab contains a number of buttons for inserting content controls in a form. Table 3.1 describes eight of them. Insert a content control by clicking the specific button in the Controls group. Several content controls, such as the plain text content control, include default placeholder text, such as *Click or tap here to enter text*. When filling in a form, the respondent clicks the placeholder text and then types the requested information.

Table 3.1 Content Control Buttons

Content Control Button	Description
Rich Text Content Control	Used to contain custom formatted text or another item, such as another content control or a table or image.
Plain Text Content Control	Used to contain plain text; cannot contain another item, such as another content control or a table or image.
Picture Content Control	Used to hold an image.
Building Block Gallery Content Control	Used to insert a placeholder from which the respondent can select a building block from a specified gallery.
Check Box Content Control	Used to insert a check box that can indicate on or off, depending on whether the respondent inserts a check mark in the check box.
Combo Box Content Control	Used to create a list of values from which the respondent can select; also allows the respondent to enter other values.
Drop Down List Content Control	Used to create a drop-down list of values from which the respondent can select; does not allow other values to be entered.
Date Picker Content Control	Used to insert a calendar from which the respondent picks a date.

Defining a Group

Quick Steps

Define a Group
1. Select text and content controls.
2. Click Developer tab.
3. Click Group button.
4. Click *Group* option.

Use the Group button on the Developer tab to define a group, which is a protected region in a form that cannot be edited or deleted by a respondent. A group can contain text, tables, graphics, and content controls. When a group is defined, the respondent can enter information in the content controls but cannot edit the other text or items in the group. To define a group, select the text and content controls, click the Group button in the Controls group on the Developer tab, and then click the *Group* option at the drop-down list.

Displaying a Form in Design Mode

When designing a form, turn on design mode by clicking the Design Mode button in the Controls group on the Developer tab. With design mode turned on, a Group starting tag and ending tag display along with starting and ending tags for content controls as shown in Figure 3.3.

When a group has been defined, the text and content controls in the group can be edited if design mode is turned on. With design mode turned off, the placeholder text can be edited but the other text in the group cannot be edited.

Figure 3.3 Form in Design Mode

1. Display the Developer tab by completing the following steps (skip the steps if the Developer tab displays on the ribbon):
   a. Click the File tab and then click *Options*.
   b. At the Word Options dialog box, click *Customize Ribbon* in the left panel.
   c. In the list box at the right, click the *Developer* check box to insert a check mark.

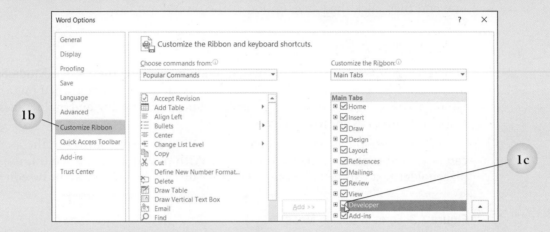

   d. Click OK to close the dialog box.
2. Create the form shown in Figure 3.2. To begin, create a template with an existing document by completing the following steps:
   a. Open **TTSLtrhd.docx** from the WL3C3 folder on your storage medium.
   b. Press the F12 function key to display the Save As dialog box.
   c. At the Save As dialog box, type XXXMailingListTemplate in the *File name* text box (typing your initials in place of the *XXX*).
   d. Click the *Save as type* option box and then click *Word Template (*.dotx)* at the drop-down list.
   e. Click the Save button.
3. At the new template, type the beginning part of the form shown in Figure 3.2 up to the colon after *First Name:* by completing the following steps:
   a. Click the Layout tab and then click the *Spacing After* measurement box down arrow in the Paragraph group two times. (This displays *0 pt* in the measurement box.)
   b. Click the Home tab, turn on bold formatting, and then change the font to Candara and the font size to 14 points.
   c. Click the Center button in the Paragraph group, type Mailing List Request, and then press the Enter key two times.
   d. Click the Align Left button in the Paragraph group and then change the font size to 12 points.
   e. Set left tabs at the 3-inch mark and 4.5-inch mark on the horizontal ruler.
   f. Type First Name: and then turn off bold formatting.
   g. Press the spacebar.

4. Insert a plain text content control by completing the following steps:
   a. Click the Developer tab.
   b. Click the Plain Text Content Control button in the Controls group.
   c. Press the Right Arrow key to deselect the content control.
5. Press the Tab key to move the insertion point to the tab at the 3-inch mark.
6. Turn on bold formatting, type Last Name:, and then turn off bold formatting.
7. Press the spacebar and then click the Plain Text Content Control button in the Controls group on the Developer tab.
8. Press the Right Arrow key to deselect the content control.
9. Press the Enter key two times.
10. Continue to type the text and insert content controls as displayed in Figure 3.2. Remember to turn off bold formatting before inserting the plain text content control. (When you enter the line that contains *City:*, *State:*, and *Zip Code:*, press the Tab key to align each item at the correct tab setting. As you type, content controls and text appear crowded and wrap to the next line. The content controls will not print when you create a document from this template.)
11. Position the insertion point one double space below the last line of the form.
12. Insert the horizontal line by pressing Shift + - (the hyphen key) three times and then pressing the Enter key. (AutoFormat will automatically change the hyphens into a vertical line.)
13. Change the font to 10-point Candara and then type the paragraph of text below the horizontal line, as shown in Figure 3.2.
14. Turn on design mode by clicking the Developer tab and then clicking the Design Mode button in the Controls group.
15. Group the text and content controls by completing the following steps:
    a. Press Ctrl + A to select all the text and content controls in the document (excluding the header and footer).
    b. Click the Group button in the Controls group and then click *Group* at the drop-down list.
16. Save and then close **XXXMailingListTemplate.dotx**.

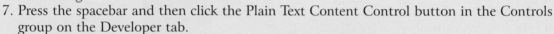

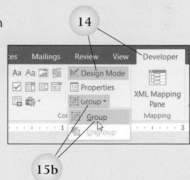

Check Your Work

Opening and Filling in a Form Document

After a form template has been created, grouped, and saved, it can be used to create a personalized form document. To begin, open a document based on the form template by clicking the File tab and then clicking the *New* option. At the New backstage area, click the *PERSONAL* option and then click the thumbnail representing the template.

When a document based on a form template is opened, the insertion point is positioned at the beginning of the document. Click in the placeholder text in the first content control to make it active and then type the required text. Press the Tab key to select the placeholder text in the next content control or press Shift + Tab to select the placeholder text in the preceding content control.

Project 1b Filling in the Mailing List Form

1. Create a form document from the template **XXXMailingListTemplate** by completing the following steps:
   a. Click the File tab and then click the *New* option.
   b. At the New backstage area, click the *PERSONAL* option.
   c. Click the *XXXMailingListTemplate* thumbnail.
2. Click in the placeholder text for the first content control (the one that displays after *First Name:*) and then type Ava.
3. Press the Tab key to advance to the next content control and continue entering the information as displayed in Figure 3.4. Make sure the labels have bold formatting applied but not the text that is typed in the content controls.
4. Save the document by completing the following steps:
   a. Press the F12 function key.
   b. At the Save As dialog box, navigate to the WL3C3 folder on your storage medium.
   c. Type 3-JacksonML in the *File name* text box and then press the Enter key.
5. Print and then close **3-JacksonML.docx**.

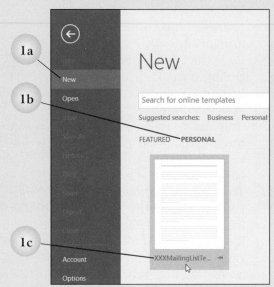

Check Your Work

Figure 3.4 Project 1b

Editing Grouped Data

Quick Steps

Edit Grouped Data
1. Open form template.
2. Click Developer tab.
3. Click Design Mode button.
4. Edit text and/or content controls.

Open a Form Template
1. Press Ctrl + F12.
2. Click *Documents* in Navigation pane.
3. Double-click *Custom Office Templates* folder.
4. Double-click form template.

When a group has been defined in a form template, the text and content controls in the group can be edited if design mode is turned on. With design mode turned off, the placeholder text can be edited but the other text in the group cannot be edited.

By default, Word saves a template in the Custom Office Templates folder. To open a template for editing, display the Open dialog box, click the *Documents* folder in the Navigation pane, double-click the *Custom Office Templates* folder in the Content pane, and then double-click the form template in the Content pane.

Project 1c Editing the Mailing List Form Template

Part 3 of 4

1. Open **XXXMailingListTemplate.dotx** by completing the following steps:
   a. Press Ctrl + F12.
   b. At the Open dialog box, click the *Documents* folder (if necessary) in the Navigation pane and then double-click the *Custom Office Templates* folder in the Content pane.
   c. Double-click **XXXMailingListTemplate.dotx** in the Content pane.

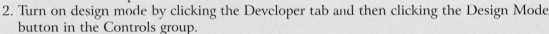

2. Turn on design mode by clicking the Developer tab and then clicking the Design Mode button in the Controls group.
3. Delete, edit, and insert a content control as shown in Figure 3.5 by completing the following steps:
   a. Select the word *Birthday*, the colon, and the plain text content control placeholder text *Click here to enter text.* and then press the Delete key.
   b. Edit the word *Telephone*, changing it to Home Phone.
   c. Move the insertion point right of the *Home Phone:* plain text content control.
   d. Press the Tab key.
   e. Turn on bold formatting, type Cell Phone:, turn off bold formatting, and then press the spacebar.
   f. Click the Plain Text Content Control button in the Controls group.
   g. Move the insertion point so it is positioned right of the ending tag for the plain text content control after *Cell Phone:*.
   h. Press the Enter key two times.
   i. Turn on bold formatting, type Email Address:, turn off bold formatting, and then press the spacebar.
   j. Click the Plain Text Content Control button in the Controls group.
4. Turn off design mode by clicking the Design Mode button.
5. Save and then close **XXXMailingListTemplate.dotx**.

Check Your Work

Figure 3.5 Project 1c

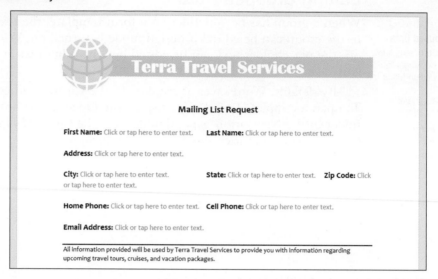

Project 1d Filling in the Edited Mailing List Form

1. Create a form document from the template **XXXMailingListTemplate.dotx** by completing the following steps:
   a. Click the File tab and then click the *New* option.
   b. At the New backstage area, click the *PERSONAL* option.
   c. Click the *XXXMailingListTemplate* thumbnail.
   d. Type the following text in the specified content controls:

   > *First Name:* Caleb
   > *Last Name:* Ellison
   > *Address:* 12302 132nd Street East
   > *City:* Decatur
   > *State:* GA
   > *Zip Code:* 30015
   > *Home Phone:* 678-555-9447
   > *Cell Phone:* 678-555-1140
   > *Email Address:* cellison@emcp.net

2. Save the document in the WL3C3 folder on your storage medium with the name **3-EllisonML**.
3. Print and then close **3-EllisonML.docx**.

Check Your Work

Project 2 **Create a Fax Template for Terra Travel Services**   **2 Parts**

You will open a fax document, save it as a template, and then insert content controls in the template.

Preview Finished Project

Inserting Specific Placeholder Text

Providing specific placeholder text for respondents who are filling in a form can aid in obtaining accurate information. When creating a form, type text in a content control placeholder that provides specific directions to respondents on what information to enter. To insert specific instructional text, click the Plain Text Content Control button in the Controls group on the Developer tab and then type the instructional text. Or type the instructional text at the location the text content control will be inserted, select the text, and then click the Plain Text Content Control button. To edit placeholder text in an existing form template, open the template, turn on design mode, select the placeholder text, and then type the specific instructional text.

Creating a Form Using a Table

The Tables feature in Word is an efficient tool for designing and creating forms. Using a table, a framework for the form can be created that provides spaces to enter data fields. Using a table also allows for easy alignment and placement of the elements of the form.

Project 2a **Inserting Content Controls in a Fax Template**   **Part 1 of 2**

1. Open **TTSFax.docx** and then save it as a template by completing the following steps:
   a. Press the F12 function key to display the Save As dialog box.
   b. At the Save As dialog box, type XXXFaxTemplate in the *File name* text box (typing your initials in place of the *XXX*).
   c. Click the *Save as type* option and then click *Word Template (*.dotx)* at the drop-down list.
   d. Click the Save button.
2. Insert after the *To:* label a plain text content control and type specific placeholder text by completing the following steps:
   a. Click the Developer tab.
   b. Click in the *To:* text box and position the insertion point one space right of the colon.
   c. Click the Plain Text Content Control button in the Controls group.
   d. Type Receiver's name.

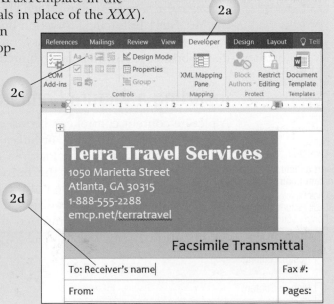

3. Complete steps similar to those in Step 2 to insert the plain text content control and placeholder text in the *Fax #:*, *From:*, *Pages:*, and *Notes:* cells, as shown in Figure 3.6. (You will insert a field for the date in the next project.)
4. Click the Save button on the Quick Access Toolbar to save the template.

Check Your Work

Figure 3.6 Project 2a

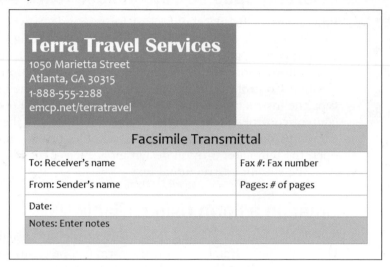

Terra Travel Services
1050 Marietta Street
Atlanta, GA 30315
1-888-555-2288
emcp.net/terratravel

Facsimile Transmittal	
To: Receiver's name	Fax #: Fax number
From: Sender's name	Pages: # of pages
Date:	
Notes: Enter notes	

Tutorial

Protecting a Form Template

Protecting a Template

A form template can be restricted so that it cannot be edited. To restrict a template from editing, click the Restrict Editing button in the Protect group on the Developer tab. This displays the Restrict Editing task pane, shown in Figure 3.7.

At the Restrict Editing task pane, click in the *Allow only this type of editing in the document* check box to insert a check mark. Click the option box arrow in the *Editing restrictions* section and then click *Filling in forms* at the drop-down list. Click the Yes, Start Enforcing Protection button in the task pane. At the Start Enforcing Protection dialog box, type a password, confirm the password, and then close the dialog box. A password is not required to protect a form.

Inserting a Picture Content Control

A picture content control can be inserted in a template that displays an image, drawing, shape, chart, table, or SmartArt graphic. Insert an image or other visual element in a form using the Picture Content Control button in the Controls group on the Developer tab. Click this button and a picture frame containing a picture icon is inserted at the location of the insertion point. Click the picture icon and the Insert Picture dialog box displays. At this dialog box, navigate to the folder containing the image to be inserted and double-click the image file; the image fills the picture content control.

Quick Steps
Protect a Template
1. Click Developer tab.
2. Click Restrict Editing button.
3. Click *Allow only this type of editing in the document* check box.
4. Click option box arrow in *Editing restrictions* section.
5. Click *Filling in forms*.
6. Click Yes, Start Enforcing Protection button.
7. Click OK.

Insert a Picture Content Control
1. Click Developer tab.
2. Click Picture Content Control button in Controls group.

 Restrict Editing

 Picture Content Control

Figure 3.7 Restrict Editing Task Pane

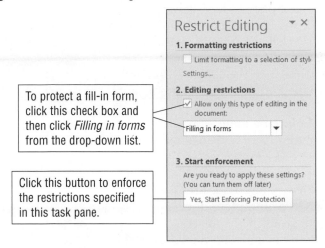

To protect a fill-in form, click this check box and then click *Filling in forms* from the drop-down list.

Click this button to enforce the restrictions specified in this task pane.

Inserting a Date Picker Content Control

Quick Steps

Insert a Date Picker Content Control
1. Click Developer tab.
2. Click Date Picker Content Control button in Controls group.

 Date Picker Content Control

A date picker content control can be inserted in a template that displays a calendar when the respondent clicks the arrow at the right side of the control. The respondent can navigate to the desired month and year and then click the date, or insert the current date by clicking the Today button. To insert a date picker content control, click the Date Picker Content Control button in the Controls group on the Developer tab.

Project 2b Inserting Picture and Date Picker Content Controls, Restricting Editing, and Filling in the Fax Form   Part 2 of 2

1. With **XXXFaxTemplate.dotx** open, insert a picture content control by completing the following steps:
   a. Click in the cell at the right in the top row.
   b. Click the Developer tab.
   c. Click the Picture Content Control button in the Controls group.
   d. Click the picture icon in the middle of the picture content control in the cell.
   e. At the Insert Pictures window, click the Browse button, navigate to the WL3C3 folder on your storage medium, and then double-click *TTSGlobe.jpg*.
2. Insert a date picker content control by completing the following steps:
   a. Click in the *Date:* cell and then position the insertion point one space right of the colon.
   b. Click the Date Picker Content Control button in the Controls group.

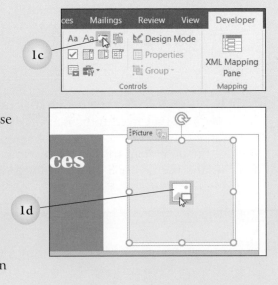

3. Protect the template by completing the following steps:
   a. Click the Restrict Editing button in the Protect group.
   b. Click the *Allow only this type of editing in the document* check box in the Restrict Editing task pane.
   c. Click the option box arrow in the *Editing restrictions* section of the task pane and then click *Filling in forms* at the drop-down list.
   d. Click the Yes, Start Enforcing Protection button.
   e. At the Start Enforcing Protection dialog box, click OK. (Creating a password is optional.)
   f. Click the Close button in the upper right corner of the Restrict Editing task pane to close the task pane.

4. Save and then close **XXXFaxTemplate.dotx**.
5. Create a form document from the template **XXXFaxTemplate.dotx** by completing the following steps:
   a. Click the File tab and then click the *New* option.
   b. At the New backstage area, click the *PERSONAL* option.
   c. Click the *XXXFaxTemplate* thumbnail (where your initials display in place of the *XXX*).
   d. Click in the text *To:*. (This selects the *To:* placeholder text *Receiver's name*.)
   e. Type Max Lopez and then press the Tab key.
   f. Type 770-555-9876 and then press the Tab key.
   g. Type Amelia Landers and then press the Tab key.
   h. Type 3 including cover and then press the Tab key.
   i. With the *Date:* content control text selected, click the arrow at the right side of the content control, click the Today button below the calendar, and then press the Tab key.

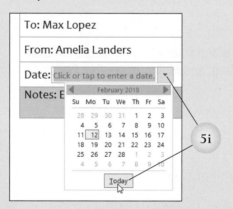

   j. Type Please review the two draft contract documents and make a note of any legal revisions that need to be made. I would like to meet with you next week to finalize these contracts.
6. Save the document in the WL3C3 folder on your storage medium and name it **3-TTSFax**.
7. Print and then close **3-TTSFax.docx**.

Check Your Work

Inserting a Drop-Down List Content Control

The designer of a form may want respondents to choose an item from a drop-down list of items, rather than type data in a content control. To make only specific items available, insert a drop-down list content control by clicking the Drop-Down List Content Control button in the Controls group on the Developer tab.

Inserting a Combo Box Content Control

Like a drop-down list content control, a combo box content control can be inserted in a form that allows the respondent to choose an item from a drop-down list. While a drop-down list content control limits the respondent to choosing an item from a drop-down list, a combo box content control allows the respondent to enter data in the content control other than items from the drop-down list. Click the Combo Box Content Control button in the Controls group to insert the content control.

Inserting a Check Box Content Control

A check box can be inserted in a form in which the respondent is asked to insert an *X* to indicate a choice. For example, check boxes can be inserted for yes and no responses. To insert a check box, click the Check Box Content Control button in the Controls group on the Developer tab. When filling in the form, the respondent clicks in the check box to insert an *X*.

Setting Content Control Properties

A content control can be customized with options at a properties dialog box. The options at the dialog box vary depending on the selected content control. For example, a list of items can be added for a drop-down list or combo box content control, a picture content control can be locked, and formatting can be specified for inserting a date with a date picker content control.

Specifying Drop-Down List Content Control Properties

Quick Steps

Specify Drop-Down List Content Control Properties

1. Select drop-down list content control.
2. Click Developer tab.
3. Click Properties button.
4. Click Add button.
5. Type choice.
6. Click OK.
7. Continue clicking Add button and typing choices.
8. Click OK to close the Content Control Properties dialog box.

 Properties

To create a list of items from which the respondent will choose, select the drop-down list or combo box content control and then click the Properties button in the Controls group on the Developer tab. Clicking a drop-down list content control will display the Content Control Properties dialog box, shown in Figure 3.8. Each content control includes properties that can be changed with options at the dialog box. The content of the dialog box varies depending on the control selected.

To add drop-down list choices, click the Add button in the dialog box. At the Add Choice dialog box, type the first choice in the *Display Name* text box and then click OK. At the Content Control Properties dialog box, click the Add button and then continue until all the choices are entered.

Create a title for the content control with the *Title* option in the Content Control Properties dialog box. Type the title text in the *Title* text box and it displays in the content control tab at the template. Having a content control title is not necessary but it can provide additional information for the person filling in the form.

A drop-down list item can be modified by clicking the item in the *Drop-Down List Properties* section and then clicking the Modify button. The position of an item in the list can also be changed by selecting the item and then clicking the Move Up or Move Down button. To remove an item from the list, select the item and then click the Remove button.

To fill in a form with a drop-down list, select the drop-down list or combo box content control, click the arrow at the right side of the content control, and then click the desired item. Another method is to press and hold down the Alt key, press the Down Arrow key until the desired item is selected, and then press the Enter key.

Figure 3.8 Content Control Properties Dialog Box for Drop-Down List Content Control

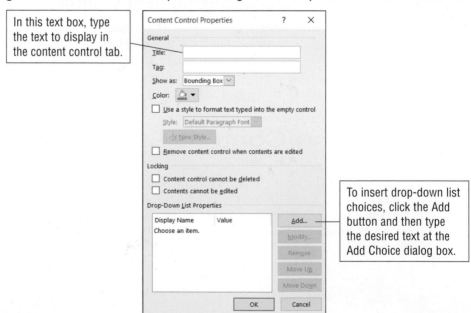

1. Open **TTSSurvey.docx** and then save it as a template by completing the following steps:
   a. Press the F12 function key to display the Save As dialog box.
   b. At the Save As dialog box, type XXXSurveyTemplate in the *File name* text box (typing your initials in place of the *XXX*).
   c. Click the *Save as type* option box and then click *Word Template (*.dotx)* at the drop-down list.
   d. Click the Save button.
2. Click in the cell immediately right of the cell containing the text *On average, how many times a year do you travel for vacation?* and then insert a drop-down list by completing the following steps:
   a. Click the Developer tab.
   b. Click the Drop-Down List Content Control button in the Controls group.
   c. With the content control selected, click the Properties button in the Controls group.

   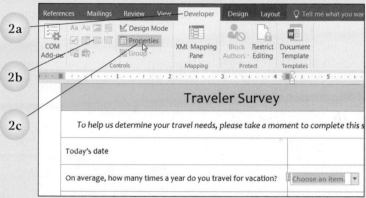

   d. At the Content Control Properties dialog box, click the Add button.
   e. At the Add Choice dialog box, type 0 in the *Display Name* text box and then click OK.
   f. Complete steps similar to those in Steps 2d and 2e to expand the drop-down list, typing the following additional choices:

      1
      2
      3 or more
3. Click in the *Title* text box and then type Frequency.

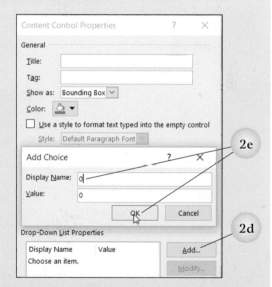

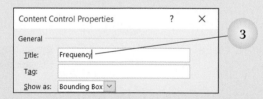

4. Click OK to close the Content Control Properties dialog box.
5. Click in the cell immediately right of the cell containing the text *What type of vacation travel most interests you?* and then insert a combo box drop-down list by completing the following steps:
   a. Click the Combo Box Content Control button in the Controls group.
   b. With the content control selected, click the Properties button in the Controls group.

c. At the Content Control Properties dialog box, click the Add button.

d. At the Add Choice dialog box, type All-inclusive resort in the *Display Name* text box and then click OK.

e. Complete steps similar to those in Steps 5c and 5d to expand the drop-down list, typing the following additional choices:

> Cruise
> Guided tour
> Eco-tour

6. Click in the *Title* text box and then type Vacation preference.

7. Click OK to close the Content Control Properties dialog box.

8. Click in the cell immediately right of the cell containing the text *Would you like one of our travel consultants to contact you with information about vacation packages?* and then insert text and check boxes by completing the following steps:

a. Click the Check Box Content Control button in the Controls group.

b. Press the Right Arrow key two times. (This moves the insertion point right of the check box content control.)

c. Press the spacebar and then type Yes.

d. Press Ctrl + Tab two times. (This moves the insertion point to a tab position within the cell.)

e. Click the Check Box Content Control button.

f. Press the Right Arrow key two times.

g. Press the spacebar and then type No.

9. Click in the cell immediately right of the cell containing the text *Are you interested in receiving our monthly travel brochure?* and then complete Steps 8a through 8g to insert check boxes and text in the cell.

10. Click the Save button on the Quick Access Toolbar to save the template.

Check Your Work

Customizing Picture Content Control Properties

Quick Steps
Lock the Picture Content Control
1. Select picture content control.
2. Click Developer tab.
3. Click Properties button.
4. Insert check mark in *Contents cannot be edited* check box.
5. Click OK.

When using a picture control in a form template, consider locking the picture. With the picture locked, the insertion point does not stop at the picture data field when the respondent presses the Tab key to move to the next data field. To lock a picture, select the picture content control and then click the Properties button in the Controls group on the Developer tab. At the Content Control Properties dialog box, shown in Figure 3.9, insert a check mark in the *Contents cannot be edited* check box. To specify that the picture content control cannot be deleted, insert a check mark in the *Content control cannot be deleted* check box.

Customizing Date Picker Content Control Properties

The date picker content control has a default format of *m/d/yyyy* for inserting the date. This date format can be customized with options at the Content Control Properties dialog box, shown in Figure 3.10. Choose the date format in the list box in the *Date Picker Properties* section of the dialog box and then click OK.

Figure 3.9 Content Control Properties Dialog Box for Picture Content Control

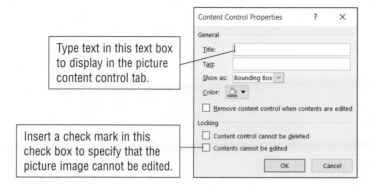

Type text in this text box to display in the picture content control tab.

Insert a check mark in this check box to specify that the picture image cannot be edited.

Figure 3.10 Content Control Properties Dialog Box for Date Picker Content Control

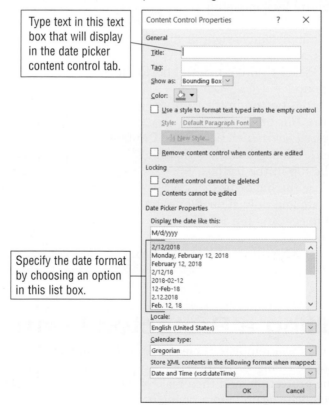

Type text in this text box that will display in the date picker content control tab.

Specify the date format by choosing an option in this list box.

1. With **XXXSurveyTemplate.dotx** open, insert a picture content control and lock the
   control by completing the following steps:
   a. Click in the cell at the right in the top row of the table.
   b. Click the Developer tab.
   c. Click the Picture Content Control button in the
      Controls group.
   d. Click the picture icon in the middle of the picture
      content control in the cell.
   e. At the Insert Pictures window, click the Browse
      button, navigate to the WL3C3 folder on your
      storage medium, and then double-click **TTSGlobe.jpg**.
   f. Click the Properties button in the Controls group.
   g. At the Content Control Properties dialog box, type
      Terra Image in the *Title* text box.
   h. Click the *Contents cannot be edited* check box to
      insert a check mark.
   i. Click OK to close the dialog box.
2. Insert a date picker content control and
   customize the control by completing the
   following steps:
   a. Click in the cell immediately right of the cell
      containing the text *Today's date*.
   b. Click the Date Picker Content Control button in
      the Controls group.
   c. Click the Properties button in the Controls group.
   d. Type Date in the *Title* text box.
   e. In the *Date Picker Properties* section of the Content
      Control Properties dialog box, click the third
      option from the top in the list box.
   f. Click OK to close the dialog box.
3. Protect the template and only allow filling in the
   form. (Refer to Project 2b, Step 3.) Close the
   Restrict Editing task pane.
4. Save and then close **XXXSurveyTemplate.dotx**.

Check Your Work

Tutorial

Editing a Form
Template

Editing a Protected Form Template

When a form template is created and then protected, the text in the template
cannot be changed. To make a change to a form template, open the template, turn
off the protection, and then make the changes. After making the changes, protect
the template again before saving it.

To turn off the protection of a form template, click the Restrict Editing button
in the Protect group on the Developer tab. At the Restrict Editing task pane, click
the Stop Protection button. If the form template was protected with a password,
enter the password and then click OK. Make the changes to the form template
and then protect it again by clicking the Yes, Start Enforcing Protection button
and then clicking OK at the Start Enforcing Protection dialog box.

1. Open **XXXSurveyTemplate.dotx** by completing the following steps:
   a. Press Ctrl + F12.
   b. At the Open dialog box, click the *Documents* folder (if necessary) in the Navigation pane and then double-click the *Custom Office Templates* folder in the Content pane.
   c. Double-click **XXXSurveyTemplate.dotx** in the Content pane.
2. Turn off protection by completing the following steps:
   a. Click the Developer tab.
   b. Click the Restrict Editing button in the Protect group.
   c. At the Restrict Editing task pane, click the Stop Protection button at the bottom of the task pane.

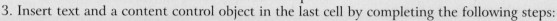

3. Insert text and a content control object in the last cell by completing the following steps:
   a. Click in the last cell. (The cell is shaded.)
   b. Type Notes: and then press the spacebar.
   c. Type the text Type additional ideas or comments here.
   d. Select *Type additional ideas or comments here.* and then click the Plain Text Content Control button in the Controls group.

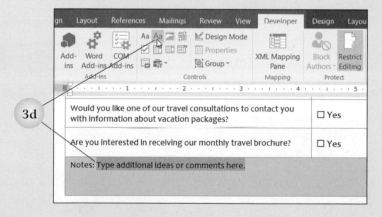

4. Protect the form template again by completing the following steps:
   a. Click the Yes, Start Enforcing Protection button.
   b. Click OK at the Start Enforcing Protection dialog box.
   c. Close the Restrict Editing task pane.
5. Save and then close **XXXSurveyTemplate.dotx**.
6. Create a form document from the template **XXXSurveyTemplate.dotx** as shown in Figure 3.11 by completing the following steps:
   a. Click the File tab and then click the *New* option.
   b. At the New backstage area, click the *PERSONAL* option.
   c. Click the *XXXSurveyTemplate* thumbnail (where your initials display in place of the *XXX*).
7. With the *Date:* content control text selected, click the arrow at the right side of the content control and then click the Today button below the calendar.
8. Press the Tab key. (This selects the drop-down list content control in the cell immediately right of the cell containing the text *On average, how many times a year do you travel for vacation?*)

9. Choose an option from the drop-down list by clicking the down-pointing arrow right of the drop-down list content control and then clicking *2*.

10. Press the Tab key to select the combo box content control.

11. Instead of choosing an item from the drop-down list, type Disney vacation. (With a combo box content control, you can type in your own entry.)

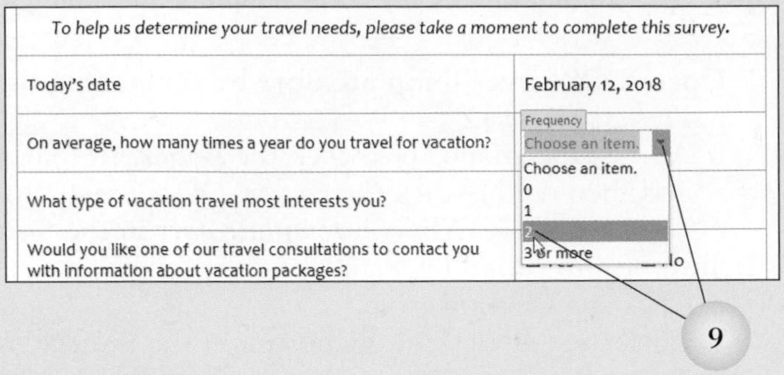

12. Click the Yes check box in the cell right of the cell containing the text *Would you like one of our travel consultations to contact you with information about vacation packages?*

13. Click the No check box in the cell right of the cell containing the text *Are you interested in receiving our monthly travel brochure?*

14. With the *Notes:* plain text content control placeholder text selected, type We are interested in a family vacation to Disneyland the summer of 2019.

15. Save the document in the WL3C3 folder on your storage medium with the name **3-TTSSurvey**.

16. Print and then close **3-TTSSurvey.docx**.

Check Your Work

Figure 3.11 Project 3c

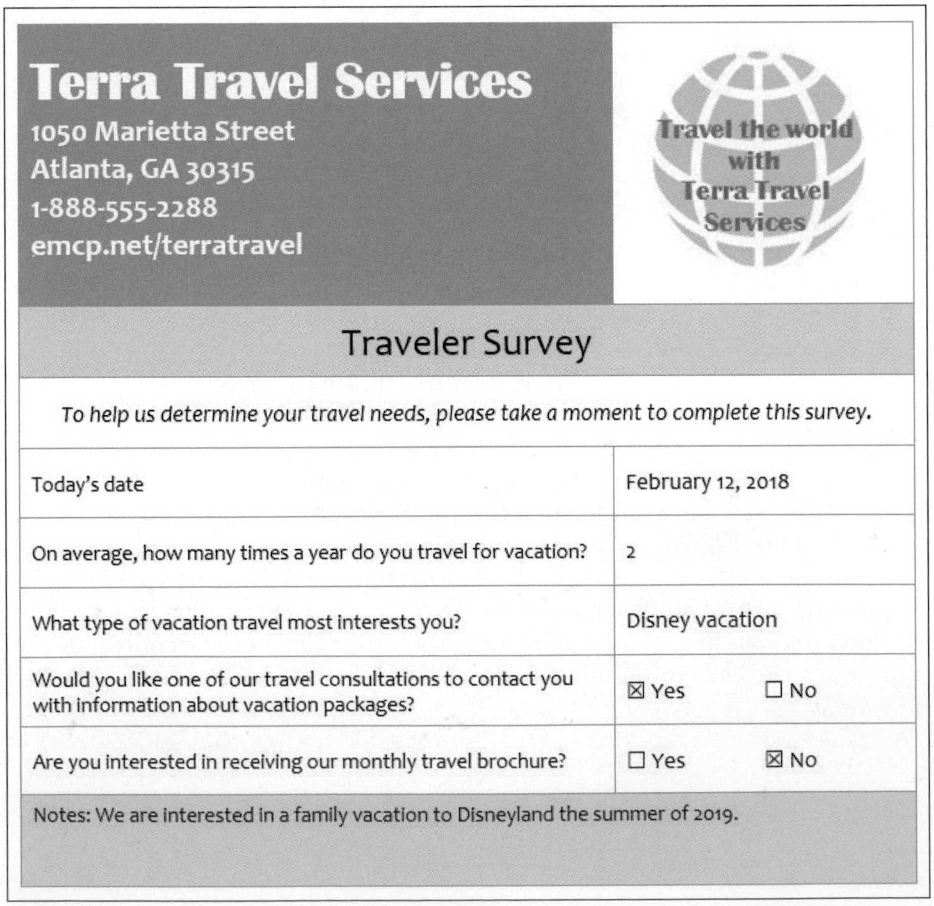

Terra Travel Services
1050 Marietta Street
Atlanta, GA 30315
1-888-555-2288
emcp.net/terratravel

Travel the world with Terra Travel Services

Traveler Survey

To help us determine your travel needs, please take a moment to complete this survey.

Today's date	February 12, 2018
On average, how many times a year do you travel for vacation?	2
What type of vacation travel most interests you?	Disney vacation
Would you like one of our travel consultations to contact you with information about vacation packages?	☒ Yes ☐ No
Are you interested in receiving our monthly travel brochure?	☐ Yes ☒ No
Notes: We are interested in a family vacation to Disneyland the summer of 2019.	

Chapter Summary

- A form is created as a template document with content controls that can be filled in with different information each time the template is used.

- Three basic steps are involved in creating a form: designing the form document based on a template and then building the structure of the form; inserting content controls in which information will be entered with the keyboard; and saving the form as a protected template.

- Save a form as a template at the Save As dialog box by changing the *Save as type* option to *Word Template (*.dotx)*. A template is automatically saved in the Custom Office Templates folder in the Documents folder on the computer's hard drive.

- The Developer tab contains buttons for creating a form. Display this tab by displaying the Word Options dialog box, clicking *Customize Ribbon* in the left panel, clicking the Developer tab check box in the list box at the right, and then clicking OK.

- Protect a region in a form from being edited by a respondent by defining a group. Define a group by selecting text and content controls, clicking the Group button on the Developer tab, and then clicking *Group* at the drop-down list.

- Turn design mode on or off by clicking the Design Mode button in the Controls group on the Developer tab. To edit text or content controls within a group, design mode must be turned on.

- Insert a content control for entering text in a form by clicking the Plain Text Content Control button in the Controls group on the Developer tab.

- Open a document based on a template by clicking the PERSONAL option at the New backstage area and then double-clicking the template thumbnail.

- Fill in a form document based on a template by clicking in the placeholder text for each content control and then typing the required text.

- To open a template for editing, display the Open dialog box, click the *Documents* folder in the Navigation pane, double-click the *Custom Office Templates* folder in Content pane, and then double-click the form template in the Content pane.

- Include instructional text in a plain text content control by inserting the content control and then typing the text. Or type the text where the content control will be inserted, select it, and then click the Plain Text Content Control button on the Developer tab.

- Use options at the Restrict Editing task pane to allow a respondent to enter information in a form but not edit the form. Display this task pane by clicking the Restrict Editing button in the Protect group on the Developer tab.

- In addition to a plain text content control, other types of content controls that can be inserted in a form include picture, date picker, drop-down list, combo box, and check box. Use buttons in the Controls group on the Developer tab to insert content controls.

- Click the Properties button in the Control group on the Developer tab to change the properties of the selected content control. This displays the Content Control Properties dialog box. The content of this dialog box varies depending on what content control is selected.

- Add drop-down list choices by clicking the Add button at the Content Control Properties dialog box, typing the first choice in the Add Choice dialog box, and then clicking OK. Continue in this manner until all choices are entered.

- Lock a picture in a picture content control by inserting a check mark in the *Contents cannot be edited* check box at the Content Control Properties dialog box.
- Change the data picker content control formatting with options in the *Date Picker Properties* section of the Content Control Properties dialog box.
- To edit a protected form template, turn off protection at the Restrict Editing task pane, make the changes, and then protect the template again.

Commands Review

FEATURE	RIBBON TAB, GROUP/OPTION	BUTTON	KEYBOARD SHORTCUT
check box content control	Developer, Controls	☑	
combo box content control	Developer, Controls		
content control properties	Developer, Controls		
date picker content control	Developer, Controls		
drop-down list content control	Developer, Controls		
New backstage area	File, *New*		
next content control			Tab
picture content control	Developer, Controls		
plain text content control	Developer, Controls	Aa	
previous content control			Shift + Tab
Restrict Editing task pane	Developer, Controls		
Word Options dialog box	File, *Options*		

Workbook

Chapter study tools and assessment activities are available in the *Workbook* ebook. These resources are designed to help you further develop and demonstrate mastery of the skills learned in this chapter.

Microsoft® Word

Creating Forms with Legacy Tools

CHAPTER 4

Performance Objectives

Upon successful completion of Chapter 4, you will be able to:

1 Create a form using legacy tools, including drop-down list, check box, and text form fields

2 Use File Explorer to open a document based on a template

3 Protect a form template

4 Fill in a form containing form fields

5 Print a form with the data or print only the data

6 Customize form field options, including drop-down list, check box, and text form fields

Precheck

Check your current skills to help focus your study.

In Chapter 3, you learned how to create forms using content controls. Content controls were first available in Word 2007, which included XML (Extensible Markup Language), a tool for storing and transporting data. Content controls are XML elements that an XML developer can program to populate a data source, such as an Access database, by binding the content control to the source. Before Word 2007, form fields were available for creating forms. Starting with Word 2007, form fields were moved to the Legacy Tools button on the Developer tab, indicating that form fields originated with earlier versions of Word.

In this chapter, you will learn how to use legacy form fields—including text, check box, and drop-down form fields—to create business forms. You will also learn how to save forms as protected documents, create documents from the forms, and enter the requested information.

Data Files

Before beginning chapter work, copy the WL3C4 folder to your storage medium and then make WL3C4 the active folder.

SNAP

If you are a SNAP user, launch the Precheck and Tutorials from your Assignments page.

Project 1 **Create and Fill in an Insurance Application Form**   **4 Parts**

You will insert form fields in an insurance application form, save the form as a template, and then open a document based on the template and insert data in the form fields.

Preview Finished Project

Tutorial

Creating a Form with Legacy Tools

 Legacy Tools

Creating a Form with Legacy Tools

Legacy form fields are available from the Legacy Tools button drop-down list. Display this list by clicking the Legacy Tools button in the Controls group on the Developer tab. The drop-down list includes three form field buttons: the Text Form Field button, the Check Box Form Field button, and the Drop-Down Form Field button. The Legacy Tools button drop-down list contains three additional buttons: the Insert Frame, Form Field Shading, and Reset Form Fields buttons. The Legacy Tools buttons are described in Table 4.1.

Opening a Document Based on a Template Using File Explorer

By default, Word saves a template in the Custom Office Templates folder in the Documents folder on the computer's hard drive. A template can also be saved to a specific folder and then a document based on the template can be opened using File Explorer, a file management application included with Microsoft Windows. For example, in Project 1a, you will save a template to the WL3C4 folder on your storage medium. If you open the template in Word from that folder, the actual template opens. To open a document based on the template, use File Explorer by clicking the File Explorer button on the taskbar, navigating to the folder containing the template, and then double-clicking the template file.

Table 4.1 Legacy Tools Buttons

Legacy Tools Button	Description
Text Form Field	Used to contain text that cannot be formatted by the respondent.
Check box	Used to insert a check box that indicates on or off, true or false, or yes or no, depending on whether the respondent inserts a check mark in the check box.
Drop-down	Used to create a drop-down list of values from which the respondent chooses.
Insert Frame	Used to insert a frame around content and hold static data.
Form Field Shading	Used to turn on or off the form field shading.
Reset Form Fields	Used to clear all entries from the form.

Inserting a Text Form Field

Quick Steps

Insert a Text Form Field
1. Click Developer tab.
2. Click Legacy Tools button.
3. Click Text Form Field button.

 Text Form Field

The text form field in the Legacy Tools button drop-down list is similar to the plain text content control. To insert a text form field, position the insertion point in the desired location, click the Legacy Tools button in the Controls group on the Developer tab, and then click the Text Form Field button. This inserts a gray shaded box in the form. This shaded box is where the respondent enters data when filling in the form. (The shading does not print when the form is printed.) The gray shading can be turned off by clicking the Form Field Shading button in the Legacy Tools button drop-down list. If the gray shading is turned off, click the button again to turn it back on.

Project 1a   Creating an Application Form Template

Part 1 of 4

1. Open **LAApp01.docx** and then save it as a template in the WL3C4 folder on your storage medium by completing the following steps:
   a. Press the F12 function key to display the Save As dialog box.
   b. At the Save As dialog box, type 4-LAApp01Form in the *File name* text box.
   c. Click the *Save as type* option box and then click *Word Template (*.dotx)* at the drop-down list.
   d. Navigate to the WL3C4 folder and then click the Save button.
2. Insert a text form field by completing the followng steps. (Figure 4.1 shows the filled-in form.)
   a. Click the Developer tab.
   b. Position the insertion point one space right of the colon after the field label *Name:* below the heading *FIRST APPLICANT*.
   c. Click the Legacy Tools button in the Controls group on the Developer tab and then click the Text Form Field button.

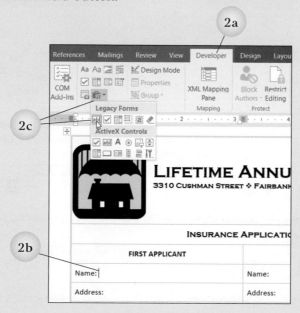

3. Complete steps similar to those in Steps 2b and 2c to insert a text form field one space right of the colon in each of the following field labels in the *FIRST APPLICANT* and *SECOND APPLICANT* sections: *Name:*, *Address:*, *Date of Birth:*, and *Occupation:*.
4. Click the Save button on the Quick Access Toolbar to save the template.

Check Your Work

Inserting a Check Box Form Field

Quick Steps
Insert a Check Box Form Field
1. Click Developer tab.
2. Click Legacy Tools button.
3. Click Check Box Form Field button.

Check Box
Form Field

A check box form field can be inserted in a form and the respondent can insert an *X* in it or leave it blank when filling in the form. Check boxes are useful in forms for indicating yes and no and for inserting options that the respondent can select by inserting check marks. To insert a check box form field, click the Legacy Tools button in the Controls group on the Developer tab and then click the Check Box Form Field button at the drop-down list.

Figure 4.1 Insurance Application Form Created in Project 1

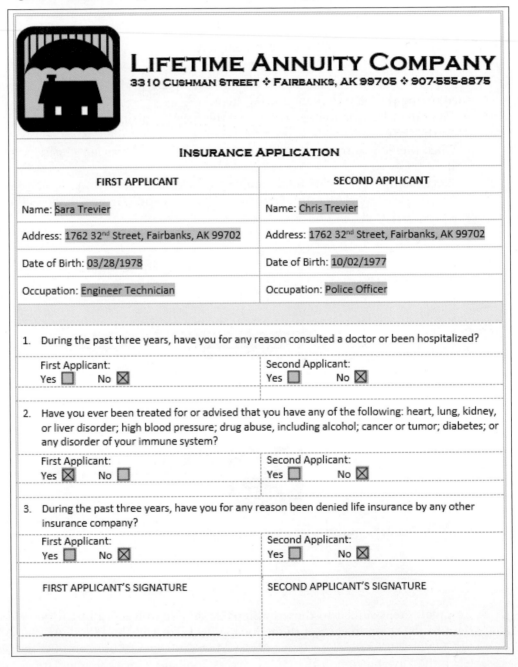

Protecting a Template

Restrict
Editing

Like a template containing content controls, a form containing form fields can be protected so that a respondent can enter information but not edit the form. To protect a template, click the Restrict Editing button on the Developer tab, click in the *Allow only this type of editing in the document* check box to insert a check mark, click the option box arrow in the *Editing restrictions* section, and then click *Filling in forms* at the drop-down list. Click the Yes, Start Enforcing Protection button in the task pane. At the Start Enforcing Protection dialog box, type a password in the *Enter new password (optional)* text box, press the Tab key, type the password again in the *Reenter password to confirm* text box, and then click OK. Protecting a template with a password is optional.

Project 1b Inserting Check Box Form Fields and Protecting a Template   Part 2 of 4

1. With **4-LAApp01Form.dotx** open, insert a check box form field by completing the following steps:
   a. Position the insertion point two spaces right of the *Yes* with the heading *First Applicant* below the first question.
   b. Make sure the Developer tab is active.
   c. Click the Legacy Tools button in the Controls group.
   d. Click the Check Box Form Field button at the drop-down list.
2. Complete steps similar to those in Steps 1c and 1d to insert the remaining check boxes for the *Yes* and *No* responses for both the *First Applicant* and *Second Applicant* sections below questions 1, 2, and 3 (refer to Figure 4.1).
3. Protect the template by completing the following steps:
   a. Click the Restrict Editing button in the Protect group.
   b. Click the *Allow only this type of editing in the document* check box in the Restrict Editing task pane to insert a check mark.
   c. Click the option box arrow in the *Editing restrictions* section of the task pane and then click *Filling in forms* at the drop-down list.
   d. Click the Yes, Start Enforcing Protection button.
   e. At the Start Enforcing Protection dialog box, type your first name all lowercase letters in the *Enter new password (optional)* text box.
   f. Press the Tab key and then type your first name again (all lowercase letters).
   g. Click OK to close the Start Enforcing Protection dialog box.
   h. Click the Close button in the upper right corner of the Restrict Editing task pane to close the task pane.
4. Save and then close **4-LAApp01Form.dotx**.

Check Your Work

Tutorial

Filling in a Form
with Form Fields

Filling in a Form with Form Fields

Fill in a form with text and check box form fields in the same manner used to fill in a form with content controls. To fill in the form, open a document based on the template and then type the information in the form fields. Press the Tab key to move to the next field or press Shift + Tab to move to the previous field. Another option is to click in the desired form field and then type the information. To insert a check mark in a check box, press the spacebar or use the mouse to click in the check box.

Project 1c **Filling in the Lifetime Annuity Form Template**   Part 3 of 4

1. Create a form document from the template **4-LAApp01Form.dotx** by completing the following steps:
   a. Click the File Explorer icon on the taskbar.
   b. At the dialog box that displays, navigate to the WL3C4 folder on your storage medium.
   c. Double-click **4-LAApp01Form.dotx** in the dialog box Content pane. (A document based on the template opens and the insertion point is positioned in the first form field after *Name:*.)
2. Type the name Sara Trevier.
3. Press the Tab key to move to the next form field.
4. Fill in the remaining text and check box form fields as shown in Figure 4.1. Press the Tab key to move to the next form field or press Shift + Tab to move to the previous form field. To insert an *X* in a check box, make the check box active and then press the spacebar.
5. When the form is completed, save the document with the name **4-LATrevierApp**.
6. Print **4-LATrevierApp.docx**.

Check Your Work

Tutorial

Printing a Form

Printing a Form

After a form document has been filled in, it can be printed in the normal manner. The form can also be printed without the filled-in data or only the data can be printed and not the entire form.

Printing only the data is useful in a situation in which a preprinted form is used and inserted in the printer. Word will print the items of data in the same locations on the page as they appear in the form document. To print only the data in a form, display the Word Options dialog box and then click the *Advanced* option in the left panel. Scroll down the dialog box and then click the *Print only the data from a form* check box in the *When printing this document* section.

When you print the form data in Project 1d, the table gridlines will print as well as the shading and image. If you do not want these elements to print, remove them from the form.

Ǭuick Steps

**Print only Data in
Form Document**
1. Click File tab.
2. Click *Options*.
3. Click *Advanced*.
4. Click *Print only the
   data from a form*
   option.
5. Click OK.
6. Click File tab.
7. Click *Print*.
8. Click Print button.

1. With **4-LATrevierApp.docx** open, print only the data by completing the following steps:
   a. Click the File tab and then click *Options*.
   b. At the Word Options dialog box, click *Advanced* in the left panel.
   c. Scroll down the dialog box to the *When printing this document* section and then click the *Print only the data from a form* check box.

   d. Click OK to close the Word Options dialog box.
   e. Click the File tab, click the *Print* option, and then click the Print button at the Print backstage area.
2. Remove the check mark from the *Print only the data from a form* check box by completing the following steps:
   a. Click the File tab and then click *Options*.
   b. At the Word Options dialog box, click *Advanced* in the left panel.
   c. Scroll down the dialog box to the *When printing this document* section and then click the *Print only the data from a form* check box to remove the check mark.
   d. Click OK to close the Word Options dialog box.
3. Save and then close **4-LATrevierApp.docx**.

Check Your Work

Project 2 Create and Fill in a Preferred Insurance Application Form   1 Part

You will insert form fields in a preferred insurance application form (including drop-down form fields), save the form as a template, and then open a document based on the template and insert data in the form fields.

Preview Finished Project

Tutorial

Customizing Form Field Options

Customizing Form Field Options

A text form field contains default settings and some of these defaults can be changed with options at the Text Form Field Options dialog box. Change default settings for a check box form field with options at the Check Box Form Field Options dialog box. Insert a drop-down list form field in a document with a button in the Legacy Tools button drop-down list. Insert a drop-down list form field and then change default settings with options at the Drop-Down Form Field Options dialog box, including typing the choices for the list.

Creating a Drop-Down List Form Field

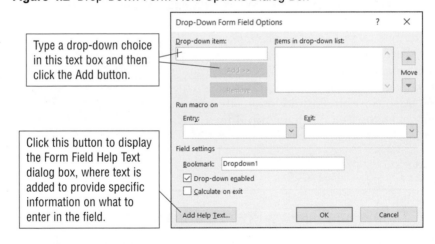

Drop-Down Form Field

To create a field that provides a number of options from which a respondent can choose when filling in the form, insert a drop-down list form field. To do this, click the Legacy Tools button in the Controls group on the Developer tab and then click the Drop-Down Form Field button at the drop-down list. To insert the choices, click the Properties button in the Controls group. This displays the Drop-Down Form Field Options dialog box, shown in Figure 4.2.

At the dialog box, type the first option in the *Drop-down item* text box and then click the Add button. This inserts the item in the *Items in drop-down list* list box. Continue in this manner until all the drop-down list items have been inserted. Remove a drop-down list item from the *Items in drop-down list* list box by clicking the item and then clicking the Remove button. When all the items have been entered in the list box, click OK to close the dialog box.

Specific information can be included in a form field to provide instructional text for a respondent who is filling in the form. To provide instructional text, click the Add Help Text button in the lower left corner of the Drop-Down Form Field Options dialog box. This displays the Form Field Help Text dialog box with the Status Bar tab selected, as shown in Figure 4.3. At the dialog box, click the *Type your own* option and then type the text that will display when the field is active. The typed text displays in the Status bar when the respondent is filling in the form.

Quick Steps

Create a Drop-Down Form Field
1. Click Developer tab.
2. Click Legacy Tools button.
3. Click Drop-Down Form Field button.
4. Click Properties button.
5. Type first list option.
6. Click Add button.
7. Continue typing choices and clicking Add button.
8. Click OK.

Figure 4.2 Drop-Down Form Field Options Dialog Box

Type a drop-down choice in this text box and then click the Add button.

Click this button to display the Form Field Help Text dialog box, where text is added to provide specific information on what to enter in the field.

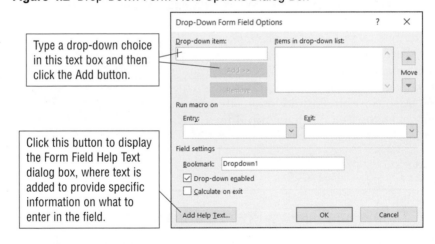

Figure 4.3 Form Field Help Text Dialog Box

Provide instructional text for the respondent by clicking the *Type your own* option and then typing the text in this text box. As the respondent fills in the form, the instructional text displays in the Status bar when the form field is active.

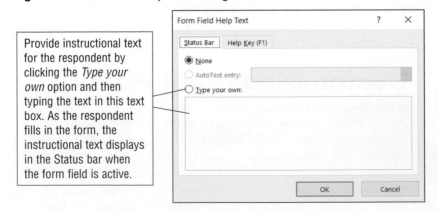

To fill in a drop-down form field, click the form field down arrow at the right side of the field and then click an option at the drop-down list. The drop-down list can also be displayed by pressing the F4 function key or pressing and holding down the Alt key and pressing the Down Arrow key.

Project 2 **Inserting Drop-Down Form Fields and Filling in a Form**   Part 1 of 1

1. Open **LAApp02.docx** and then save the document as a template with the name **4-LAApp02Form** in the WL3C4 folder on your storage medium.
2. Insert a drop-down form field by completing the following steps. (Figure 4.4 shows the filled-in form.)
   a. Position the insertion point one space right of the colon after *Nonprofit Employer:*.
   b. Click the Developer tab.
   c. Click the Legacy Tools button in the Controls group and then click the Drop-Down Form Field button.

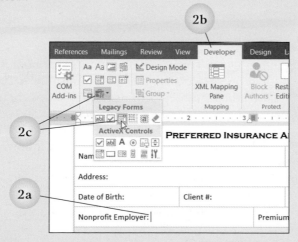

3. Insert the drop-down list choices and create instructional text by completing the following steps:
   a. With the insertion point positioned immediately right of the drop-down form field, click the Properties button in the Controls group on the Developer tab.
   b. At the Drop-Down Form Field Options dialog box, type College in the *Drop-down item* text box.
   c. Click the Add button.
   d. Type Public school in the *Drop-down item* text box.
   e. Click the Add button.
   f. Type Private school in the *Drop-down item* text box.
   g. Click the Add button.
   h. Click the Add Help Text button in the lower left corner of the dialog box.

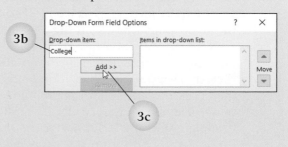

i. At the Form Field Help Text dialog box with the Status Bar tab selected, click the *Type your own* option.

j. In the text box, type the text Click the Nonprofit Employer form field down arrow and then click the employer at the drop-down list.

k. Click OK to close the Form Field Help Text dialog box.

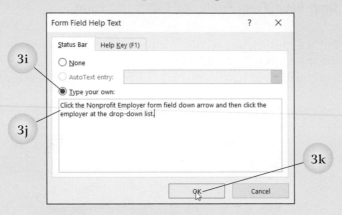

l. Click OK to close the Drop-Down Form Field Options dialog box.

4. Insert a drop-down form field one space after the colon that follows *Premium Payments:* and then complete steps similar to those in Step 3 to insert the following items at the Drop-Down Form Field Options dialog box: *Annually*, *Semiannually*, and *Quarterly*.

5. Insert text form fields (using the Text Form Field button from the Legacy Tools button drop-down list) one space following the colon after each of the following: *Name:*, *Date:*, *Address:*, *Date of Birth:*, and *Client #:*.

6. Insert check box form fields two spaces right of *Female* and *Male* following *Gender:* and right of *Yes* and *No* in the questions.

7. Protect the template to allow only filling in the form and use your last name (all lowercase letters) as the password. (Refer to Project 1b, Step 3.)

8. Save and then close **4-LAApp02Form.dotx**.

9. Create a form document from the template **4-LAApp02Form.dotx** and fill in the form as shown in Figure 4.4 by completing the following steps:

a. Click the File Explorer button on the taskbar.

b. At the dialog box that displays, navigate to the WL3C4 folder on your storage medium and then double-click **4-LAApp02Form.dotx** in the dialog box Content pane.

c. In the document based on the template, enter the data in the form fields as shown in Figure 4.4. (To insert *Public school* in the *Nonprofit Employer* drop-down form field, click the *Nonprofit Employer* form field down arrow and then click *Public school* at the drop-down list. [Notice the instructional text that displays in the Status bar.] Complete similar steps to insert *Quarterly* in the *Premium Payments* drop-down form field.)

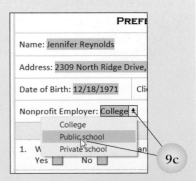

10. When the form is completed, save the document with the name **4-LAReynoldsApp**.

11. Print and then close **4-LAReynoldsApp.docx**.

Check Your Work

Figure 4.4 Preferred Insurance Application Form Created in Project 2

LIFETIME ANNUITY COMPANY
3310 Cushman Street ✧ Fairbanks, AK 99705 ✧ 907-555-8875

PREFERRED INSURANCE APPLICATION

Name: Jennifer Reynolds   Date: 03/08/2018

Address: 2309 North Ridge Drive, Fairbanks, AK 99708

| Date of Birth: 12/18/1971 | Client #: 210-322 | Gender: Female ☒   Male ☐ |

Nonprofit Employer: Public school   Premium Payments: Quarterly

1. Will this insurance replace any existing insurance or annuity?
    Yes ☒   No ☐

2. Within the past three years has your driver's license been suspended or revoked, or have you
    been convicted for driving under the influence of alcohol or drugs?
    Yes ☐   No ☒

3. Do you have any intention of traveling or residing outside the United States or Canada within the
    next twelve months?
    Yes ☐   No ☒

APPLICANT'S SIGNATURE: DATE:

_____   _____

Project 3 Create and Fill in an Application for Benefits Change Form   2 Parts

You will insert form fields in an application for benefits change form, customize the form fields, save the form as a template, and then open a document based on the template and insert data in the form fields.

Preview Finished Project

Customizing Check Box Form Field Options

Customize check box form field options at the Check Box Form Field Options dialog box, shown in Figure 4.5. Display this dialog box by inserting or selecting an existing check box form field and then clicking the Properties button in the Controls group on the Developer tab.

Figure 4.5 Check Box Form Field Options Dialog Box

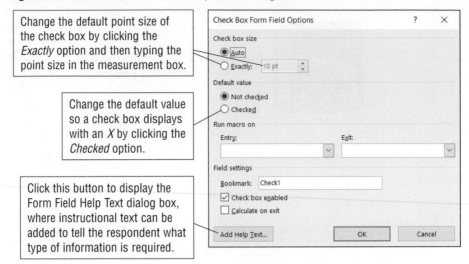

Change the default point size of the check box by clicking the *Exactly* option and then typing the point size in the measurement box.

Change the default value so a check box displays with an *X* by clicking the *Checked* option.

Click this button to display the Form Field Help Text dialog box, where instructional text can be added to tell the respondent what type of information is required.

By default, Word inserts a check box in a form template that is the same size as the adjacent text. To change the default point size, click the *Exactly* option and then type the point size in the measurement box or use the measurement box up or down arrow to increase or decrease the point size.

A check box form field is empty by default. This default can be changed so the check box displays with an *X* by clicking the *Checked* option in the *Default value* section of the dialog box.

Project 3a   Inserting and Customizing Check Box Form Fields

Part 1 of 2

1. Open **LAApp03.docx** and then save the document as a template with the name **4-LAApp03Form** in the WL3C4 folder on your storage medium.
2. Insert a check box that contains a check mark by completing the following steps: (Figure 4.6 shows the filled-in form.)
   a. Position the insertion point two spaces right of the *Yes* below the *Are you currently working?* question.
   b. Click the Developer tab, click the Legacy Tools button in the Controls group, and then click the Check Box Form Field button at the drop-down list.
   c. With the insertion point positioned immediately right of the check box form field, click the Properties button in the Controls group.
   d. At the Check Box Form Field Options dialog box, click the *Checked* option in the *Default value* section.
   e. Click OK.

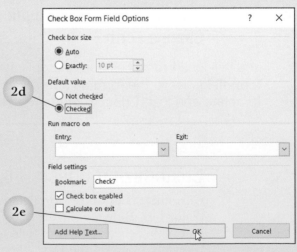

3. Complete steps similar to those in Step 2 to insert a check box that contains a check mark right of *Yes* below the *Do you work full time?* question.
4. Insert the remaining check boxes for questions 1, 2, and 3 (without check marks).
5. Insert a drop-down form field two spaces after the question mark that ends question 4 and insert the following items at the Drop-Down Form Field Options dialog box: *Standard, Premium, Gold,* and *Platinum.*
6. Insert a drop-down form field two spaces after the question mark that ends question 5 and insert the following items at the Drop-Down Form Field Options dialog box: *Standard, Premium, Gold,* and *Platinum.*
7. Save **4-LAApp03Form.dotx**.

Check Your Work

Figure 4.6 Application for Benefits Change Form Created in Project 3

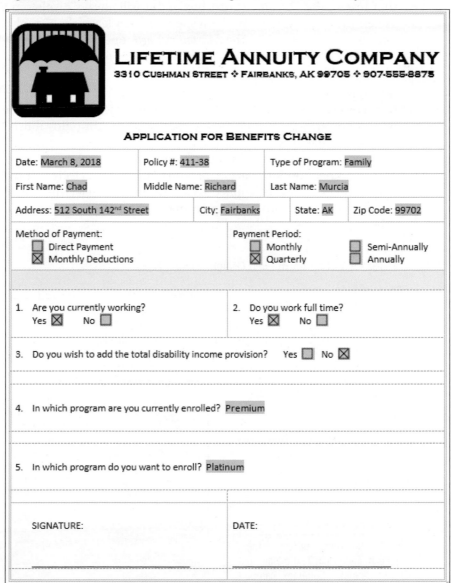

Customizing Text Form Fields

To change options for a text form field, select the form field (or position the insertion point immediately right of the form field) and then click the Properties button in the Controls group on the Developer tab. This displays the Text Form Field Options dialog box, shown in Figure 4.7.

Change the type of text to be inserted in the form field with the *Type* option at the Text Form Field Options dialog box. The default setting is *Regular text* and it can be changed to *Number*, *Date*, *Current date*, *Current time*, or *Calculation*. If the *Type* option is changed, Word displays an error message if the wrong type of information is entered in the form field. For example, if the *Type* option is changed to *Number*, a respondent filling in the form can only enter a number. If the respondent tries to enter something other than a number, Word displays an error message, selects the entry, and keeps the insertion point in the form field until a number is entered.

If a particular text form field generally requires the same information, type that text in the *Default text* text box and it will always display in the form field. When the form is filled in, the respondent can leave the default text in the form field or type over it. Use the *Maximum length* option at the dialog box to specify a maximum number of characters for the form field. This option has a default setting of *Unlimited*.

Apply formatting to text in a form field with options in the *Text format* option box. For example, to display text in all uppercase letters, click the *Text format* option box arrow and then click *Uppercase* at the drop-down list. When the respondent has typed text in the form field, that text is automatically converted to uppercase letters as soon as the respondent presses the Tab key or the Enter key. The *Text format* options vary depending on what is selected in the *Type* option box. Formatting can also be applied to a form field by selecting the form field, applying the formatting, and then using Format Painter to apply the same formatting to other form fields.

Figure 4.7 Text Form Field Options Dialog Box

Use the *Type* option to specify the type of information that can be entered in the form field. Click the option box arrow to display a drop-down list of options.

If the same information is generally required in a text form field, type the text in the *Default text* text box.

Use the *Maximum length* option box to specify the number of characters that can be entered in the text form field.

Click this button to display the Form Field Help Text dialog box, where instructional text can be added to tell the respondent what type of information is required.

1. With **4-LAApp03Form.dotx** open, create a custom text form field by completing the following steps:
   a. Position the insertion point one space right of the colon after *Type of Program:*.
   b. Insert a text box form field by clicking the Legacy Tools button in the Controls group and then clicking the Text Form Field button at the drop-down list.
   c. Most employees are enrolled in a family insurance program. Reflect this by making *Family* the default setting for the text form field. To do this, make sure the insertion point is positioned immediately right of the text form field and then click the Properties button.
   d. At the Text Form Field Options dialog box, type Family in the *Default text* text box.
   e. Click OK to close the dialog box.

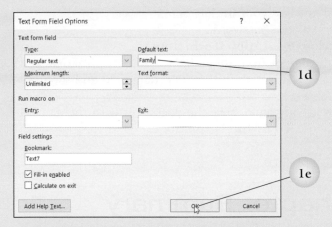

2. Create a custom text form field for the *State:* form field that specifies that the field must contain two uppercase letters by completing the following steps:
   a. Position the insertion point one space right of the colon after *State:*.
   b. Insert a text box form field by clicking the Legacy Tools button in the Controls group and then clicking the Text Form Field button at the drop-down list.
   c. Click the Properties button.
   d. At the Text Form Field Options dialog box, click the *Maximum length* measurement box up arrow until *2* displays.
   e. Click the *Text format* option box arrow and then click *Uppercase* at the drop-down list.

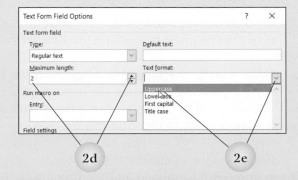

   f. Click OK to close the Text Form Field Options dialog box.
3. Complete steps similar to those in Step 2 to create a custom text form field for the *Zip Code:* form field that specifies a maximum length of five characters.
4. Complete steps similar to those in Step 2 to create a custom text form field for the *Policy #:* form field that specifies a maximum length of six characters.

5. Customize the text form field right of *Date:* by completing the following steps:
   a. Click the text form field shaded box that displays right of *Date:*.
   b. Click the Properties button in the Controls group.
   c. At the Text Form Field Options dialog box, click the *Type* option box arrow and then click *Current date* at the drop-down list.
   d. Click the *Date format* option box arrow and then click the *MMMM d, yyyy* option at the drop-down list.
   e. Click OK to close the dialog box.
6. Protect the template to allow only filling in the form and and use your initials (all uppercase letters) as the password.
7. Save and then close **4-LAApp03Form.dotx**.
8. Create a form document from the template **4-LAApp03Form.dotx** and fill in the form as shown in Figure 4.6. (Type ak in the *State:* data field and then press the Tab key; the text changes to uppercase letters.)
9. When the form is completed, save the document with the name **4-LAMurciaApp**.
10. Print and then close **4-LAMurciaApp.docx**.

Check Your Work

Chapter Summary

- The Legacy Tools button in the Controls group on the Developer tab contains buttons for inserting text, check box, and drop-down form fields into a form.

- Use File Explorer to open a document based on a template that is saved in a folder other than the Custom Office Templates default folder. Open File Explorer by clicking the File Explorer button on the taskbar.

- A text form field is similar to a plain text content control. Insert a text form field by clicking the Legacy Tools button in the Controls group on the Developer tab and then clicking the Text Form Field button at the drop-down list.

- Insert a check box form field in a form in which the respondent is to choose an option by inserting an *X* in the check box.

- Protect a form containing form fields with options at the Restrict Editing task pane. Display the task pane by clicking the Restrict Editing button on the Developer tab.

- Print a filled-in form in the normal manner, print the form without the data, or print only the data. To print only the data, display the Word Options dialog box, click the *Advanced* option in the left panel, scroll down the dialog box, and then insert a check mark in the *Print only the data from a form* check box in the *When printing this document* section.

- Create a drop-down list of choices from which the respondent can select by inserting a drop-down form field and then typing the choices at the Drop-Down Form Field Options dialog box. Display this dialog box by inserting a drop-down form field and then clicking the Properties button in the Control group on the Developer tab.

- To fill in a form with a drop-down form field, the respondent clicks the form field down arrow and then clicks an option at the drop-down list. Another way to display the drop-down list is to press the F4 function key or to press and hold down the Alt key and then press the Down Arrow key.
- Customize check box form field options at the Check Box Form Field Options dialog box. Display this dialog box by inserting a check box form field and then clicking the Properties button in the Control group on the Developer tab.
- Customize text form field options at the Text Form Field Options dialog box. Display this dialog box by inserting a text form field and then clicking the Properties button in the Controls group on the Developer tab.

Commands Review

FEATURE	RIBBON TAB, GROUP	BUTTON, OPTION	KEYBOARD SHORTCUT
check box form field	Developer, Controls		
Check Box Form Field Options dialog box	Developer, Controls		
drop-down list form field	Developer, Controls		
Drop-Down List Form Field Options dialog box	Developer, Controls		
Legacy Tools button drop-down list	Developer, Controls		
next data field			Tab
previous data field			Shift + Tab
Restrict Editing task pane	Dveloper, Controls		
text form field	Developer, Controls		
Text Form Field Options dialog box	Developer, Controls		

Workbook

Chapter study tools and assessment activities are available in the *Workbook* ebook. These resources are designed to help you further develop and demonstrate mastery of the skills learned in this chapter.

Microsoft®

Word

Using Outline View and Creating a Table of Authorities

Performance Objectives

Upon successful completion of Chapter 5, you will be able to:

1 Display a document in Outline view

2 Collapse, expand, promote, demote, and assign levels in Outline view

3 Organize a document in Outline view

4 Assign levels at the Paragraph dialog box

5 Navigate in a document with assigned levels

6 Collapse and expand levels in Normal view

7 Move collapsed text

8 Collapse levels by default

9 Create a master document

10 Open and close a master document and its subdocuments

11 Expand, collapse, edit, insert, unlink, split, and merge subdocuments

12 Create, insert, and update a table of authorities

Use Outline view to display specific titles, headings, and body text in a Word document. In this view, you can quickly see an overview of a document by collapsing parts of it so only specific titles and headings display. With the titles and headings collapsed, you can perform editing functions, including moving and deleting sections of a document.

For some documents, such as books and procedures manuals that contain many parts or sections, consider creating master documents and subdocuments. For example, if several people are working on one large document, each person can prepare a document and then those documents can be combined into a master document. Word provides options for creating a table of authorities, which is a list of citations that appears in a legal brief or other legal document. In this chapter, you will learn how to use Outline view, create master documents and subdocuments, and how to create, insert, and update a table of authorities.

SNAP

Data Files ▶

Before beginning chapter work, copy the WL3C5 folder to your storage medium and then make WL3C5 the active folder.

You will open a document on computer security issues, display the document
in Outline view, expand and collapse levels, promote and demote levels, assign
levels to text, and organize data in the document.

Preview Finished Project

Managing a Document
in Outline View

When working in a large or complex document, consider using Outline view
to display heading levels, turn on or off the display of heading text formatting,
show only the first line of body text in the outline, and collapse or expand levels.
Outline view is useful for displaying the structure of the document and for
rearranging document content.

A title or heading formatted with the Heading 1 style displays as a level 1
heading in Outline view. A heading formatted with the Heading 2 style displays
as a level 2 heading, a heading formatted with the Heading 3 style displays as a
level 3 heading, and so on. If titles and headings in a document have not been
formatted with heading styles, heading level formatting can be applied in Outline
view with the *Outline Level* option box.

Displaying a Document in Outline View

To switch to Outline view, click the View tab and then click the Outline button in
the Views group. Figure 5.1 shows a document in Outline view that has heading
styles applied to the titles and headings. The figure also identifies the Outlining
tab, which contains options and buttons for working in Outline view.

Figure 5.1 Document in Outline View

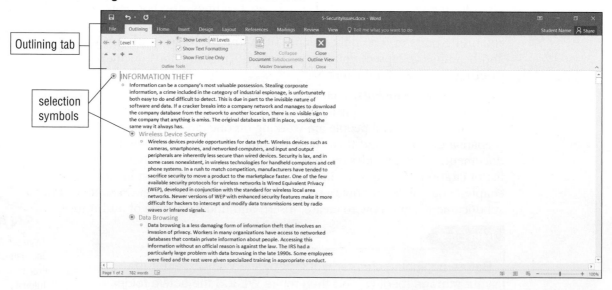

Outlining tab

selection
symbols

In Figure 5.1, the title *INFORMATION THEFT* is identified as a level 1 heading because the Heading 1 style was applied it. The heading *Wireless Device Security* is identified as a level 2 heading because the Heading 2 style was applied to it. The paragraphs of text that follow the title and heading are identified as body text. Each heading shown in Figure 5.1 displays with a selection symbol (a gray circle containing a plus [+] symbol) immediately left of it. Click this symbol to select text in that particular heading.

Use buttons and options on the Outlining tab in Outline view to assign levels, promote and demote levels, show only specific levels, turn off the display of text formatting, and show only the first line of body text below a level. The buttons and options on the Outlining tab are described in Table 5.1.

Table 5.1 Outlining Tab Buttons and Options

Button/Option	Name	Action
	Promote to Heading 1	Promotes text to the highest level of the outline.
	Promote	Promotes a heading (and its body text) by one level; promotes body text to the heading level of the preceding heading.
Level 1	Outline Level	Assigns and displays the current level of text.
	Demote	Demotes a heading by one level; demotes body text to the heading level below the preceding heading.
	Demote to Body Text	Demotes a heading to body text.
	Move Up	Moves the selected item up within the outline.
	Move Down	Moves the selected item down within the outline.
	Expand	Expands the first heading level below the currently selected heading.
	Collapse	Collapses body text into a heading and then collapses the lowest heading levels into higher heading levels.
Show Level: All Levels	Show Level	Displays all headings through the lowest level chosen.
✓ Show Text Formatting	Show Text Formatting	Displays the outline with or without character formatting.
✓ Show First Line Only	Show First Line Only	Switches between displaying all body text or only the first line of each paragraph.

Collapsing and Expanding Levels

One of the major advantages of working in Outline view is being able to see a condensed outline of the document without all the text between the titles, headings, and subheadings. A level in an outline can be collapsed so that any text or subsequent lower levels temporarily do not display. Being able to collapse and expand headings in an outline provides flexibility in managing a document. With the levels collapsed, moving from one part of a document to another is faster. Collapsing levels is also helpful for maintaining consistency between titles and headings.

To collapse an entire document, click the *Show Level* option box arrow in the Outline Tools group on the Outlining tab and then click the desired level at the drop-down list. For example, if the document contains three levels, click *Level 3* at the drop-down list. Figure 5.2 shows the document used in Project 1 collapsed so that only level 1 and level 2 headings display. When a heading that is followed by text is collapsed, a gray horizontal line displays beneath the title or heading, as shown in the figure. To redisplay all the text in the document, click the *Show Level* option box arrow and then click *All Levels* at the drop-down list.

In addition to the *Show Level* option box, the Collapse and Expand buttons on the Outlining tab can be used to hide and show specific headings and body text, respectively. Use the Collapse button on the Outlining tab to hide the body text below a heading and any lower level headings. Click the Expand button to display the body text below a heading and any lower level headings.

Figure 5.2 Collapsed Document

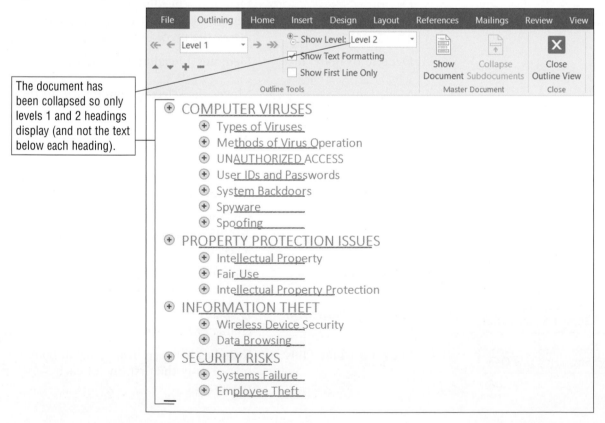

The document has been collapsed so only levels 1 and 2 headings display (and not the text below each heading).

1. Open **Security01.docx** and then save it with the name **5-SecurityIssues**.
2. Apply the Heading 1 style to the two titles: *INFORMATION THEFT* and *COMPUTER VIRUSES*.
3. Apply the Heading 2 style to the four headings: *Wireless Device Security*, *Data Browsing*, *Types of Viruses*, and *Methods of Virus Operation*.
4. Press Ctrl + Home to move the insertion point to the beginning of the document. Display the document in Outline view by clicking the View tab and then clicking the Outline button in the Views group.

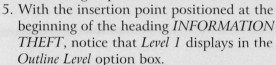

5. With the insertion point positioned at the beginning of the heading *INFORMATION THEFT*, notice that *Level 1* displays in the *Outline Level* option box.
6. Display only level 1 headings by clicking the *Show Level* option box arrow and then clicking *Level 1* at the drop-down list.
7. Display level 1 and level 2 headings by clicking the *Show Level* option box arrow and then clicking *Level 2* at the drop-down list.
8. Turn off the display of heading style formatting by clicking the *Show Text Formatting* check box to remove the check mark.
9. Redisplay the formatting by clicking the *Show Text Formatting* check box to insert a check mark.
10. Show all the heading levels by clicking the *Show Level* option box arrow and then clicking *All Levels* at the drop-down list.
11. Click in the first paragraph of text below the heading *INFORMATION THEFT* and notice that *Body Text* displays in the *Outline Level* option box.
12. If necessary, display all the body text by clicking the *Show First Line Only* check box to remove the check mark.
13. Click in the heading *INFORMATION THEFT* and then collapse the body text as well as the body text below the level 2 headings by clicking the Collapse button in the Outline Tools group.
14. Click in the heading *Types of Viruses* and then collapse the body text by clicking the Collapse button.
15. Click the Expand button to expand the body text below the heading *Types of Viruses*.
16. Click in the heading *INFORMATION THEFT* and then click the Expand button.
17. Close Outline view by clicking the Close Outline View button on the Outlining tab.
18. Save **5-SecurityIssues.docx**.

Check Your Work

Promoting and Demoting Heading Levels

Quick Steps

Promote a Level
1. Display document in Outline view.
2. Click in heading.
3. Click Promote to Heading 1 button or Promote button.

Demote a Level
1. Display document in Outline view.
2. Click in heading.
3. Click Demote button.

💡 **Hint** Alt + Shift + Left Arrow is the keyboard shortcut to promote text to the next higher level.

💡 **Hint** Alt + Shift + Right Arrow it the keyboard shortcut to demote text to the next lower level.

Levels are assigned to titles and headings in Outline view based on the heading styles applied. Level 1 is assigned to titles and headings with the Heading 1 style applied, level 2 is assigned to headings with the Heading 2 style applied, and so on. The assigned level can be changed by promoting or demoting it. Use the Promote to Heading 1 button on the Outlining tab to promote text to level 1, and click the Promote button to promote a heading and its body text by one level. Click the Demote button to demote a heading by one level and click the Demote Body Text button to demote a heading to body text.

Another method for promoting or demoting a heading in Outline view is to drag the selection symbol immediately left of the heading 0.5 inch to the left or right. The selection symbol for a level heading displays as a gray circle containing a plus symbol, and the selection symbol for body text displays as a smaller gray circle. For example, to demote text identified as level 1 to level 2, position the arrow pointer on the heading selection symbol immediately left of the level 1 text until the pointer turns into a four-headed arrow. Click and hold down the left mouse button, drag right with the mouse until a gray vertical line displays down the screen, and then release the mouse button. Complete similar steps to promote a heading. In addition, a heading can be promoted with the keyboard shortcut Alt + Shift + Left Arrow key and demoted with Alt + Shift + Right Arrow key.

Project 1b Promoting and Demoting Heading Levels   Part 2 of 4

1. With **5-SecurityIssues.docx** open, press Ctrl + Home to move the insertion point to the beginning of the document and then use the *Text from File* option at the Object button drop-down list on the Insert tab to insert the document **Security02.docx**. (This document has heading styles applied to all the headings.)
2. Press Ctrl + Home to move the insertion point to the beginning of the document and then display the document in Outline view by clicking the View tab and then clicking the Outline button.
3. With the insertion point positioned at the beginning of the heading *SECURITY RISKS*, click the Promote to Heading 1 button to promote the heading to level 1.
4. Click in the heading *Systems Failure* and then click the Promote button to promote the heading to level 2.

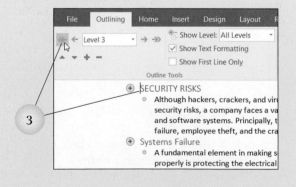
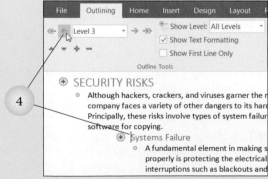

5. Click in the heading *Employee Theft* and then click the Demote button to demote the heading to level 2.

6. Promote the heading *PROPERTY PROTECTION ISSUES* using the mouse by completing the following steps:

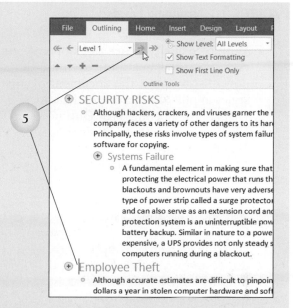

   a. Position the mouse pointer on the selection symbol immediately left of the heading *PROPERTY PROTECTION ISSUES* until the mouse pointer turns into a four-headed arrow.

   b. Click and hold down the left mouse button, drag with the mouse to the left until a gray vertical line displays near the left side of the page (as shown in the image at the right), and then release the mouse button. (When you release the mouse button, check to make sure *Level 1* displays in the *Outline Level* option box.)

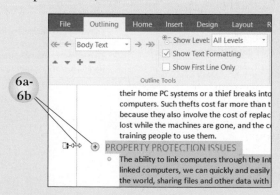

7. Click in the heading *Intellectual Property* and then demote it to level 2 by pressing Alt + Shift + Right Arrow.

8. Click in the heading *Fair Use* and then promote it to level 2 by pressing Alt + Shift + Left Arrow.

9. Click in the heading *Intellectual Property Protection* and then click the Demote button to demote the heading to level 2.

10. Click the Close Outline View button on the Outlining tab.

11. Save **5-SecurityIssues.docx**.

Check Your Work

Assigning Levels

Quick Steps

Assigning Levels
1. Display document in Outline view.
2. Click *Outline Level* option box arrow.
3. Click level at drop-down list.

If heading styles have not been applied in a document, assigning heading levels in Outline view will apply them to the heading text. For example, assigning level 1 to a heading will apply the Heading 1 style. Assign a level by clicking the *Outline Level* option box arrow and then clicking a level at the drop-down list. Promoting and demoting also assigns levels.

1. With **5-SecurityIssues.docx** open, press Ctrl + End to move the insertion point to the end of the document and then use the *Text from File* option at the Object button drop-down list to insert the document **Security03.docx**. (This document does not have heading styles applied to the title or headings.)
2. Display the document in Outline view.
3. Click in the heading *UNAUTHORIZED ACCESS* and then click the Promote to Heading 1 button.
4. Click in the heading *User IDs and Passwords*, click the *Outline Level* option box arrow, and then click *Level 2* at the drop-down list.
5. Click in the heading *System Backdoors*, click the *Outline Level* option box arrow, and then click *Level 2* at the drop-down list.
6. Click in the heading *Spoofing* and then click the Promote button.
7. Click in the heading *Spyware*, click the *Outline Level* option box arrow, and then click *Level 2* at the drop-down list.
8. Click the Close Outline View button on the Outlining tab. (Notice that heading styles have been applied to the headings.)
9. Save **5-SecurityIssues.docx**.

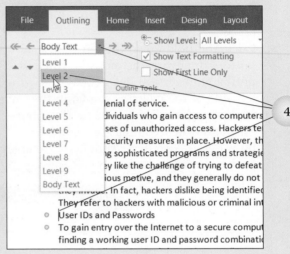

Check Your Work

Organizing a Document in Outline View

Collapsing and expanding headings within an outline is only one of the useful features of Outline view. Outline view can also be used to organize a document. Move a heading level and any body text or lower heading levels move with the heading. Move a heading level with the Move Up button or Move Down button in the Outline Tools groups on the Outlining tab. For example, to move a level 2 heading below other level 2 headings, collapse the outline, click in the level 2 heading to be moved, and then click the Move Down button in the Outline Tools group until the level 2 heading is in the desired position.

A heading level can also be moved to a new location by dragging it with the mouse pointer. To do this, position the mouse pointer on the selection symbol immediately left of the heading until the pointer turns into a four-headed arrow, click and hold down the left mouse button, drag the heading to the new location, and then release the mouse button. As the heading is being moved, a gray horizontal line with an arrow attached displays. Use this horizontal line to help position the heading in the new location.

1. With **5-SecurityIssues.docx** open, press Ctrl + Home to move the insertion point to the beginning of the document.
2. Display the document in Outline view.
3. Click the *Show Level* option box arrow and then click *Level 1* at the drop-down list.
4. Move the heading *COMPUTER VIRUSES* to the beginning of the document by clicking in the heading and then clicking the Move Up button three times.
5. Move the heading *SECURITY RISKS* to the end of the document by clicking in the heading and then clicking the Move Down button three times.
6. Click the *Show Level* option box arrow and then click *Level 2* at the drop-down list.
7. Move the *Spoofing* heading below *Spyware* by completing the following steps:

   a. Position the mouse pointer on the selection symbol immediately left of the heading *Spoofing* until the pointer turns into a four-headed arrow.
   b. Click and hold down the left mouse button, drag down with the mouse until the gray horizontal line with the arrow attached is positioned below *Spyware*, and then release the mouse button.
8. Save and then print the document. (This will print the collapsed outline, not the entire document.)
9. Click the *Show Level* option box arrow and then click *All Levels* at the drop-down list.
10. Click the Close Outline View button.
11. Save, print, and then close **5-SecurityIssues.docx**.

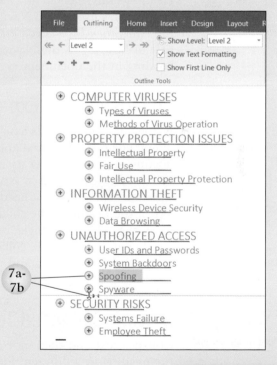

Check Your Work

Project 2   Assign Levels to a Resume Document   2 Parts

You will use options at the Paragraph dialog box to assign levels to a resume document and then collapse and expand the levels, move a level, and then specify that specific levels open collapsed by default.

Preview Finished Project

Assigning Levels at the Paragraph Dialog Box

Assigning a level to text in Outline view applies a heading style. In some situations, the headings in a document may contain specific formatting that should not be overwritten by heading styles. Assign a level to text that does not apply a heading style with the *Outline level* option box at the Paragraph dialog box. To use this option, position the insertion point in a heading and then click the Paragraph group dialog box launcher on the Home tab. At the Paragraph dialog box, click the *Outline level* option box arrow and then click a level option at the drop-down list. The drop-down list contains nine level options and a body text option.

Ḋuick Steps

Assign Levels at the Paragraph Dialog Box

1. Position insertion point in heading.
2. Click Paragraph group dialog box launcher.
3. Click *Outline level* option box arrow.
4. Click level at drop-down list.

💡 **Hint** Use the *Outline level* option box to assign levels to titles and headings without applying heading styles.

Navigating in a Document with Assigned Levels

When levels are assigned to titles and headings with the *Outline level* option box at the Paragraph dialog box, the levels display in the Navigation pane with the Headings tab selected and can be used to navigate to specific locations in the document. Display the Navigation pane by clicking the View tab and then clicking the *Navigation Pane* check box in the Show group to insert a check mark. Click a title or heading in the Navigation pane to move the insertion point to that title or heading in the document.

Collapsing and Expanding Levels in Normal View

A document with levels assigned with the *Outline level* option box at the Paragraph dialog box can be viewed and edited in Outline view in the same manner as a document with heading styles applied. In addition to Outline view, levels can be collapsed or expanded in Normal view. To collapse levels in Normal view, position the mouse pointer on a heading level and a collapse triangle displays immediately left of the heading. The collapse triangle displays as a small, solid, dark triangle. Click the collapse triangle and any body text and lower level heading and body text below the level will collapse. To expand a collapsed level, position the mouse pointer on the heading and then click the expand triangle immediately left of the heading. The expand triangle displays as a small, hollow, right-pointing triangle.

Ḋuick Steps

Collapse a Level in Normal View

1. Position mouse pointer on heading level.
2. Click collapse triangle left of heading.

Expand a Level in Normal View

1. Position mouse pointer on heading level.
2. Click expand triangle left of heading.

Move Collapsed Text

1. Select collapsed heading.
2. Position mouse pointer in selected text.
3. Click and hold down left mouse button.
4. Drag to new position and then release mouse button.

Moving Collapsed Text

Collapse text and then move the heading and any body text or lower levels below the heading to a different location in the document. To move collapsed text, select the collapsed heading and then position the mouse pointer in the selected text. Click and hold down the left mouse button and then drag with the mouse. When dragging with the mouse, a thick, black vertical line displays indicating where the text will be moved. Drag with the mouse until the vertical line displays in the desired position and then release the mouse button.

1. Open **Resumes.docx** and then save it with the name **5-Resumes**.
2. Assign level 1 to the two titles in the document by completing the following steps:
    a. With the insertion point positioned at the beginning of the title *RESUME STYLES*, click the Paragraph group dialog box launcher.
    b. At the Paragraph dialog box, click the *Outline level* option box arrow and then click *Level 1* at the drop-down list.
    c. Click OK to close the dialog box.
    d. Scroll down the document, click in the title *RESUME WRITING*, and then press the F4 function key to repeat the last command.

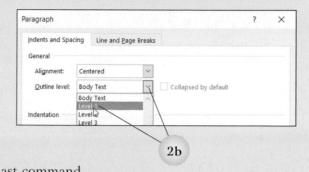

3. Assign level 2 to the five headings in the document by completing the following steps:
    a. Scroll up the document and then click in the heading *The Chronological Resume*.
    b. Click the Paragraph group dialog box launcher.
    c. At the Paragraph dialog box, click the *Outline level* option box arrow and then click *Level 2* at the drop-down list.
    d. Click OK to close the dialog box.
    e. Click in the heading *The Functional Resume* and then press the F4 function key.
    f. Click in the heading *The Hybrid Resume* and then press the F4 function key.
    g. Click in the heading *The Right Mix* and then press the F4 function key.
    h. Click in the heading *Information about the Job* and then press the F4 function key.
4. Press Ctrl + Home to move the insertion point to the beginning of the document.
5. Collapse the body text below the title by positioning the mouse pointer on the title *RESUME STYLES* and then click the collapse triangle immediately left of the title.

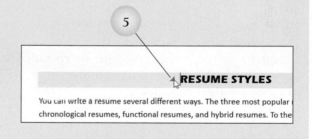

6. Collapse the body text below the second title by positioning the mouse pointer on the title *RESUME WRITING* and then clicking the collapse triangle immediately left of the title.
7. Move the title *RESUME* WRITING and all the body text and level 2 headings by completing the following steps:
    a. Select the title *RESUME WRITING*.
    b. Position the mouse pointer on the selected title and click and hold down the left mouse button.
    c. Drag up with the mouse until a thick, black vertical line displays left of the title *RESUME STYLES* and then release the mouse button.

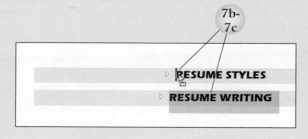

8. Expand the text below the title *RESUME STYLES* by positioning the mouse pointer on the title and then clicking the expand triangle immediately left of it.

9. Expand the text below the title *RESUME WRITING* by positioning the mouse pointer on the title and then clicking the expand triangle immediately left of it.

10. Navigate in the document by completing the following steps:
    a. Click the View tab and then click the *Navigation Pane* check box in the Show group.
    b. Click the heading *The Functional Resume* in the Navigation pane to move the insertion point to the beginning of the heading.

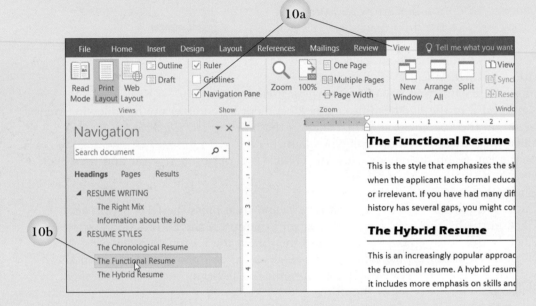

c. Click the title *RESUME WRITING* in the Navigation pane to move the insertion point to the beginning of the title.
    d. Close the Navigation pane by clicking the *Navigation Pane* check box in the Show group on the View tab to remove the check mark.

11. Save **5-Resumes.docx**.

Check Your Work

Collapsing Levels by Default

Quick Steps

Collapse a Level by Default
1. Position insertion point in title or heading.
2. Click Paragraph group dialog box launcher.
3. Click *Collapsed by default* check box to insert check mark.
4. Click OK.

If a collapsed document is closed and then opened, it opens with all the levels expanded. The Paragraph dialog box contains the *Collapsed by default* check box, which can be used to specify that a specific title or heading level should open in a collapsed manner. To use this option, position the insertion point in the title or heading, display the Paragraph dialog box, insert a check mark in the *Collapsed by default* check box, and then close the dialog box. Save and then close the document and each time the document is opened, it opens with the specific title or heading level collapsed.

1. With **5-Resumes.docx** open, make sure the insertion point is positioned at the beginning of the document.
2. Specify that all the body text and levels below the title *RESUME WRITING* should open collapsed by completing the following steps:

   a. Click the Paragraph group dialog box launcher.

   b. At the Paragraph dialog box, click the *Collapsed by default* check box to insert a check mark.

   c. Click OK to close the dialog box. (The body text and levels are collapsed below the title.)

   2b

   Paragraph   ?   ✕

   Indents and Spacing   Line and Page Breaks

   General

   Alignment: Centered

   Outline level: Level 1   ☑ Collapsed by default

3. Click in the title *RESUME STYLES* and then complete steps similar to those in 2a through 2c to specify that the title should open collapsed.
4. Save and then close **5-Resumes.docx**.
5. Open **5-Resumes.docx** and notice that the body text and levels below both titles are collapsed.
6. Print and then close **5-Resumes.docx**. (Only the two headings will print.)

Check Your Work

Project 3   **Create a Master Document and Subdocuments with a Graphic Software Report**   **2 Parts**

You will create a master document from an existing document containing information on graphic and multimedia software and then create subdocuments with text in the master document. You will expand and collapse the document in Outline view and also edit a subdocument.

Preview Finished Project

Creating a Master Document

For a project that contains many parts or sections—such as a reference guide, procedures manual, or book—consider using a master document. A master document contains a number of separate documents referred to as *subdocuments*.

Creating a master document is useful in a situation in which several people are working on one project. Each person prepares a document for part of the project and then all the documents are combined in a master document. Working with a master document also allows for easier editing. Rather than work in one large document, changes are made in several subdocuments and then all the edits are reflected in the master document.

Creating a Master Document from an Existing Document

An existing document can be created as a master document. Text in the master document can be divided into subdocuments, which removes the subdocument text from the original document, creates new documents for the individual subdocuments, and inserts hyperlinks to the subdocuments in the master document. In this way,

Quick Steps

Create a Master Document from an Existing Document
1. Display document in Outline view.
2. Assign levels.
3. Click Show Document button.
4. Select headings and text to be divided into subdocuments.
5. Click Create button.

Show Document

Create

each subdocument can be assigned to an individual for editing. Any edits made to text in the subdocuments are automatically reflected in the master document.

To create a master document from an existing document, open the document; switch to Outline view; assign heading levels to titles and headings within the document, if necessary; and then click the Show Document button in the Master Document group. Select the headings and text to be divided into subdocuments and then click the Create button in the Master Document group. Text specified as a subdocument is enclosed within a box formed by thin gray lines and a subdocument icon displays in the upper left corner of the border.

Word creates a subdocument for each heading at the top level within the selected text. For example, if the selected text begins with level 1 text, Word creates a new subdocument at each level 1 heading in the selected text. Save the master document in the same manner as a normal document. Word automatically assigns a document name to each subdocument using the first characters in the subdocument heading.

Opening and Closing a Master Document and Its Subdocuments

Open a master document at the Open dialog box in the same manner as a normal document. Subdocument text in a master document displays collapsed in the master document, as shown in Figure 5.3. This figure displays the master document, which you will create in Project 3a. Notice that Word automatically converts subdocument names into hyperlinks. To open a subdocument, press and hold down the Ctrl key, click the subdocument hyperlink, and then release the Ctrl key.

Close a subdocument in the normal manner and if changes were made, a confirmation message will display. Closing a subdocument redisplays the master document and the subdocument hyperlink displays in a different color, identifying that the hyperlink has been used.

Figure 5.3 Master Document

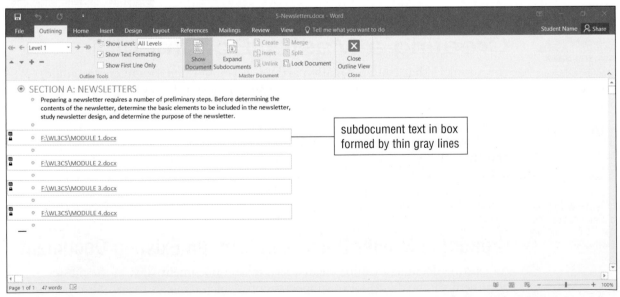

Expanding and Collapsing Subdocuments

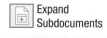
Expand Subdocuments

Collapse Subdocuments

Open a master document and its subdocuments automatically collapse. To expand the subdocuments, click the Expand Subdocuments button in the Master Document group on the Outlining tab. This expands the subdocuments and also changes the Expand Subdocuments button to the Collapse Subdocuments button.

Project 3a Creating a Master Document and Expanding and Collapsing Subdocuments   Part 1 of 2

1. Open **GraphicSoftware.docx** and then save it with the name **5-GraphicSoftware**. (This document contains a title with the Heading 1 style applied and four headings with the Heading 2 style applied.)
2. Display the document in Outline view.
3. Create a subdocument for each level 2 heading and body text by completing the following steps:

   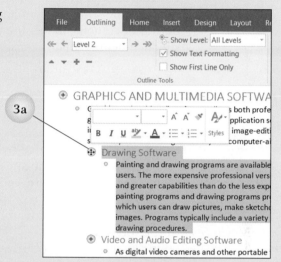

   a. Using the mouse, click the selection symbol immediately left of the heading *Drawing Software*. (This selects the heading and the body text below the heading.)
   b. Scroll down the document to the heading *CAD Software*.
   c. Press and hold down the Shift key, click the selection symbol immediately left of the heading *CAD Software*, and then release the Shift key.
   d. With all of the level 2 headings and body text selected, click the Show Document button in the Master Document group on the Outlining tab.
   e. Click the Create button in the Master Document group.

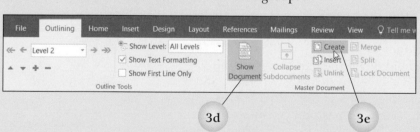

4. Save the document by clicking the Save button on the Quick Access Toolbar.
5. Click the Collapse Subdocuments button. (This collapses the subdocuments and also changes the name of the button to Expand Subdocuments.)
6. Click the Close Outline View button.
7. Print the document. At the question asking if you want to open the subdocuments, click No. (The document will print collapsed, as displayed on the screen.)
8. Save and then close **5-GraphicSoftware.docx**.

Check Your Work

Editing a Subdocument

The subdocuments created within a master document do not reside in the master document. Each subdocument is saved as an individual document and the master document contains a hyperlink to each one. Edit a subdocument by opening the subdocument, making changes, and then saving and closing it. The changes made to the subdocument are reflected in the subdocument text in the master document. Another method for editing a subdocument is to open the master document, click the subdocument hyperlink, make the changes, and then save and close the subdocument.

💡 **Hint** Edits made to a subdocument are reflected in the master document.

When subdocuments are created in a master document, the subdocument files are saved in the same location as the master document. The hyperlink to each subdocument in the master document reflects the location of the subdocument. For this reason, moving a subdocument to a different location will remove the link between the subdocument and the master document. When working with a master document, make sure the location of the master document and subdocuments remains consistent.

Project 3b Editing Subdocuments

Part 2 of 2

1. Open **Drawing Software.docx** from the WL3C5 folder on your storage medium. (This was one of the subdocuments created by Word in Project 3a. Word used the names of the headings as the names of the subdocuments.)
2. Select and then delete the last sentence in the paragraph of text (the sentence that begins *Programs typically include a variety*).
3. Save and then close **Drawing Software.docx**.
4. Open **5-GraphicSoftware.docx**.
5. Open the subdocument **Drawing Software.docx** by pressing and holding down the Ctrl key and then clicking the F:\WL3C5\Drawing Software.docx hyperlink.
6. Notice that the last sentence in the paragraph of text has been deleted and then close **Drawing Software.docx**.
7. Press and hold down the Ctrl key, click the F:\WL3C5\CAD Software.docx hyperlink, and then release the Ctrl key.
8. In the subdocument, position the insertion point immediately left of the first occurrence of *software* in the first sentence, type (CAD), and then press the spacebar.
9. Save and then close **CAD Software.docx**.
10. Display the master document in Outline view.
11. Click the Expand Subdocuments button.
12. Scroll through the text and notice that the edits made to two of the subdocuments are reflected in the subdocuments.
13. Close Outline view.
14. Save, print, and then close **5-GraphicSoftware.docx**.

> **GRAPHICS AND MULTIMEDIA SOFTWARE**
>
> Graphics and multimedia software allows both professional a
> video, and audio. A variety of application software is focused
> software, image-editing software, video and audio editing sof
> computer-
> file:///f:\wl3c5\drawing software.docx
> **Ctrl+Click to follow link**
> F:\WL3C5\Drawing Software.docx
> F:\WL3C5\Video and Audio Editing Software.docx

⑤

⑧

> CAD Software
> Computer-aided design (CAD) software is a sophistic
> enable professionals to create architectural, engine
> use the software to design buildings or bridges, and

Check Your Work

Preview Finished Project

Inserting a Subdocument

In the previous project, headings and body text in an existing document were divided into subdocuments. Another method for working with a master document is to insert documents in it as subdocuments. To insert a document as a subdocument, position the insertion point above or below the existing subdocument headings where the subdocument is to be inserted. (A subdocument cannot be inserted within body text.) Click the Insert button in the Master Document group on the Outlining tab. At the Insert Subdocument dialog box, navigate to the folder containing the document to be inserted and then double-click the document.

> **Hint** Use the Insert button to assemble existing documents into a master document.

Project 4a **Creating a Master Document and Inserting Subdocuments**   **Part 1 of 2**

1. Open **Newsletters.docx** and then save it with the name **5-Newsletters**.
2. Display the document in Outline view.
3. Create a subdocument for each level 2 heading and body text by completing the following steps:
   a. Using the mouse, click the selection symbol immediately left of the heading *MODULE 1: DEFINING NEWSLETTER ELEMENTS*. (This selects the heading, the level 3 headings, and the body text below the headings.)
   b. Scroll down the document to the heading *MODULE 2: PLANNING A NEWSLETTER*.
   c. Press and hold down the Shift key and then click the selection symbol immediately left of the heading *MODULE 2: PLANNING A NEWSLETTER*.
   d. Click the Show Document button in the Master Document group on the Outlining tab.
   e. Click the Create button in the Master Document group.
4. Insert subdocuments in the master document by completing the following steps:
   a. Press Ctrl + End to move the insertion point to the end of the document.
   b. Click the Insert button in the Master Document group on the Outlining tab.

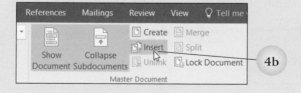

c. At the Insert Subdocument dialog box, navigate to the WL3C5 folder on your storage medium and then double-click **MODULE 3.docx**.

   d. Click the Insert button.

   e. At the Insert Subdocument dialog box, double-click **MODULE 4.docx**.

5. Click the Save button on the Quick Access Toolbar.

6. Click the Collapse Subdocuments button in the Master Document group.

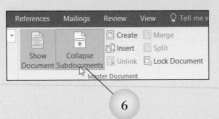

7. Close the Outline view.

8. Print the collapsed document. (At the question asking if you want to open the subdocuments, click No.)

9. Save and then close **5-Newsletters.docx**.

Check Your Work

Unlinking a Subdocument

Each subdocument is linked to the master document. A subdocument can be unlinked from the master document, which deletes the link and inserts the subdocument contents in the master document. To unlink a subdocument from the master document, expand the subdocuments, click anywhere in the subdocument to be unlinked, and then click the Unlink button in the Master Document group.

Splitting a Subdocument

A subdocument can be split into smaller subdocuments. To split a subdocument, expand the subdocuments, select the specific text within the subdocument, and then click the Split button in the Master Document group on the Outlining tab. Word assigns a document name based on the first characters in the subdocument heading.

Merging Subdocuments

Several subdocuments in a master document can be merged into one subdocument. To merge subdocuments, expand the subdocuments and then click the subdocument icon of the first subdocument to be merged. Press and hold down the Shift key, click the subdocument icon of the last subdocument, and then release the Shift key. (The subdocuments must be adjacent.) With the subdocuments selected, click the Merge button in the Master Document group. Word saves the combined subdocuments with the name of the first subdocument.

Hint When subdocuments are merged, Word saves the merged subdocument with the name of the first subdocument.

 Unlink

 Split

1. Open **5-Newsletters.docx** and then display the document in Outline view.
2. Insert a subdocument by completing the following steps:
   a. Click the Show Document button.
   b. Click the Expand Subdocuments button.
   c. Position the insertion point on the blank line below the paragraph of text below the title *DESIGNING NEWSLETTERS*.
   d. Click the Insert button in the Master Document group on the Outlining tab.

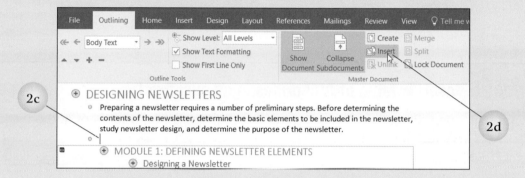

   e. At the Insert Subdocument dialog box, navigate to the WL3C5 folder on your storage medium and then double-click *NwsltrConsistency.docx*.
3. Unlink the new subdocument so it becomes part of the master document by completing the following steps:
   a. Click in the paragraph of text below the heading *MAINTAINING CONSISTENCY*.
   b. Click the Unlink button in the Master Document group.
   c. Select and then delete the heading *MAINTAINING CONSISTENCY*. (The paragraphs should be separated only by a blank line.)
4. Delete the module 2 subdocument by completing the following steps:
   a. Click the selection symbol immediately left of the heading *MODULE 2: PLANNING A NEWSLETTER*.
   b. Press the Delete key.
5. Split the module 1 subdocument by completing the following steps:
   a. In the subdocument, edit the heading *Defining Basic Newsletter Elements* so that it displays as *MODULE 2: DEFINING BASIC ELEMENTS*.
   b. Click the heading *MODULE 2: DEFINING BASIC ELEMENTS* and then click the Promote button to change the heading from level 3 to level 2.

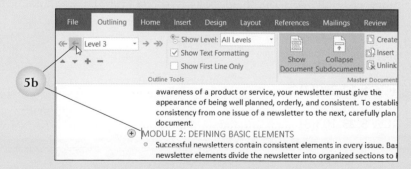

   c. Position the mouse pointer on the selection symbol immediately left of the heading *MODULE 2: DEFINING BASIC ELEMENTS* until the pointer turns into a four-headed arrow and then click the left mouse button.

Check Your Work

Project 5 **Insert a Table of Authorities in a Legal Brief** **1 Part**

You will open a legal brief, mark citations, and then insert a table of authorities.

Preview Finished Project

Tutorial

Inserting and Updating a Table of Authorities

Hint A table of authorities provides a list of all sources cited in a legal document.

Creating a Table of Authorities

A table of authorities is a list of citations that appears in a legal brief or other legal document as well as the page numbers on which the citations appear. Word provides many common categories under which citations can be organized: *Cases, Statutes, Other Authorities, Rules, Treatises, Regulations*, and *Constitutional Provisions.* Within each category, Word alphabetizes the citations. Figure 5.4 shows an example of a table of authorities.

Figure 5.4 Table of Authorities

TABLE OF AUTHORITIES

Cases

Mansfield v. Rydell, 72 Wn.2d 200, 433 P.2d 723 (1993) 3
State v. Fletcher, 73 Wn.2d 332, 124 P.2d 503 (2006) 5
Yang v. Buchwald, 21 Wn.2d 385, 233 P.2d 609 (2012) 7

Statutes

RCW 8.12.230(2) 4
RCW 6.23.590 7
RCW 5.23.103(3) 10

Creating a table of authorities requires thought and planning. Before marking any text in a legal document for inclusion in such a table, first determine what section headings to use and what listing to include within each section. When marking the text for the table, find the first occurrence of each citation, mark it as a full citation with the complete name, and then specify a short citation.

Mark Citation

To mark a citation for a table of authorities, select the first occurrence of the citation, click the References tab, and then click the Mark Citation button or press Alt + Shift + I. At the Mark Citation dialog box, shown in Figure 5.5, edit and format the text in the *Selected text* text box as it should appear in the table of authorities. Edit and format the text in the *Short citation* text box so it matches the short citation Word should search for in the document. Click the *Category* option box and then click the category at the drop-down list that applies to the citation. Click the Mark button to mark the selected citation or click the Mark All button to mark all the long and short citations in the document that match those displayed in the Mark Citation dialog box.

The Mark Citation dialog box remains open to mark other citations. Click the Next Citation button to find the next citation in the document. Word searches the document for the next occurrence of text commonly found in a citation, such as *in re* or *v*. Continue marking citations and, when finished, click the Close button to close the Mark Citation dialog box.

Inserting a Table of Authorities

Insert Table of Authorities

After marking citations in a document, insert the table of authorities. A table of authorities is inserted in a document in a manner similar to a table of contents or figures. A table of authorities generally appears at the beginning of a document on a separate page. To insert a table of authorities in a document that contains text marked as citations, click the References tab and then click the Insert Table of Authorities button. This displays the Table of Authorities dialog box, shown in Figure 5.6. At this dialog box, make any necessary changes and then click OK to close the dialog box.

Hint Word inserts codes around marked citations that can be displayed by turning on the display of nonprinting characters.

Figure 5.5 Mark Citation Dialog Box

Edit and format the text in this text box as it should appear in the table of authorities.

Edit and format the text in this text box so it matches the short citation that Word searches for in the document.

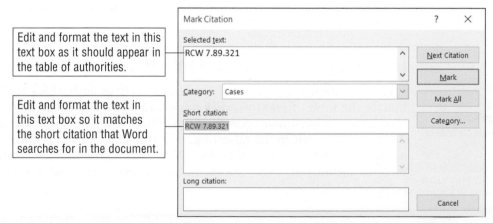

Figure 5.6 Table of Authorities Dialog Box

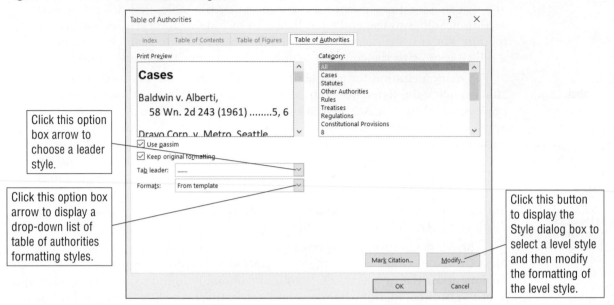

Click this option box arrow to choose a leader style.

Click this option box arrow to display a drop-down list of table of authorities formatting styles.

Click this button to display the Style dialog box to select a level style and then modify the formatting of the level style.

💡 **Hint** The citations marked in a document are organized in the table of authorities in the order in which they appear in the *Category* list box in the Table of Authorities dialog box.

Like the Table of Contents dialog box and Table of Figures dialog box, the Table of Authorities dialog box contains options for formatting a table of authorities. The *Use passim* check box contains a check mark by default, which tells Word to replace five or more page references to the same authority with *passim*. With the *Keep original formatting* check box active, Word retains the formatting of the citation as it appears in the document. Click the *Tab leader* option to change the leader character. When a table of authorities is inserted, Word includes a heading for each of the seven categories by default. To insert citations for only a specific category, select that category at the *Category* drop-down list.

The formatting of a heading level style for a table of authorities can be modified. To do this, click the Modify button in the Table of Authorities dialog box, click *Table of Authorities* in the *Styles* list box, and then click the Modify button. At the Modify Style dialog box, apply the desired formatting and then click OK.

Updating or Deleting a Table of Authorities

Ōuick Steps

Update a Table of Authorities
1. Click in the table of authorities.
2. Click References tab.
3. Click Update Table of Authorities button or press F9 function key.

 Update Table

If changes are made to a document after a table of authorities has been inserted, update the table. To do this, click anywhere in the table and then click the Update Table button or press the F9 function key. To edit a citation, edit it in the document and not in the table of authorities. If a citation is edited in the table of authorities, the changes will be lost the next time the table is updated. To delete a table of authorities, select the entire table using the mouse or keyboard and then press the Delete key.

1. Open **LarsenBrief.docx** and then save it with the name **5-LarsenBrief**.
2. Mark *RCW 7.89.321* as a statute citation by completing the following steps:
   a. Select *RCW 7.89.321*. (This citation is located near the middle of the second page.) *Hint: Use the **Find feature to help you locate this citation.***
   b. Click the References tab.
   c. Click the Mark Citation button in the Table of Authorities group.
   d. At the Mark Citation dialog box, click *Category* option box arrow and then click *Statutes* at the drop-down list.
   e. Click the Mark All button. (This turns on the display of nonprinting characters.)
   f. Click the Close button to close the Mark Citation dialog box.

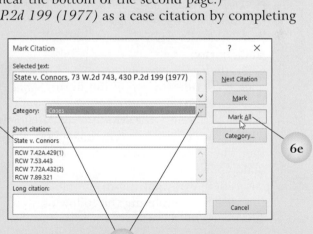

3. Complete steps similar to those in Step 2 to mark all instances of *RCW 7.53.443* as a statute citation. (This citation is located near the middle of the second page.)
4. Complete steps similar to those in Step 2 to mark all instances of *RCW 7.72A.432(2)* as a statute citation. (This citation is located near the bottom of the second page.)
5. Complete steps similar to those in Step 2 to mark all instances of *RCW 7.42A.429(1)* as a statute citation. (This citation is located near the bottom of the second page.)
6. Mark *State v. Connors, 73 W.2d 743, 430 P.2d 199 (1977)* as a case citation by completing the following steps:
   a. Select *State v. Connors, 73 W.2d 743, 430 P.2d 199 (1977)*. (This citation is located near the middle of the second page.) *Hint: Use the Find feature to help you locate this citation.*
   b. Press Alt + Shift + I.
   c. At the Mark Citation dialog box, type State v. Connors in the *Short citation* text box.
   d. Click the *Category* option box arrow and then click *Cases* at the drop-down list.
   e. Click the Mark All button.
   f. Click the Close button to close the Mark Citation dialog box.
7. Complete steps similar to those in Step 6 to mark all instances of *State v. Bertelli, 63 W.2d 77, 542 P.2d 751 (1974)* as a case citation. Type State v. Bertelli as the short citation. (This citation is located near the middle of the second page.)
8. Complete steps similar to those in Step 6 to mark all instances of *State v. Landers, 103 W.2d 432, 893 P.2d 2 (1987)* as a case citation. Type State v. Landers as the short citation. (This citation is located near the bottom of the second page.)

9. Insert page numbering by completing the following steps:
   a. Position the insertion point at the beginning of the document and then press the Enter key.
   b. Position the insertion point immediately left of the *S* in *STATEMENT OF CASE* and then insert a section break that begins a new page. (To insert a section break that begins a new page, click the Layout tab, click the Breaks button in the Page Setup group, and then click *Next Page* at the drop-down list.)
   c. With the insertion point positioned below the section break, insert a page number at the bottom center of each page and change the starting number to 1. (Insert a page number with the Page Number button on the Insert tab. Change the starting number at the Page Number Format dialog box. Display this dialog box by clicking the *Format Page Numbers* option at the Page Number button drop-down list.)
10. Double-click in the document to make it active and complete the following steps:
    a. Press Ctrl + Home to move the insertion point to the beginning of the document.
    b. Make sure bold and center formatting is active and then type TABLE OF AUTHORITIES.
    c. Press the Enter key, turn off bold formatting, and change to left alignment.
11. Modify and insert the table of authorities by completing the following steps:
    a. Click the References tab.
    b. Click the Insert Table of Authorities button in the Table of Authorities group.
    c. At the Table of Authorities dialog box, make sure *All* is selected in the *Category* list box and then click the Modify button.
    d. At the Style dialog box, click *Table of Authorities* in the *Styles* list box and then click the Modify button.

    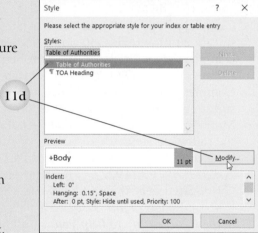

    11d

    e. At the Modify Style dialog box, click the Italic button.
    f. Click the *Font Color* option box arrow and then click *Dark Blue* (ninth option in the *Standard Colors* section).
    g. Click OK to close the Modify Style dialog box, click OK to close the Style dialog box, and then click OK to close the Table of Authorities dialog box.
12. Apply different formatting to the table of authorities by completing the following steps:
    a. Click the Undo button on the Quick Access Toolbar to remove the table of authorities. (If this does not remove the table of authorities, select the *Cases* entries and *Statutes* entries and then press the Delete key.)
    b. Click the Insert Table of Authorities button.
    c. At the Table of Authorities dialog box, click the *Formats* option box arrow and then click *Distinctive* at the drop-down list.
    d. Click the *Tab leader* option box arrow and then click the hyphen symbols at the drop-down list (second option from the bottom of the list).
    e. Click OK to close the Table of Authorities dialog box.

    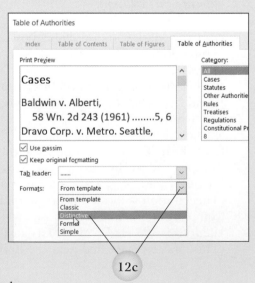

    12c

13. With the insertion point positioned anywhere in the table of authorities, change the page numbering format to lowercase roman numerals. (Change to lowercase roman numerals at the Page Number Format dialog box.)
14. Turn off the display of nonprinting characters.
15. Make sure the table of authorities displays the correct page numbers by selecting all the entries in the *Cases* section and the *Statutes* section, and then clicking the Update Table button in the Table of Authorities group.
16. Save **5-LarsenBrief.docx** and then print the table of authorities page.
17. Close **5-LarsenBrief.docx**.

Check Your Work

Chapter Summary

- Display a document in Outline view by clicking the View tab and then clicking the Outline button in the Views group.

- A title or heading formatted with a heading style applied displays as that level in Outline view. For example, a title or heading formatted with the Heading 1 style displays as a level 1 heading.

- Use buttons on the Outlining tab in Outline view to display heading levels, turn on or off the display of heading text formatting, show only the first line of body text, collapse or expand levels, promote and demote heading levels, and assign levels.

- One of the major advantages of working in Outline view is being able to see a condensed outline of a document without all the text between titles, headings, and subheading. Another advantage of working in Outline view is being able to maintain consistency between titles and headings.

- To collapse an entire document, use the *Show Level* option box to specify a level. For example, if a document contains two levels, click the *Level 2* option. To redisplay all the document, click the *All Levels* option at the drop-down list.

- To collapse all the text beneath a particular heading, click the Collapse button in the Outline Tools group on the Outlining tab. Click the Expand button to display all the text.

- Promote or demote a title or heading in Outline view using the Promote to Level 1 button, Promote button, or Demote button or by dragging the selection symbol immediately left of a title or heading.

- If heading styles have not been applied to the titles or headings in a document, assigning levels in Outline view will apply styles. Use the *Outline Level* option box to assign a specific level.

- The contents of a document can be rearranged in Outline view. To move a heading and the body text below it, select the heading and then click the Move Down or Move Up button in the Outline Tools group. A heading and the body text below it can also be moved by dragging the selection symbol immediately left of the heading to the desired position.

- Assign a level to text that does not apply a style using the *Outline level* option box at the Paragraph dialog box.

- When levels are assigned to titles and headings using the *Outline level* option at the Paragraph dialog box, the levels display in the Navigation pane with the Headings tab selected and can be used to navigate to specific locations in the document.

- A level can be collapsed in Normal view by clicking the collapse triangle that displays immediately left of the level text. The collapse triangle displays as a small, solid, dark triangle and appears left of level text when the mouse pointer is positioned over the text.

- Expand a collapsed level in Normal view by clicking the expand triangle immediately left of the level text. The expand triangle displays as a small, hollow, right-pointing triangle.

- Collapsed text can be moved by selecting the collapsed heading and then dragging the heading with the mouse until a thick, black vertical line displays in the new position.

- Specify that a level remain collapsed when a document is opened using the *Collapsed by default* check box at the Paragraph dialog box.

- A master document contains a number of separate documents called *subdocuments*. Create a master document or format an existing document as a master document in Outline view.

- Open a master document in the same manner as a normal document. To open a subdocument, open the master document, hold down the Ctrl key, click the subdocument hyperlink, and then release the Ctrl key.

- Clicking the Show Document button and then clicking the Create button—both located in the Master Document group on the Outlining tab—causes Word to create a subdocument for each heading at the top level within the selected text.

- Save a master document in the same manner as a normal document. Word automatically assigns a document name to each subdocument using the first characters in the subdocument heading.

- Use buttons in the Master Document group on the Outlining tab to create, insert, unlink, expand, collapse, merge, and split subdocuments.

- A table of authorities is a list of the citations in a legal brief or other legal document and the pages on which the citations appear.

- When marking text for a table of authorities, find the first occurrence of a citation, mark it as a full citation with the complete name, and then specify a short citation at the Mark Citation dialog box.

- Display Mark Citation dialog box by clicking the Mark Citation button on the References tab or pressing Alt + Shift + I.

- Insert a table of authorities in a document with the Insert Table of Authorities button in the Table of Authorities group on the References tab.

- A table of authorities generally appears at the beginning of a document.

- Delete a table of authorities by selecting the entire table and then pressing the Delete key.

Commands Review

FEATURE	RIBBON TAB, GROUP	BUTTON	KEYBOARD SHORTCUT
create master document	Outlining, Master Document		
collapse outline	Outlining, Outline Tools		Alt + Shift + _
collapse subdocuments	Outlining, Master Document		
demote to body text	Outlining, Outline Tools		
demote to next lower level	Outlining, Outline Tools		Alt + Shift + Right Arrow
expand outline	Outlining, Outline Tools		Alt + Shift + +
expand subdocuments	Outlining, Master Document		
insert subdocument	Outlining, Master Document		
Mark Citation dialog box	References, Table of Authorities		Alt + Shift + I
move down outline level	Outlining, Outline Tools		Alt + Shift + Down Arrow
move up outline level	Outlining, Outline Tools		Alt + Shift + Up Arrow
Outline view	View, Views		Alt + Ctrl + O
Paragraph dialog box	Home, Paragraph		
promote to heading 1	Outlining, Outline Tools		
promote to next higher level	Outlining, Outline Tools		Alt + Shift + Left Arrow
show document	Outlining, Master Document		
split subdocument	Outlining, Master Document		
Table of Authorities dialog box with Table of Authorities tab selected	References, Table of Authorities		
unlink subdocument	Outlining, Master Document		

Workbook

Chapter study tools and assessment activities are available in the *Workbook* ebook. These resources are designed to help you further develop and demonstrate mastery of the skills learned in this chapter.

Word

Sharing Documents and Customizing Word Options

Performance Objectives

Upon successful completion of Chapter 6, you will be able to:

1   Check the accessibility of a document

2   Improve the accessibility of a document by adding alternate text
    for a picture or table, wrapping a picture inline with text, deleting a
    blank row in a table, removing spaces in a heading, and removing a
    watermark

3   Share documents among programs, computers, and websites and
    as email attachments

4   Customize Word options

5   Customize and display account information

Word's accessibility checker checks a document for content that may be difficult
for someone with a disability, such as a visual impairment, to read and understand.
In this chapter, you will learn how to correct content identified by the accessibility
checker as an error, a warning, or a tip.

The Share backstage area provides options for sharing documents among
programs, websites, and other computers and as email attachments. In this chapter,
you will learn how to use options at the Share backstage area and how to use the
Present Online feature to share a document with others over the Internet.

The Word Options dialog box provides a variety of options for customizing
Word. You will learn how to use options in the left panel to customize Word and
display account information.

Preview Finished Project

Tutorial

Tutorial Review: Checking the Accessibility and Compatibility of a Document

Check for Issues

Managing the Accessibility of a Document

As explained in Level 2, Chapter 8, Word's accessibility checker checks documents for content that someone with a disability, such as a visual impairment, might find difficult to read. Check the accessibility of a document by clicking the Check for Issues button at the Info backstage area and then clicking *Check Accessibility*.

In addition to checking an image for alternate text, the accessibility checker examines a document for the most common accessibility problems and groups them into three categories: errors—content that is very difficult or impossible for people with disabilities to understand; warnings—content that makes a file difficult for people with disabilities to understand; tips—content that people with disabilities can understand but that can be better organized. Examples of these three types of accessibility issues are explained in Table 6.1.

Quick Steps

Check Accessibility
1. Click File tab.
2. Click Check for Issues button at Info backstage area.
3. Click *Check Accessibility*.

The accessibility checker examines the document, closes the Info backstage area, and displays the Accessibility Checker task pane. At the Accessibility Checker task pane, unreadable errors are grouped in the *Errors* section, content that is difficult to read is grouped in the *Warnings* section, and content that may or may not be difficult to read is grouped in the *Tips* section. Select an issue in one of the sections and an explanation of why the issue should be fixed and how to fix it displays at the bottom of the task pane.

Creating Alternate Text for an Image or Table

The first item in the *Errors* section, *Alt text*, refers to a text-based representation of an image. For example, if a document contains a picture, alternate text can be added that describes the picture. To create alternate text for an image, right-click the image in the document and then click *Format Picture* at the shortcut menu. At the Format Picture task pane, click the Layout & Properties icon and then click *Alt Text* to expand the options. Type a title for the image in the *Title* text box and type a description of the image in the *Description* text box.

Create alternate text for a table by right-clicking in the table in the document and then clicking *Table Properties* at the shortcut menu. At the Table Properties dialog box, click the Alt Text tab and then a title for the table in the *Title* text box and a description in the *Description* text box.

When creating alternate text for an object, describe the object accurately and succinctly and avoid phrases such as "Image of. . ." and "This is. . .". The alternate text for an image will display when a screen reader is used to view the document or when the document is saved in a file format such as HTML

(Hypertext Markup Language) or DAISY (Digital Accessible Information System). If a document is saved in a format that is easy to share or publish, such as PDF (portable document format) or XML (Extensible Markup Language), then all the changes made to make it accessible are included.

Table 6.1 Accessibility Checker Issues

Errors

Alt text: All objects have alternate text. Objects include pictures, clip art images, tables, SmartArt, shapes, charts, embedded objects, and video and audio files. Providing alternate text for an object helps readers understand the information presented by the object.

Table headers: Tables specify column header information. A table header row provides context and helps readers navigate the data in a table.

Document structure: Long documents use styles to provide structure. Headings and/or a table of contents are used to help organize the content. Creating a structure helps readers find information in the document.

Warnings

Meaningful hyperlink text: Hyperlink text includes a ScreenTip and matches the hyperlink target. Hyperlink text should provide a description of the destination, not just the URL.

Simple table structure: Tables have a simple structure that does not include nested tables or merged or split cells. Tables should have a simple two-dimensional structure to be easily navigated and understood by readers.

Blank cells: Tables do not use blank cells for formatting or contain entirely blank rows or columns. Encountering blank cells may lead readers to think they have reached the end of the table.

Blank characters: Repeated blank characters (such as a series of blank spaces, tabs, or paragraphs) are avoided. Blank characters may lead readers to think they have reached the end of the document. Do not separate paragraphs of text with blank lines; apply paragraph styles.

Heading length: Headings do not contain too much information. Rather, they are short (fewer than 20 words). Short, concise headings help readers navigate the document more easily.

Floating objects: The use of floating objects is avoided. Text wrapping for objects should be set to *Inline with Text*, *Square*, or *Top and Bottom*. Documents with floating objects are difficult to navigate.

Tips

Closed captions: Closed captions are included for inserted audio and video files. Without closed captions, important information in audio or video files may not be accessible for people with disabilities.

Table layout: Tables are structured for easy navigation and follow the appropriate reading order. For English, data in a table is read from left to right and top to bottom. Tabbing through the cells in a table will determine whether the information is presented in a logical order.

Watermarks: No watermark images are used in the document. Watermark images may not be understood by people with visual disabilities.

Heading order: All headings appear in the correct order. Use correct heading levels so readers can find information and navigate easily in the document.

Establishing a Header Row

Properties

The first row in a table should be established as a header row, so if the table flows onto a second page, the first row is repeated at the top. A header row helps identify the contents of the table. Specify the first row of a table as a header row by inserting a check mark in the *Repeat as header row at the top of each page* check box at the Table Properties dialog box with the Row tab selected. Display this dialog box by clicking the Table Tools Layout tab and then clicking the Properties button in the Table group.

Using Built-In Styles

💡*Hint* Keep headings relatively short and apply heading styles.

💡*Hint* In a long document, consider including a heading every two pages at a minimum.

When preparing accessible documents, use the built-in heading styles to identify headings. Screen readers used by people with visual impairments recognize text with a heading style applied as a heading. Text with direct formatting applied, such as a larger font size or bold formatting, is not recognized as a heading by screen readers. Another advantage to applying built-in heading styles is that the person preparing the document can increase the font size of heading text by modifying the heading styles.

In addition to applying heading styles to make documents more accessible, apply body text styles. As with headings, the person preparing the document can modify the size of the body font and all the text in the document with that style applied will increase in size. Increasing the font size of text in a document makes the text easier to read for people with visual impairments.

Project 1 Improving the Accessibility of a Document   Part 1 of 1

1. Open **BTZTAdventures.docx** and then save it with the name **6-BTZTAdventures**.
2. Check the accessibility of the document by completing the following steps:
   a. Click the File tab.
   b. At the Info backstage area, click the Check for Issues button and then click *Check Accessibility* at the drop-down list.
   c. Notice the Accessibility Checker task pane at the right side of the screen. The task pane displays *Errors*, *Warnings*, and *Tips* sections.

2c

3. Add alternate text to the picture by completing the
   following steps:
   a. Click *Picture 3* in the *Errors* section in the Accessibility
      Checker task pane. (This selects the picture in the
      document.)
   b. Read the information near the bottom of the task pane
      that describes why the error should be fixed and how
      to fix it.
   c. Right-click the picture in the document and then click
      Format Picture at the shortcut menu.
   d. At the Format Picture task pane, click the Layout &
      Properties icon.
   e. Click *Alt Text* to expand the options.
   f. Click in the *Title* text box and then type Penguins in
      Antarctica.
   g. Click in the *Description* text box and then type Adelie
      penguins on an iceberg in Antarctica.
   h. Click the Close button in the upper right
      corner of the Format Picture task pane.
4. Add alternate text to the table in the document
   by completing the following steps:
   a. Click *Table* below *Missing Alt Text* in the *Errors*
      section of the Accessibility Checker task pane.
      (This selects the table in the document.)
   b. Read the information near the bottom of
      the task pane that describes why the error
      should be fixed and how to fix it.
   c. Right-click the table in the document and
      then click *Table Properties* at the
      shortcut menu.
   d. At the Table Properties dialog box,
      click the Alt Text tab.
   e. Click in the *Title* text box and then
      type Zenith Adventures.
   f. Click in the *Description*
      text box and then type
      Four adventures offered by
      Zenith Adventures including
      number of days and price.
   g. Click OK.
5. Specify a header row for the table by
   completing the following steps:
   a. Click *Table* below *No Header Row
      Specified* in the *Errors* section of the
      Accessibility Checker task pane.
      (This selects the first row in the
      table.)
   b. Click the Table Tools Layout tab.
   c. Click the Properties button in the Table group.

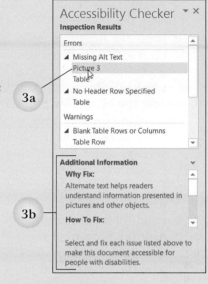

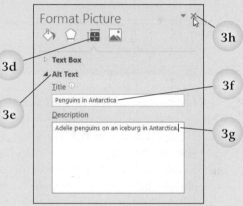

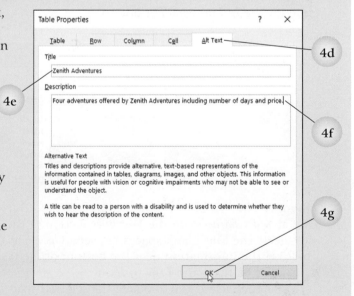

d. At the Table Properties dialog box, click the Row tab.

e. Click the *Repeat as header row at the top of each page* check box to insert a check mark.

f. Click OK.

6. Delete the blank row in the table by completing the following steps:

a. Click *Table Row* in the *Warnings* section of the Accessibility Checker task pane. (This selects the blank row in the table.)

b. Read the information near the bottom of the task pane that describes why the issue should be fixed and how to fix it.

c. If necessary, click the Table Tools Layout tab.

d. Click the Delete button in the Rows & Columns group and then click *Delete Rows* at the drop-down list.

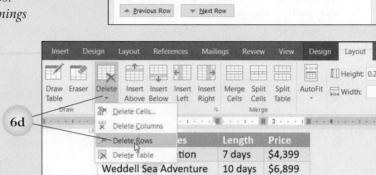

7. Format the picture to be in line with the text by completing the following steps:

a. Click *Picture 3* in the *Warnings* section of the Accessibility Checker task pane. (This selects the picture in the document.)

b. Read the information near the bottom of the task pane that describes why the issue should be fixed and how to fix it.

c. Click the Layout Options button outside the upper right corner of the picture and then click the *In Line with Text* option.

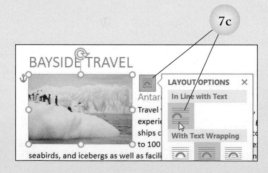

8. Remove blank spaces in the heading *Upcoming Adventures* by completing the following steps:

a. Click *4 Characters* in the *Warnings* section of the Accessibility Checker task pane. (This selects the four blank spaces between *Upcoming* and *Adventures*.)

b. Read the information near the bottom of the task pane that describes why the issue should be fixed and how to fix it.

c. Press the Delete key to delete the selected spaces and then press the spacebar to insert a space.

9. The last item in the Accessibility Checker task pane is *Using Image Watermark*, which displays in the *Tips* section. Remove the watermark in the document by completing the following steps:

   a. Click the Design tab.

   b. Click the Watermark button in the Page Background group and then click *Remove Watermark* at the drop-down list.

10. Notice that the Accessibility Checker task pane now displays a message indicating that no accessibility issues were found. Close the Accessibility Checker task pane.

11. The headings in the document have heading styles applied and the text has the *Body Text* style applied. Increase the sizes of the fonts in the heading styles by completing the following steps:

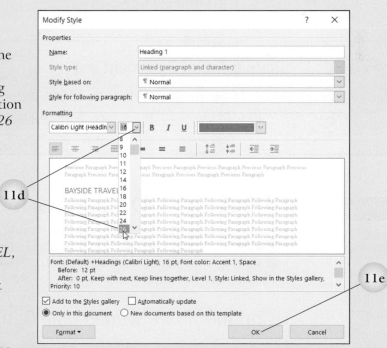

   a. Press Ctrl + Home to move the insertion point to the beginning of the document (the insertion point will be positioned immediately left of the title *BAYSIDE TRAVEL*).

   b. Click the Home tab.

   c. Right-click the *Heading 1* style in the Styles group and then click *Modify* at the shortcut menu.

   d. At the Modify Style dialog box, click the *Font Size* option box arrow and then click *26* at the drop-down list.

   e. Click OK to close the Modify Style dialog box.

   f. With the insertion point still positioned at the beginning of the title *BAYSIDE TRAVEL*, click the *Heading 1* style. (This applies the new font size to the text.)

   g. Right-click the *Heading 2* style in the Styles group and then click *Modify* at the shortcut menu.

   h. At the Modify Style dialog box, click the *Font Size* option box arrow and then click *20* at the drop-down list.

   i. Click OK to close the Modify Style dialog box.

12. Increase the size of the body text font by completing the following steps:

a. Click anywhere in the paragraph of text below the heading *Antarctic Zenith Adventures*.

b. Click the More Styles button in the Styles group.

c. Click *Apply Styles* at the drop-down gallery.

d. At the Apply Styles window, make sure *Body Text* displays in the *Style Name* text box. If not, select the text in the *Style Name* text box, type Body Text, and then press the Enter key.

e. Click the Modify button in the Apply Styles window.

f. At the Modify Style dialog box, make sure that *Body Text* displays in the *Name* text box.

g. Click the *Font Size* option box arrow and then click *14* at the drop-down list.

h. Click OK to close the Modify Style dialog box.

i. Close the Apply Styles window.

13. Save, print, and then close **6-BTZTAdventures.docx**.

Check Your Work

Project 2 **Share a Travel Document**   **3 Parts**

You will save a travel document to your OneDrive account and then share the document with others. You will also send the document as an email attachment and present the document online.

Preview Finished Project

Tutorial

Sharing a Document

Sharing a Document

Word provides a number of options for sharing documents among programs, websites, and other computers and as email attachments. Options for sending and sharing documents are available at the Share backstage area. Display this backstage area by clicking the File tab and then clicking the *Share* option.

Using the *Share with People* Option

Use the *Share with People* option at the Share backstage area to invite people to view a Word document. To use this option, the Word document must be saved to a OneDrive account or a shared location, such as a website or SharePoint library. (Microsoft SharePoint is a collection of products and software that includes a number of components. If a company or organization uses SharePoint, a document can be saved in a library on the organizations SharePoint site so colleagues have a central location for accessing documents.)

Share with People

To share a Word document, open the document from a OneDrive account (or other shared location) and then click the Share with People button at the Share backstage area. This closes the backstage area and the document displays with the Share task pane at the right side of the screen, similar to what is shown in Figure 6.1. Another method for displaying the Share task pane is to click the Share button in the upper right corner of the screen below the Close button.

If a document is open that is not saved to a OneDrive account (or other shared location), the information at the right side of the Share backstage area will specify that the document needs to be saved and a Save to Cloud button displays. Or, clicking the Share button in the upper right corner of the screen displays the Share task pane with a Save to Cloud button. To save the document to a OneDrive account, click the Save to Cloud button and double-click the OneDrive account at the Save As backstage area. At the Save As dialog box with the OneDrive account folder active and the document name in the *File name* text box, click the Save button. With the document saved to the OneDrive account, click the Share button in the upper right corner of the screen or click the File tab, click the *Share* option, and then click the Share with People button. This displays the Share task pane at the right side of the screen.

Save to Cloud

In the *Invite people* text box in the Share task pane, type the names or email addresses of people to invite them to view and/or edit the document. Use semicolons to separate multiple names or email addresses. The option box below the *Invite people* text box contains the default setting *Can edit*. At this setting, the people invited will be able to edit the document. Change this option to *Can view* if the invited people should only be able to view the document.

Hint The person sharing the document is the only person who can change the settings for individuals in the group.

When all names or email addresses are entered, click the Share button. An email is sent to the email address or addresses typed and in a few moments the name or names display in the Share task pane. Any time the document is opened in the future, clicking the Share button in the upper right corner of the screen or displaying the Share backstage area and then clicking the Share with People

Figure 6.1 Share Task Pane

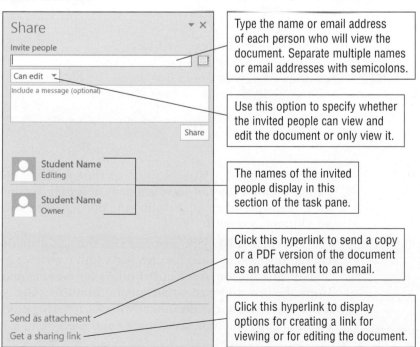

button will open the Share task pane in the document. To stop sharing the document with someone, right-click his or her name in the Share task pane and then click *Remove User* at the shortcut menu.

Project 2a   Inviting People to View Your Document

Note: To complete this optional project, you need to be connected to the Internet and have a OneDrive account.

1. Open **6-BTZTAdventures.docx** and then save it with the name **6-BTZTAdvs**.
2. Save **6-BTZTAdvs.docx** to your OneDrive account folder and name it **6-BTZTAdvs-Shared**. (To do this, click the File tab, click the *Save As* option, and then double-click the OneDrive account in the middle panel. At the Save As dialog box with the OneDrive account folder active, type 6-BTZTAdvs-Shared in the *File name* text box and then click the Save button.)
3. With **6-BTZTAdvs-Shared.docx** open, click the File tab and then click the *Share* option.
4. At the Share backstage area with the *Share with People* option selected, click the Share with People button.
5. Type the email address for your instructor and/or a a classmate or friend in the *Invite people* text box in the Share task pane.
6. Click the option box arrow for the option box containing the text *Can edit* and then click *Can view* at the drop-down list.
7. Click the Share button.
8. After a few moments, notice the name or names that display in the Share task pane.
9. Check with your instructor, classmate, and/or friend to see if he or she could open the email containing the link to your document.
10. Remove the name (or one of the names) that displays in the Share task pane by right-clicking the name and then clicking *Remove User* at the shortcut menu.
11. Close the Share task pane.
12. Close **6-BTZTAdvs-Shared.docx** saved to your OneDrive account folder and then open **6-BTZTAdvs.docx** from your removable device.

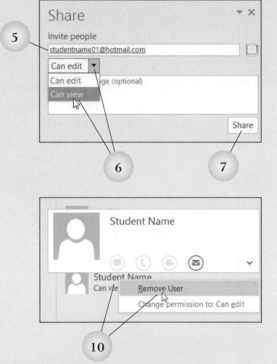

Use the Send as attachment hyperlink near the bottom of the Share task pane to send a copy of the document or a PDF version of the document as an attachment to an email. Sending the document as an attachment requires having an Outlook account.

The Share task pane also contains the Get a sharing link hyperlink that when clicked displays options for creating a link for viewing or editing. Click the Create an edit link button and a link displays for viewing and editing the document. Copy the link and paste it an email, instant message, or social media site. To paste a link for viewing the document without allowing editing, click the View-only link button. Copy the link that displays and then paste it in the specific locations.

Using the *Email* Option

Click the *Email* option at the Share backstage area and options display for sending a copy of the document as an attachment to an email, sending a link to the document, attaching a PDF or XPS copy of the open document to an email address, and sending an email as an Internet fax.

As mentioned earlier, sending the document as an attachment requires having an Outlook email account. To create an email that contains a link to the document, the document must be saved to a OneDrive account or a shared location, such as a website or SharePoint library.

 Send as PDF

Click the Send as PDF button and the document is converted to a PDF file and attached to the email. Click the Send as XPS button and the document is converted to XPS format and attached to the email. (XPS [XML paper specification] is a Microsoft file format for publishing content in an easily viewable format.)

Send as XPS

Send as Internet Fax

Click the Send as Internet Fax button to fax the current document without using a fax machine. Using this button requires having an account with a fax service provider.

Project 2b **Sending a Document as an Email Attachment**   **Part 2 of 3**

Note: Before completing this optional project, check with your instructor to determine if Outlook is your email provider.

1. With **6-BTZTAdvs.docx** open, click the File tab and then click the *Share* option.
2. At the Share backstage area, click the *Email* option and then click the Send as Attachment button.

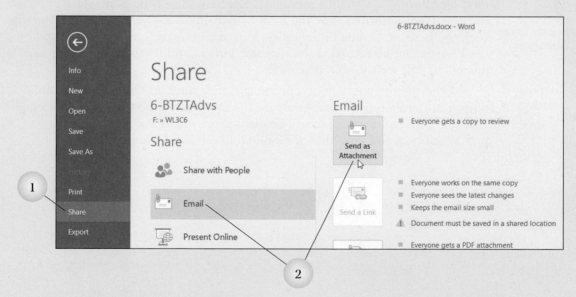

3. At the Outlook window, type your instructor's email address in the *To* text box.
4. Click the Send button.

Presenting a Document Online

Word includes the Present Online feature for sharing a document with others over the Internet by sending a link to the people who will view the document in their own browsers. Using this feature requires having a network service to host the document. Microsoft provides the Office Presentation Service, which is available to anyone with a Windows Live ID (such as a OneDrive account), and Microsoft Office 2016.

 Present Online

To present a document online, click the *Present Online* option at the Share backstage area and then click the Present Online button. At the Present Online window that displays, click the CONNECT button, and enter your Windows Live ID user name and password if necessary. When Word has connected to an account and prepared the document, the Present Online window will display with a unique link that Word created for the document. Click the Copy Link hyperlink in the Present Online window to copy the link and then paste it into an email that will be sent to the people who will view the document. If the person presenting the document online has an Outlook account, clicking the Send in Email hyperlink opens Outlook and the link can be pasted in the message window.

After everyone has opened the document link in a web browser, click the START PRESENTATION button in the Present Online window. People viewing the document do not need to have Word installed on their computers to view the document because the document displays through their web browsers.

Edit

When presenting a document online, the Present Online tab displays with options for sharing the document through OneNote, displaying the unique link to send to more people, editing the document, and ending the document presentation. When presenting a document online, make edits to it by clicking the Edit button in the Present Online group on the Present Online tab. A yellow message bar displays to indicate that the presentation is paused. Make edits to the document and then click the Resume button on the yellow message bar or click the Resume Online Presentation button in the Present Online group on the Present Online tab. Click the Resume button and the people viewing the document will see the edited version.

Resume Online Presentation

End Online Presentation

To end the presentation of a document, click the End Online Presentation button in the Present Online group on the Present Online tab. At the message indicating that all the people will be disconnected and asking if the online presentation should end, click the End Online Presentation button.

Note: To complete this optional project, you must have a Windows Live ID account. Depending on your system configuration and what services are available, the following steps will vary.

1. With **6-BTZTAdvs.docx** open, click the File tab and then click the *Share* option.
2. At the Share backstage area, click the *Present Online* option and then click the Present Online button.

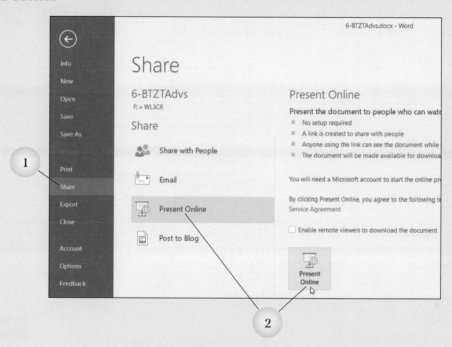

3. At the Present Online window that displays, click the CONNECT button. (If a CONNECT button does not appear, skip to Step 5.)
4. Type your user name and password in the Windows Security dialog box.
5. At the Present Online window with the unique link selected, click the Copy Link hyperlink.
6. Send the link to colleagues by opening the desired email account, pasting the link into a new message window, and then sending the email to the viewers. If you are using Microsoft Outlook, click the Send in Email hyperlink and Microsoft Outlook opens in a new message window with the link inserted in the message. In Outlook, send the link to the people you want to view the document.
7. When everyone has received the link, click the START PRESENTATION button at the Present Online window.

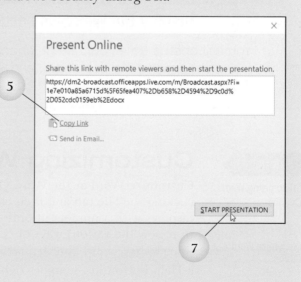

8. Edit one of the prices in the table by completing the following steps:

   a. Click the Edit button in the Present Online group on the Present Online tab.

   b. Drag the button on the Zoom slider bar so the document displays at 100% view.

   c. Scroll through the document to display the table.

   d. Change the Antarctic Exploration adventure price from *$4,399* to *$3,500*.

   e. Click the Resume button on the yellow message bar.

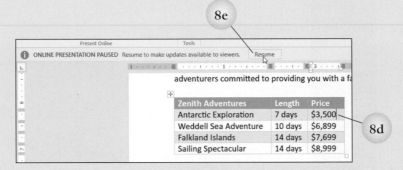

9. Click the End Online Presentation button on the Present Online tab.

10. At the message that displays stating that all remote viewers will be disconnected if you continue, click the End Online Presentation button.

11. Increase the zoom of the document back to 100%.

12. Save, print, and then close **6-BTZTAdvs.docx**.

Check Your Work

Project 3 **Customize Word and Account Options and Display the Windows Feedback Window** **5 Parts**

You will open a travel document, change options at the Word Options dialog box, make changes to the document, and then restore the default options at the Word Options dialog box. You will also customize and display account options.

Preview Finished Project

Tutorial

Customizing Word Options

Customizing Word Options

Customize Word at the Word Options dialog box. Display the dialog box by clicking the File tab and then clicking *Options*. The Word Options dialog box displays with a number of options in the left panel. Click each option one by one to review the various ways of customizing Word.

The Word Options dialog box, like many other dialog boxes in Word, contains a Help button in the upper right corner. Click this button and the Word Help window displays with information about the options in the dialog box.

Quick Steps

Customize Word Options

1. Click File tab.
2. Click *Options*.
3. Click option in left panel.
4. Make customization choices.
5. Click OK.

Customizing *General* Options

By default, the Word Options dialog box displays with *General* selected in the left panel, as shown in Figure 6.2. Use options in the Word Options dialog box with *General* selected to turn the Mini toolbar and live preview features on or off, specify the ScreenTip style, change user information, choose a different Office background and theme, and specify start up options.

When Word opens, the Word start screen displays by default. This screen contains a Recent list and templates for creating a document. To have Word open directly to a blank document, remove the check mark from the option *Show the Start screen when this application starts*.

Figure 6.2 Word Options Dialog Box with *General* Selected

Click the options in this panel to display customization features and commands.

With *General* selected in the left panel, options display for customizing the user interface, personalizing Microsoft Office, start up, and real-time collaboration.

Word Options ? ✕

| General |
| Display |
| Proofing |
| Save |
| Language |
| Advanced |
| Customize Ribbon |
| Quick Access Toolbar |
| Add-ins |
| Trust Center |

General options for working with Word.

User Interface options

☑ Show Mini Toolbar on selection ⓘ
☑ Enable Live Preview ⓘ
☑ Update document content while dragging ⓘ

ScreenTip style: Show feature descriptions in ScreenTips ▼

Personalize your copy of Microsoft Office

User name: Student Name
Initials: SN
☐ Always use these values regardless of sign in to Office.

Office Background: No Background ▼
Office Theme: Colorful ▼

Start up options

Choose the extensions you want Word to open by default: Default Programs...
☑ Tell me if Microsoft Word isn't the default program for viewing and editing documents.
☑ Open e-mail attachments and other uneditable files in reading view ⓘ
☑ Show the Start screen when this application starts

Real-time collaboration options

When working with others, I want to automatically share my changes: Ask Me ▼
☐ Show names on presence flags

OK   Cancel

1. At a blank document, customize Word options by completing the following steps:
   a. Click the File tab and then click *Options*.
   b. At the Word Options dialog box with *General* selected in the left panel, click the *Show Mini Toolbar on selection* check box to remove the check mark.
   c. Click the *Enable Live Preview* check box to remove the check mark.
   d. Make a note of the name in the *User name* text box and then select the name and type Sylvia Porter.
   e. Make a note of the initials in the *Initials* text box and then select the initials and type SP.
   f. Click the *Always use these values regardless of sign in to Office* check box to insert a check mark.
   g. Click the *Office Background* option box arrow and then click *Calligraphy* at the drop-down list.
   h. Click the *Office Theme* option box arrow and then click *Dark Gray* at the drop-down list.
   i. Click the *Show the Start screen when this application starts* check box to remove the check mark.
   j. Click OK to close the dialog box.

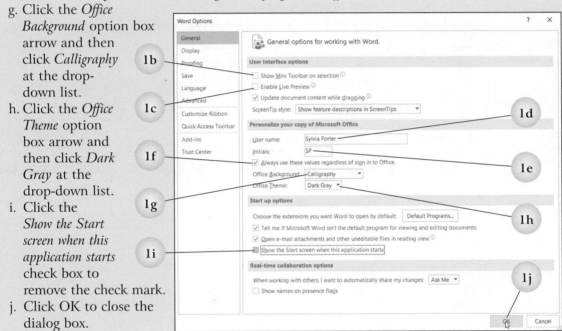

2. Close Word and then reopen Word. Notice that a blank document displays, rather than the Word Start screen.
3. Open **BTAfricaStudy.docx** and then save it with the name **6-BTAfricaStudy**.
4. Select text in the document and notice that the Mini toolbar does not display because this feature is turned off.
5. With the text still selected, click the *Font* option box arrow and then hover the mouse pointer over the font options that display at the drop-down gallery. Because the live preview feature is turned off, the text in the document does not display the font that the mouse pointer is hovering over.
6. Insert a user name field by completing the following steps:
   a. Press Ctrl + End to move the insertion point to the end of the document.
   b. Click the Insert tab.
   c. Click the Quick Parts button in the Text group and then click *Field* at the drop-down list.
   d. At the Field dialog box, scroll to the bottom of the *Field names:* list box and then double-click *UserName*.
7. Save **6-BTAfricaStudy.docx**.

Check Your Work

Customizing *Display* Options

Click the *Display* option in the left panel and the Word Options dialog box displays options for how document content appears on the screen and when it is printed, as shown in Figure 6.3

Chapter 4 in Level 1 contained information on turning on and off the display of white space that separates pages in Print Layout view by double-clicking the white space or the line separating two pages. The display of white space between pages can also be turned on or off with the *Show white space between pages in Print Layout view* option at the dialog box. The display of highlighting and ScreenTips can also be turned on or off at the dialog box.

Customizing *Proofing* Options

Click the *Proofing* option in the left panel and the Word Options dialog box displays options for customizing AutoCorrect and the spelling and grammar checker. Some of these options were used in previous chapters.

Figure 6.3 Word Options Dialog Box with *Display* Selected

With *Display* selected in the left panel, options display for customizing page and printer options and showing formatting marks.

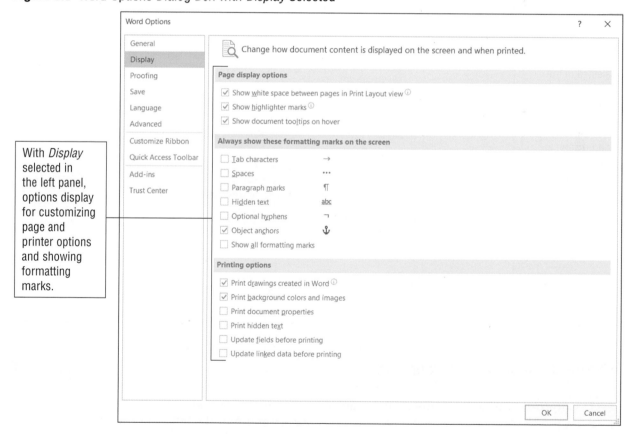

Customizing *Save* Options

Click the *Save* option in the left panel and the Word Options dialog box displays options for customizing how and where documents are saved, as shown in Figure 6.4. You can change the format in which files are saved from the default *Word Document (*.docx)* to another format, such as a previous version of Word, Word template, web page, or plain text. You can also change the default locations for saving documents and AutoRecover files. These save options are also available with the *Save as type* option at the Save As dialog box. The difference is that changing the file save format with the *Save files in this format* option at the Word Options dialog box with *Save* selected changes the default for all future documents.

Figure 6.4 Word Options Dialog Box with *Save* Selected

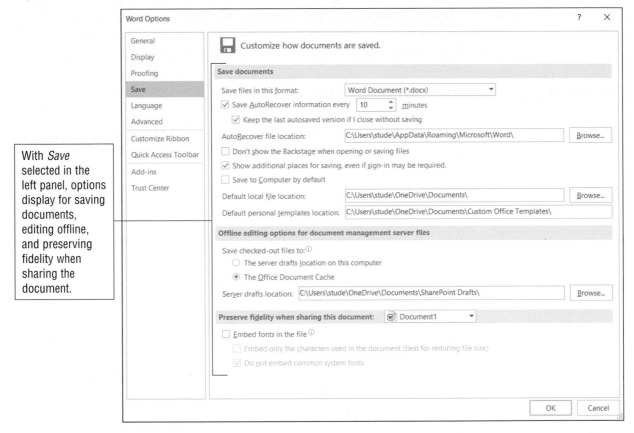

With *Save* selected in the left panel, options display for saving documents, editing offline, and preserving fidelity when sharing the document.

Project 3b Customizing *Save* Options

Part 2 of 5

1. With **6-BTAfricaStudy.docx** open, click the File tab and then click *Options*.
2. At the Word Options dialog box, click the *Display* option in the left panel and then look at the options available.
3. Click the *Proofing* option in the left panel and then look at the options available.

4. Click the *Save* option in the left panel.
5. Change the default local file location by completing the following steps:
   a. Make note of the current default local file location.
   b. Click the Browse button right of the *Default local file location* option box.

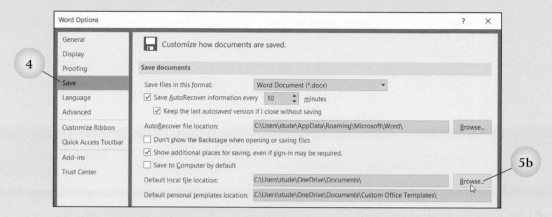

c. At the Modify Location dialog box, click Desktop to navigate to the desktop.

   d. Click OK.
6. Click OK to close the Word Options dialog box.
7. Save, print, and then close **6-BTAfricaStudy.docx**.
8. Close Word and then reopen Word.
9. At a blank document, press the F12 function key to display the Save As dialog box. (Notice that the default save location is the desktop.)
10. Click the Cancel button to remove the Save As dialog box.

Check Your Work

Customizing *Advanced* Options

Figure 6.5 shows the Word Options dialog box with the *Advanced* option selected. With the *Advanced* option selected, the Word Options dialog box displays a number of sections that identify ways to customize Word. Included are sections for changing editing options; specifying how text is cut, copied, and pasted in a document; specifying what document content to show; and customizing the display and printing of a document, among others.

Figure 6.5 Word Options Dialog Box with *Advanced* Selected

With *Advanced* selected in the left panel, options display for customizing editing and pasting options; specifying image size and quality; showing document content; and customizing display, print, save, layout, and general options.

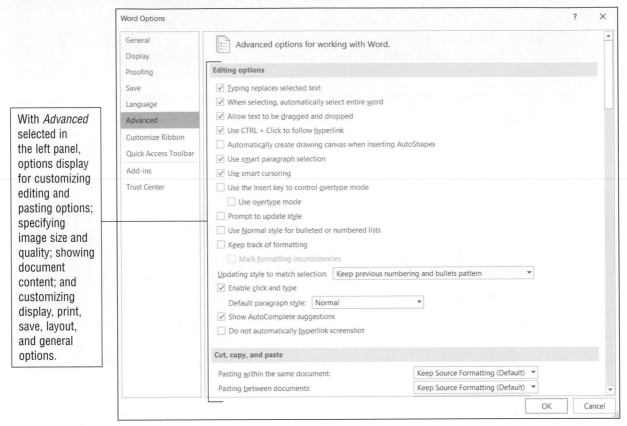

Project 3c Customizing Advanced Options

1. Open **6-BTAfricaStudy.docx**.
2. Click the File tab and then click *Options*.
3. At the Word Options dialog box, click the *Advanced* option in the left panel.

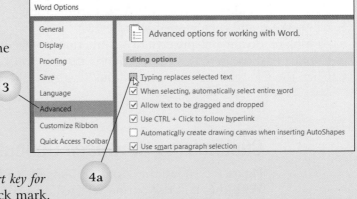

4. Make the following changes to the options in the dialog box:
   a. Click the *Typing replaces selected text* check box in the *Editing options* section to remove the check mark.
   b. Scroll down the dialog box to the *Cut, copy, and paste* section and then click the *Use the Insert key for paste* check box to insert a check mark.
   c. Scroll down the dialog box to the *Show document content* section and then click the *Show text boundaries* check box to insert a check mark.
   d. Scroll down the dialog box to the *Display* section, select the current number in the *Show this number of Recent Documents* measurement box, and then type 5.
5. Click OK to close the dialog box.
6. At the document, notice the boundary lines around paragraphs of text. These lines display because a check mark was inserted in the *Show text boundaries* check box.

7. Double-click the word *African* in the heading *African Study Adventure*, type Bayside Travel, and then press the spacebar. (The typed text did not replace the selected word, *African*. This is because the check mark was removed from the *Typing replaces selected text* check box.)

8. Copy and paste text by completing the following steps:

   a. Select text from the beginning of the heading *Disneyland Adventure* and the four bulleted items that follow it and then press Ctrl + C.

   b. Position the insertion point at the beginning of the heading *Cancun Adventure* and then press the Insert key. (The Insert key pastes the copied text because a check mark was inserted in the *Use the Insert key for paste* check box.)

9. Save, print, and then close **6-BTAfricaStudy.docx**.

Check Your Work

Customizing *Add-Ins and Trust Center* Options

Click the *Add-Ins* option and the Word Options dialog box displays add-ins, which are supplemental options that add custom commands and specialized features to Office 2016 applications. With the *Trust Center* option selected in the left panel of the Word Options dialog box, the Microsoft Trustworthy Computing hyperlink displays. Click this hyperlink to display the Trustworthy Computing web page at the microsoft.com website. Click the Trust Center Settings button and the Trust Center dialog box displays with options for specifying macro settings.

Project 3d **Displaying Add-In and Trust Center Options and Returning Options to the Default**   **Part 4 of 5**

1. At a blank document, click the File tab and then click *Options*.
2. At the Word Options dialog box, click the *Add-ins* option and then look at the options available in the dialog box.
3. Click the *Trust Center* option and then click the Microsoft Trustworthy Computing hyperlink.

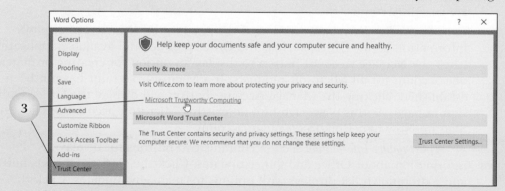

4. Look at the information that displays on the Trustworthy Computing web page and then close the web browser.

Word Level 3   Chapter 6 | Sharing Documents and Customizing Word Options   **167**

5. At the Word Options dialog box, click the *General* option.
6. Click the *Show Mini Toolbar on selection* check box to insert a check mark.
7. Click the *Enable Live Preview* check box to insert a check mark.
8. Click the *Show the Start screen when this application starts* check box to insert a check mark.
9. Select the current name in the *User name* text box and then type the original name.
10. Select the current initials in the *Initials* text box and then type the original initials.
11. Click the *Office Background* option box arrow and then click *No Background* at the drop-down list.
12. Click the *Office Theme* option box arrow and then click *Colorful* at the drop-down list.
13. Click the *Always use these values regardless of sign in to Office* check box to remove the check mark.
14. Change the default file location back to the original setting by completing the following steps:
    a. Click the *Save* option in the left panel of the Word Options dialog box.
    b. Click the Browse button right of the *Default local file location* option box.
    c. At the Modify Location dialog box, navigate to the original location.
    d. Click OK.
15. Click the *Advanced* option in the left panel of the Word Options dialog box and then make the following changes:
    a. Click the *Typing replaces selected text* check box to insert a check mark.
    b. Scroll down the dialog box to the *Cut, copy, and paste* section and then click the *Use the Insert key for paste* check box to remove the check mark.
    c. Scroll down the dialog box to the *Show document content* section and then click the *Show text boundaries* check box to remove the check mark.
    d. Scroll down the dialog box to the *Display* section, select the current number in the *Show this number of Recent Documents* measurement box, and then type 20.
16. Click OK to close the Word Options dialog box.

Customizing Account Information

Click the File tab and then the *Account* option and account information displays in the Account backstage area, similar to what is shown in Figure 6.6. The *User Information* section contains hyperlinks for changing the user photo and information, signing out of all Office applications, and switching accounts. The *Office Background* and *Office Theme* options in the Account backstage area are the same as the options at the Word Options dialog box with *General* selected. The *Connected Services* section displays any services, such as a OneDrive account, that are currently connected.

Quick Steps

Display Account Information
1. Click File tab.
2. Click *Account* option.

The *Product Information* section of the Account backstage area displays information about Office, such as the Office product and available applications. Click the Manage Account button to display an option for creating or managing one account for all Microsoft products. If a Microsoft account has not been established, clicking the Manage Account button will display the Office Online sign in page. At this page, sign into an existing Microsoft account or click the Sign up Now hyperlink to create an account.

 Update Options

The *Product Information* section contains two buttons for displaying information about Office and Office updates. Click the Update Options button and a drop-down list displays with options for managing updates. Click the *Update Now* option to check for and apply updates and click the *Disable Updates* option to specify whether updates should be performed automatically. Click the *View Updates* option to display a web page with information on new and

Figure 6.6 Account Backstage Area

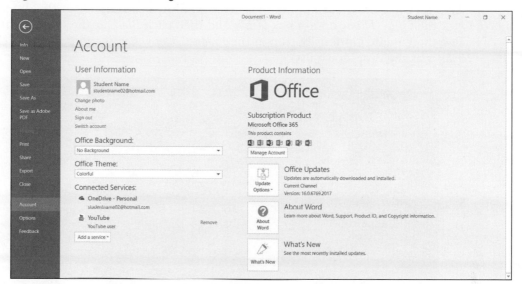

 About Word

improved features in Office 2016 and Office 365. Display information about updates by clicking the *About Updates* option. Click the About Word button to display information about the Word version, product identification number, and Microsoft software license terms. If an update has been installed, a What's New button may appear in the Account backstage area. Click this button to display information on the most recently installed update.

Project 3e Customizing and Displaying Account Information

Part 5 of 5

Note: Before completing this project, check with your instructor to determine if you have access to account information on the computer.

1. Make sure a blank document displays.
2. Click the File tab and then click the *Account* option.
3. At the Account backstage area, click the <u>About me</u> hyperlink in the *User Information* section. If you are signed into an account, a profile page will display with options for changing the photo, managing profiles, and adding a phone number. If you are not signed in, a sign in page will display.
4. Close the profile page or sign in page.

5. Click the *Office Background* option box arrow and then click *Spring* at the drop-down list.
6. Click the *Office Theme* option box arrow and then click *Black* at the drop-down list.
7. Click the Update Options button in the *Product Information* section and then click *View Updates* at the drop-down list.

8. View the information that displays in a web browser on new and improved features in Office 2016 and Office 365 and then close the web browser.
9. Click the Update Options button and then click *About Updates* at the drop-down list.
10. Read the information in the Automatic Updates window and then click OK to close the window.
11. Click the About Word button, look at the information that displays about Word, and then click OK to close the window.
12. Click the Back button to return to the blank document.
13. Change back to the Office default background and colors by completing the following steps:
   a. Click the File tab and then click the *Account* option.
   b. Click the *Office Background* option box arrow and then click the *No Background* option at the drop-down list.
   c. Click the *Office Theme* option box arrow and then click the *Colorful* option at the drop-down list.
14. Close the blank document without saving changes.

Chapter Summary

- The accessibility checker reviews a document to identify content that people with disabilities might find difficult to read or understand. Run the accessibility checker by clicking the Check for Issues button at the Info backstage area and then clicking *Check Accessibility* at the drop-down list.

- The accessibility checker examines a document and then displays information in the Accessibility Checker task pane. Content is grouped into three sections in the task pane. The *Error* section displays content that is very difficult or impossible for people with disabilities to understand, the *Warnings* section displays content that make a file difficult for people with disabilities to understand, and the *Tips* section displays content that people with disabilities can understand but that can be better organized.

- Create alternate text for a table with options at the Table Properties dialog box with the Alt Text tab selected. Display the dialog box by right-clicking a table, clicking *Table Properties* at the shortcut menu, and then clicking the Alt Text tab.

- Identify the first row in a table as a header row with options at the Table Properties dialog box with the Row tab selected. Display this dialog box by clicking the Table Tools Layout tab, clicking the Properties button in the Table group, and then clicking the Row tab.

- Apply built-in heading styles to identify headings and apply body text styles to text when preparing accessible documents.

- Apply built-in heading styles and body text styles when preparing an accessible document.

- Use options at the Share backstage area to invite people to view and/or edit a document, send a document as an email attachment in PDF or XPS format, send a document as a fax, and present a document online.

- Invite people to view a Word document with the *Share with People* option at the Share backstage area. To share a document, it must be saved to a shared location such as a OneDrive account.

- Click the Share with People button at the Share backstage area with the *Share with People* option selected and the Share task pane displays with options for inviting people to view and/or edit the document. Enter the names or email addresses at the Share task pane and then click the Share button.

- Send a copy of the document or a PDF version of the document as an attachment with the Send as attachment hyperlink at the Share task pane. Click the Get a sharing link hyperlink to create a link for viewing or editing the document.

- Click the *Email* option at the Share backstage area to display options for sending a copy of a document as an attachment to an email, sending a link to the document, attaching a PDF or XPS copy of the document, and sending an email as an Internet fax.

- Use the Present Online feature to share a document with others over the Internet. Send a link to the people to view a document in a web browser.

- Customize Word options at the Word Options dialog box. Display the dialog box by clicking the File tab and then clicking *Options*.

- Use options at the Word Options dialog box with *General* selected to turn the Mini toolbar and live preview features on or off, specify the ScreenTip style, change user information, choose a different Office background and theme, and specify start up options.

- The Word Options dialog box with *Display* selected contains options for specifying how document content appears on the screen and when it is printed.
- Use options at the Word Options dialog box with *Proofing* selected to customize AutoCorrect and the spelling and grammar checker.
- The Word Options dialog box with *Save* selected contains options for customizing how and where documents are saved.
- Click *Advanced* in the left panel of the Word Options dialog box to display a number of sections for identifying ways to customize Word such as changing editing options; specifying how text is cut, copied, and pasted; what document content to show; and customizing the display and printing of a document.
- The Word Options dialog box with *Add-Ins* selected, displays options for adding custom commands and specialized features to Office 2016 applications.
- The Account backstage area contains options for changing user information and the Office background and theme. It also contains product information, Office updates, and information about Word. Display this backstage area by clicking the File tab and then clicking the *Account* option.

Commands Review

FEATURE	RIBBON TAB, OPTION	BUTTON, OPTION
accessibility checker	File	, *Check Accessibility*
Account backstage area	File, *Account*	
Share backstage area	File, *Share*	
Word Options dialog box	File, *Options*	

Workbook

Chapter study tools and assessment activities are available in the *Workbook* ebook. These resources are designed to help you further develop and demonstrate mastery of the skills learned in this chapter.

Capstone assessment activities are also available in the *Workbook*. These activities are designed to help you demonstrate mastery of the skills learned in Chapters 1 through 6.

Index

A

Access, merging main document with Access database table source file, 25

accessibility of document
Accessibility Checker errors, warnings, tips, 148, 149
Check for Issues button, 148
creating alternate text for image or table, 148–149
establishing header row in tables, 150
improving example, 150–154
overview of, 148
using built-in heading styles, 150

Account backstage area, 168–170

account information, customizing and displaying, 168–170

Add-Ins options, customizing, 167–168

Advanced options, customizing, 165–167

alternate text for image or table, 148–149

assigned levels at Paragraph dialog box
assigning, 128–130
collapsing and expanding levels in Normal view, 128
collapsing levels by default, 130
moving collapsed text, 128
navigating in document with, 128

attachment, sending document as, 156

AutoCorrect, customizing, 163

automatic macros, 26–28

B

body fonts, finding and replacing, 15–17

C

character formatting, 2–10
adjusting character spacing, 2–4
applying OpenType features, 4–7
applying Text Effects, 7–8
change default font, 9–10
finding and replacing, special characters, 14–15
finding/replacing, using wildcard characters, 17–19
finding/replacing characters and fonts, 13–19
kerning, 3–4

character spacing, adjusting, 2–4

Check box button, 102

check box content control, inserting, 91

Check Box Content Control button, 91

check box form field
customizing, 111–113
inserting in form, with Legacy Tools, 104–105

Check Box Form Field Options dialog box, 111–112

Check for Issues button, 148

citations, creating table of authorities, 138–143

closing, master documents and subdocuments, 132

Collapse button, 121

Collapse Subdocuments button, 133

collapsing
levels
in Normal view, 128
in Outline view, 122–123
subdocuments, 133

combo box content control, inserting, 91

Combo Box Content Control button, 91

content control
content control button, 80

inserting

check box content control, 91
combo box content control, 91
date picker content control, 89–90
drop-down list content control, 91
picture content control, 88–90

inserting controls in survey template, 93–94

setting properties, 91–96
customizing date picker content, 95–96
customizing picture content controls, 94, 96
specifying drop-down list for, 92–94

Content Control Properties dialog box, 92, 94–96

contextual alternates, 6–7

copying, macros between documents and templates, 33–34

copyrighted intellectual property, 10–11

Create button, 132

Create New Style from Formatting Dialog Box, 44–46, 59, 63

Customize Keyboard dialog box, 47

customizing
account information, 168–170
Word Options, 160–168
Add-Ins options, 167–168
Advanced options, 165–167
Display option, 163
General options, 161–162
Proofing options, 163
Save options, 164–165
Trust Center options, 167–168

Custom Office Templates folder, 37–38
custom style sets
    changing default setting, 57
    deleting, 58
    saving, 56–58

D

data, editing grouped data, 85
data source file, merging main
    document
    with Access database table
        source file, 25
    with Excel worksheet data
        source file, 23–24
    with Word table data source
        file, 22–23
date picker content control
    customizing, 95–96
    inserting, 89–90
Date Picker Content Control
    button, 89
default style set, changing, 57
Define New List Style dialog
    box, 59
Demote button, 121, 124
Demote to Body Text button,
    121, 124
demoting heading levels, 124–
    125
Design Mode, displaying form
    in, 81
Design Mode button, 81
Developer tab, 78
    displaying, 80
Display option, customizing,
    163
documents
    accessibility management,
        148–154
    copying macros between
        documents and templates,
        33–34
    copying styles between
        templates and, 72–74
    creating master document,
        131–138

managing in Outline view,
    120–131
master document, 131–138
navigating, with assigned
    levels, 128
opening and filling form
    document, 83–84
opening document based
    on template using File
    Explorer, 102
save as template, 52
saving macro-enabled, 32–34
sharing, 154–160
subdocuments, 131–138
using File Explorer to open
    document based on
    template, 37–38
Drop-down button, 102
Drop-Down Form Field button,
    108
Drop-Down Form Field Options
    dialog box, 108
drop-down list content control
    inserting, 91
    specifying, 92–94
Drop-Down List Content
    Control button, 91
drop-down list form field,
    creating with Legacy Tools,
    108–111

E

Edit button, 158
editing, subdocuments, 134
Email option, for sharing
    document, 157
em dash, 11–12
en dash, 11–12
End Online Presentation
    button, 158
Excel, merging main document
    with Excel worksheet data
    source file, 23–24
Expand button, 121
expanding
    levels
        in Normal view, 128
        in Outline view, 122–123

subdocuments, 133
Expand Subdocuments button,
    133

F

Field dialog box, 35
fields
    check box form field, 104–
        105
    check box form field options,
        111–113
    drop-down list form field,
        108–111
    inserting If...Then...Else...
        field, 20–22
    Merge Record # field, 20
    recording macro with Fill-in
        field, 35–37
    text form field, 103
    text form fields, 114–116
File Explorer, to open document
    based on template, 37–38
Fill-in field
    recording macro with, 35–37
    running macro with, 38
finding and replacing
    body and heading fonts,
        15–17
    special characters, 14–15
    styles, 15–17
    using wildcard characters,
        17–19
Font dialog box, advanced tab
    selected, 2–3
fonts
    adjusting character spacing,
        2–4
    changing default, 9–10
    contextual alternates, 6–7
    finding and replacing, styles,
        15–17
    finding/replacing, body and
        heading fonts, 15–17
    Ligature, 4–6
    stylistic sets, 6–7
    Text Effects, 7–8
form
    creating

defining group, 81, 82–83
designing form, 78–79
displaying Developer tab, 80
displaying form in Design Mode, 81
editing grouped data, 85–86
editing protected form template, 96–98
form template, 79–80
inserting
  check box content control, 91
  combo box content control, 91
  content controls, 80
  date picker content control, 89–90
  drop-down list content control, 91
  picture content control, 88–90
  specific placeholder text, 87
mailing list form template, 82–83
opening and filling in form document, 83–84
protecting template, 88
setting content control properties, 91–96
using table to, 87–88
creating with Legacy Tools, 101–116
customizing
  check box form field options, 111–113
  drop-down list form field, 108–111
  text form fields, 114–116
inserting
  check box form field, 104–105
  form fields, 106
  text form field, 103
opening document based on template using File Explorer, 102
protecting template, 105

form template, editing protected, 96–98
printing, only data in form document, 106–107
Format Text Effects dialog box, 7–8
formatting
character formatting, 2–10
  adjusting character spacing, 2–4
  applying OpenType features, 4–7
  applying Text Effects, 7–8
  change default font, 9–10
finding/replacing
  body and heading fonts, 15–17
  special characters, 14–15
  styles, 15–17
  using wildcard characters, 17–19
finding/replacing characters and fonts, 13–19
inserting symbols and special characters
  hyphens, 11–12
  intellectual property symbols, 10–11
macros
  assigning macro to Quick Access Toolbar, 29–31
  copying macros between documents and templates, 33–34
  recording macro with Fill-in field, 35–37
  running macro automatically, 26–28
  saving macro-enabled document/template, 32–34
  specifying macro security settings, 31–34
  using File Explorer to open document based on template, 37–38
merging
  inserting If…Then…Else… field, 20–22

inserting Merge Record # field, 20
  with other data source files, 22–25
with styles, 43–74
  creating style, 44–50
  displaying all styles, 54–55
  managing styles, 69–74
  modifying predesigned style, 50–54
  multilevel list style, 59–62
  revealing style formatting, 55–56
  saving custom style set, 56–58
  Style Inspector task pane, 67–69
  table style, 63–67
Form Field Help Text dialog box, 108
Form Field Shading button, 102, 103

G

General options, customizing, 161–162
group
  defining, 81–83
  editing grouped data, 85
Group button, 81

H

header row, establishing, 150
heading fonts, finding and replacing, 15–17
heading levels, in Outline view
  assigning levels, 125–126
  expanding and collapsing, 122–123
  moving, 126
  overview of, 120, 121
  promoting and demoting, 124–125
headings, in Outline view, assigned levels at Paragraph dialog box
assigning, 128–130

collapsing and expanding levels in Normal view, 128

collapsing levels by default, 130

moving collapsed text, 128

navigating in document with, 128

heading styles, using built-in, 150

hyperlink, sharing document with, 156

hyphen

em and en dashes, 11–12

nonbreaking, 11

optional, 11

regular, 11

Hyphenation button, 11

hyphens, inserting, 11–12

I

If…Then…Else… field, 20–22

images, creating alternate text for, 148–149

Insert button, 135

Insert Frame button, 102

inserting

check box content control, 91

combo box content control, 91

content controls, 80

date picker content control, 89–90

drop-down list content control, 91

form fields, 106

hyphens, 11–12

intellectual property symbols, 10–11

nonbreaking spaces, 12–13

picture content control, 88–90

specific placeholder text, 87

subdocuments, 135–136

table of authorities, 139–143

text form field, 103

Insert Table of Authorities button, 139

Insert Word Field: IF Dialog Box, 20

intellectual property symbols, inserting, 10–11

Internet Fax, sending document as, 157

Invite people text box, 155–156

K

kerning, 3–4

keyboard short cuts

assigning style to, 47–50

inserting intellectual property symbols, 10–11

marking citation, 139

promoting and demoting heading levels, 124

revealing style formating, 55

update table of authorities, 140

L

Legacy Tools, creating forms, 101–116

customizing

check box form field options, 111–113

drop-down list form field, 108–111

text form fields, 114–116

inserting

check box form field, 104–105

form fields, 106

text form field, 103

opening document based on template using File Explorer, 102

protecting template, 105

Legacy Tools button, 102

creating forms with, printing only data in form document, 106–107

Ligature

applying, 5–6

categories of, 4

M

macros

assigning macro to Quick Access Toolbar, 29–31

copying macros between documents and templates, 33–34

recording, 26–28

with Fill-in field, 35–37

running macro automatically, 26–28

saving macro-enabled document/template, 32–34

specifying macro security settings, 31–34

storage of, 26

using File Explorer to open document based on template, 37–38

Macros button, 26

Macro Security button, 31

mail merge

inserting If…Then…Else… field, 20–22

inserting Merge Record # field, 20

merging main document

with Access database table source file, 25

with Excel worksheet data source file, 23–24

with Word table data source file, 22–23

Manage Styles dialog box, 69–71

Mark Citation button, 138

Mark Citation dialog box, 139

master document, 131–138

creating, from existing document, 131–133

opening and closing, 132

subdocuments

editing, 134

expanding and collapsing, 133

inserting, 135–136

merging, 136–138

splitting, 136–138

unlinking, 136–138
uses/benefits of, 131
Match Fields button, 23
Merge button, 136
Merge Record # field, 20
merging. *See also* mail merge
subdocuments, 136–138
Modify Style dialog box, 50–51
More Styles button, 44
Move Down button, 121, 126
Move Up button, 121, 126
multilevel list style
creating, 59–62
modifying, 66

N

navigating, document with
assigned levels, 128
Nonbreaking Hyphen option,
11
nonbreaking spaces, inserting,
12–13
Normal view, collapsing and
expanding levels in, 128
numbers, spacing, 4–6
Number spacing option, 4–5

O

OneDrive, save document to,
154–155
opening
document based on template,
52
master documents and
subdocuments, 132
OpenType font file format
applying Ligature and
Number form, 5–6
applying stylistic set and
contextual alternates, 6–7
Ligature categories, 4
overview of, 4
Organizer dialog box, 33, 34,
72–73
Outline button, 120
buttons and options in
Outlining tab, 121

Outline Level option, 121
Outline view
assigned levels at Paragraph
dialog box
assigning, 128–130
collapsing and expanding
levels in Normal view,
128
collapsing levels by default,
130
moving collapsed text, 128
navigating in document
with, 128
assigning levels, 125–126
benefits/uses of, 119, 120
collapsing levels, 122–123
demoting heading levels,
124–125
display document in, 120–
121, 123
expanding levels, 122–123
moving headings, 126
organizing document in,
126–127
promoting heading levels,
124–125
Outlining tab, buttons and
options in, 121

P

Paragraph dialog box, assigned
levels
assigning, 128–130
collapsing and expanding
levels in Normal view, 128
collapsing levels by default,
130
moving collapsed text, 128
navigating in document with,
128
Paragraph formatting option
box, 67–69
Paragraph Spacing button, 69
PDF file, sending document as,
157
picture content control
customizing, 94, 96
inserting, 88–90

Picture Content Control button,
88
placeholder text, inserting
specific, 87
Plain Text Content Control
button, 87
predesigned style, modifying,
50–51
Present Online button, 158
Present Online feature, 158–160
printing, only data in form
document, 106–107
Product Information section,
168
Promote button, 121, 124
Promote to Heading 1 button,
121, 124
promoting heading levels,
124–125
Proofing options, customizing,
163
Properties button, 92, 150

Q

Quick Access Toolbar, assigning
macro to, 29–31
Quick Parts button, 35

R

Record Macro button, 26
Record Macro dialog box, 26, 27
registered trademark symbol,
10–11
Rename button, 72
Reset Form Fields button, 102
Restrict Editing button, 88, 105
Restrict Editing task pane,
88–89
Resume Online Presentation
button, 158
Rules button, adding fields to
main document with, 20

S

Save options, customizing,
164–165

Save to Cloud button, 155
saving
　to cloud, 155
　custom style set, 56–58
　macro-enabled document or
　　template, 32–34
　to OneDrive account, 154–
　　155
　styles in template, 52–53
Scale options, 3
security, specifying macro
　　security settings, 31–34
Send as Internet Fax button,
　157
Send as PDF button, 157
Send as XPS button, 157
Set as Default button, 57
Set As Default button, 9
SharePoint, 154
Share task pane, 155
Share with People button, 155
Share with People option, using,
　154–156
sharing document
　email option, 157
　inviting people to view your
　　document, 155–156
　presenting document online,
　　158–160
　Share with People option,
　　154–156
Show Document button, 132
Show First Line Only option,
　121
Show Level option, 121, 122
Show Text Formatting option,
　121
spacing
　adjusting character spacing
　　and kerning, 2–4
　inserting nonbreaking spaces,
　　12–13
special characters. *See* symbols
　and special characters
spelling and grammar checker,
　customizing, 163
Split button, 136
splitting, subdocuments, 136–
　138

START PRESENTATION
　button, 158
Style Inspector task pane,
　67–69
Style Pane Options dialog box,
　54–55
styles, 43–74
　copying between documents
　　and templates, 72–74
　creating
　　assigning keyboard shortcut
　　　to style, 47–50
　　based on existing
　　　formatting, 44–45
　　based on existing style, 44
　　new style, 45–46, 48–50
　custom style sets
　　changing default setting, 57
　　deleting, 58
　　saving, 56–58
　displaying all styles, 54–55
　finding and replacing, 15–17
　managing, 69–72
　modifying applied style, 54
　modifying predesigned style,
　　50–51
　multilevel list style
　　creating, 59–62
　　modifying, 66
　renaming, 72
　revealing style formating,
　　55–56
　saving in template, 52–53
　Style Inspector task pane,
　　67–69
　table style
　　creating, 63–66
　　modifying, 66–67
　updating template with
　　updated style, 60
stylistic set, 6–7
subdocuments
　defined, 131
　editing, 134
　expanding and collapsing,
　　133
　inserting, 135–136
　merging, 136–138
　opening and closing, 132

　splitting, 136–138
　unlinking, 136–138
survey form template, editing
　　and filling in, 97–98
symbols and special characters
　finding and replacing, 14–15
　finding/replacing, using
　　wildcard characters, 17–19
　inserting
　　hyphens, 11–12
　　intellectual property
　　　symbols, 10–11
　　nonbreaking spaces, 12–13

T

table of authorities
　creating, 138–139
　deleting, 140
　example of, 138
　inserting, 139–143
　updating, 140
Table of Authorities dialog box,
　139–140
tables
　creating alternate text for,
　　148–149
　establishing header row, 150
Tables feature, creating form
　　using, 87
table style
　creating, 63–66
　modifying, 66–67
templates
　copying macros between
　　documents and templates,
　　33–34
　copying styles between
　　documents and, 72–74
　creating application form,
　　103
　form template
　　creating, 79
　　editing protected, 96–98
　　mailing list form template,
　　　82–83
　　protecting, 88
　open document based on, 52

opening document based on template using File Explorer, 102
protecting, with Legacy Tools, 105
saving macro-enabled, 32–34
saving styles in, 52–53
survey template
editing and filling in, 97–98
inserting controls in, 93–94
updating, with updated styles, 60
using File Explorer to open document based on template, 37–38
text, creating alternate text for image or table, 148–149
Text effects, applying, 7–8
Text Effects and Typography button, 4
Text Effects button, 7
text form field
customizing with Legacy Tools, 114–116
inserting in form, with Legacy Tools, 103

Text Form Field button, 102, 103
Text Form Field Options dialog box, 114
Text level formatting option box, 67
trademark symbol, 10–11
Trust Center dialog box, 31–32
Trust Center options, customizing, 167–168

U

Unlink button, 136
unlinking, subdocuments, 136–138
Update Options button, 168
Update Table button, 140
updating, table of authorities, 140
User Information section, 168–170

W

white space separating pages, turning on and off, 163

wildcard characters
finding and replacing using, 17–19
functions of common, 18
Word, merging main document with Word table data source file, 22–23
Word Options, customizing, 160–168
Add-Ins options, 167–168
Advanced options, 165–167
Display option, 163
General options, 161–162
Proofing options, 163
Save options, 164–165
Trust Center options, 167–168
Word Options dialog box, 160–161

X

XPS format, sending document as, 157